~~Norman Clark~~ Dale Barclay

Bodie Bonanza

Nevada Publications
Paperback Edition, 1989
ISBN 0-913814-32-6

Proudly printed in the USA

Bodie Bonanza

The True Story of a Flamboyant Past

by

Warren Loose

Published by Stanley Paher

Nevada Publications
Box 15444
Las Vegas, Nevada 89114

WHEN YOU VISIT

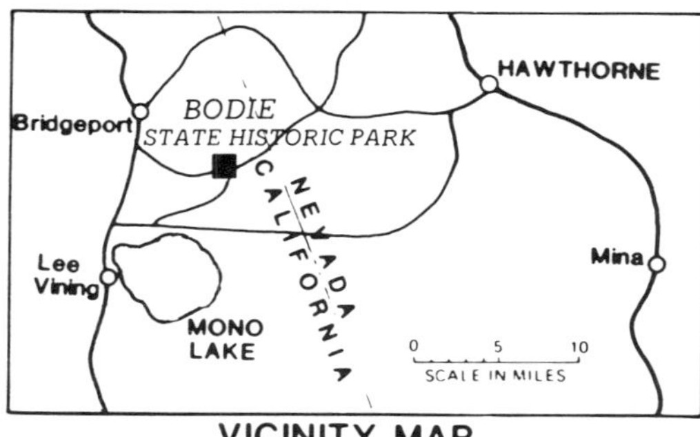

VICINITY MAP

Bodie State Historic park is best visited during the summer. At other times the weather is unpredictable. Off-season visitors are cautioned to check at the Mono County Sheriff's office in Bridgeport for road and weather conditions before making the trip. Roads are often difficult; trailers are not advised. Over-snow equipment (snowmobiles, skis, snow shoes, etc.) may be required to reach the park during the winter months.

The Park is open year-round; 9:00 a.m. to 7:00 p.m. in the summer months and 9:00 a.m. to 4:00 p.m. the rest of the year. An entrance fee is charged year-round.

For more information about Bodie SHP you may contact the park either by writing to:

BODIE STATE HISTORIC PARK
Post Office Box 515
Bridgeport, California 93517
or by calling the park directly at:
(619) 647-6445

PLEASE HELP US

- DON'T TOUCH ANYTHING: leave every rock and rusty can in place for our grandchildren to see.
- WATCH OUT: this is a real ghost town; splinters, nails and broken glass are everywhere.
- DON'T SMOKE: except in the parking lot.
- The Mill Area is hazardous; please stay out.
- Unless otherwise noted, all buildings are closed to the public.

DEPARTMENT OF PARKS & RECREATION
State of California – The Resources Agency
P.O. Box 942896 Sacramento, CA 94296-0838

The Friends of Bodie is a group dedicated to the preservation of the gold mining ghost town of Bodie. It is a chapter of the Tahoe-Sierra State Parks Association. This is a volunteer, non-profit organization which helps preserve and interpret state parks in the Sierra District of the State Department of Parks and Recreation.

In 1962 Bodie became a state historic park. This did not automatically insure all structures and artifacts would be properly preserved. Within the state Park System Bodie must compete with other parks for funding and priority projects. Likewise, the Department of Parks and Recreation must compete with all other state agencies for limited amounts of funding.

The Friends of Bodie can help raise funds and provide volunteer support to insure that Bodie is properly preserved.

Financial support and volunteer workers are vital in preserving Bodie. Should you wish to participate in this effort please contact:

THE FRIENDS OF BODIE
Post Office Box 515
Bridgeport, CA 93517

This Book Is Dedicated to All
The Argonauts of All Time

Contents

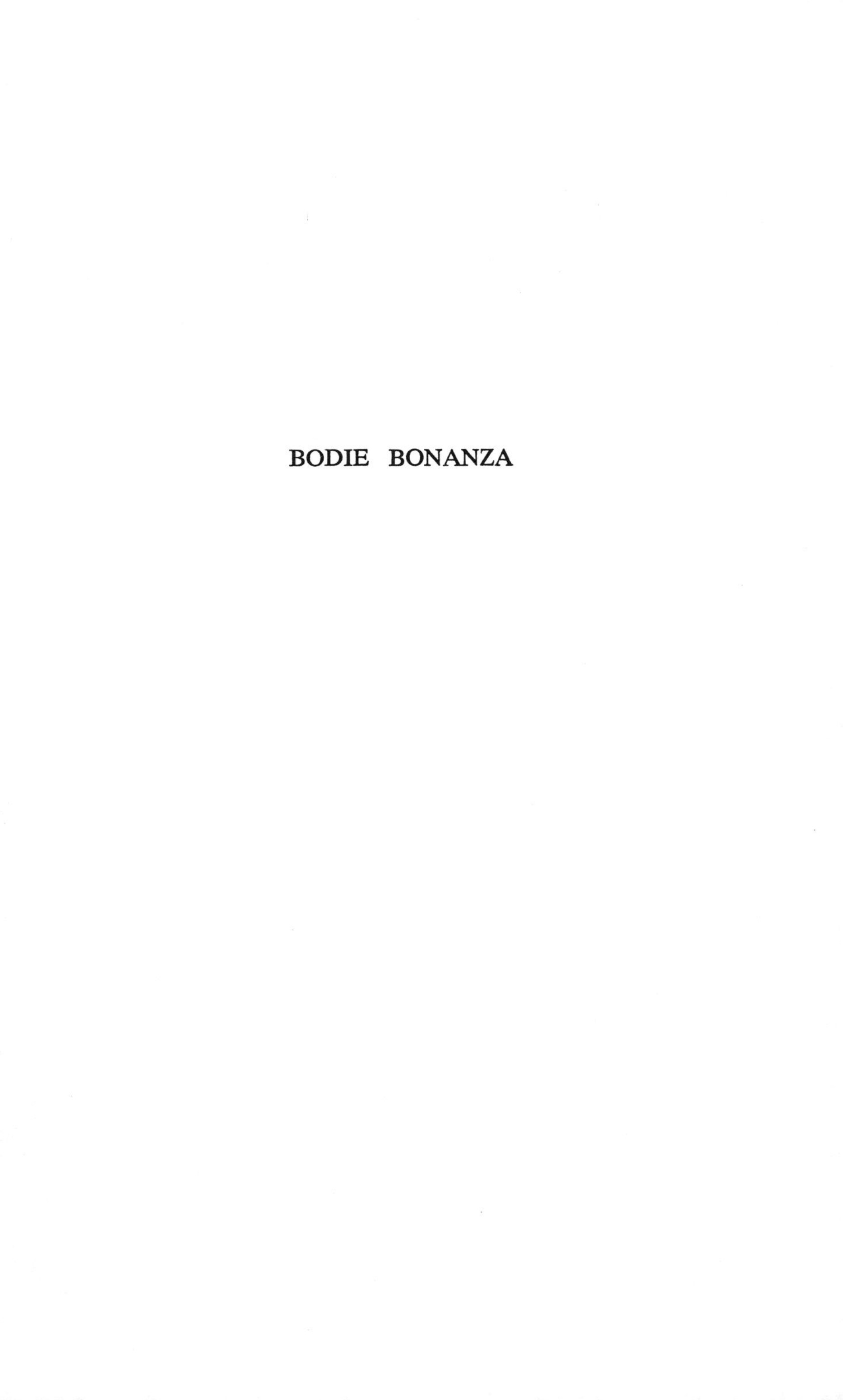

BODIE BONANZA

CHAPTER I

The Two Discoveries - 1859

It had been eleven years since Sutter's Mill and the cry of "Gold! Gold!" brought the Argonauts surging west to California. They prospected the rivers and tributaries of the Tuolumne, the Mokelumne, the Sacramento, the Yuba, the Feather, and others. Many found gold; on some Dame Fortune smiled and they gleaned fortunes from the rich channels and bars. A few kept their riches; most lost it in further fruitless search, bad investments, and sampling the fleshpots of the time. Some, after indifferent success, turned from the lure of the yellow dust to the business of agriculture, stock raising, or trade. But there was a hard core of the restless miners who failed to find it in a big way. They carried their little hand rockers up the strange branches and tributaries of the westward-flowing river systems. These men were the seekers who persevered year after year. Thus it was, in the spring of 1859, that stories of possible rich placer "diggin's" seeped westward over the Sierras. Weary overland travelers, cattlemen, cavalrymen, and Indian scouts carried tales of men panning gold on the eastern slope of the Sierras. It was said that rich pans could be had in the Washoe District and a hundred miles further south where the mountain streams tumbled through their canyons and emptied into the dead sea of Mono.

Two discoveries were made in the year of 1859 that will live for all time in the stirring annals of the West. Both were made when the West was raw and the wild Indian and the buffalo ruled and roamed its wasteland and there were hardly twenty miles of railroad, and very few miles of uncertain telegraph wire, in a vast territory that stretched from the Rockies to the Golden Gate—one, the fabulous Virginia City on the Comstock Lode; the other, Bodie on its high, bleak sage-covered plateau. Virginia City became one of the richest silver camps in the history of the world. Bodie in its heyday (1878-80) was the biggest excitement in the West, and it came on as the big bonanzas of the Comstock Lode faded. For a brief period the production of gold bullion from the Bodie Mine and the Standard Mine was ranked first and second respectively among all the Drift Mines in California (1878).

Bodie during its zenith was on the minds and lips of the turbulent West. Its fame blazed across the mining firmament like the passing of a giant comet. Its aura drew both good men and bad. Journalists like Bret Harte helped to make "The Bad Man From Bodie" a national character.

DISCOVERY OF THE COMSTOCK LODE

Early that spring Peter O'Riley and Patrick McLaughlin, who had been trying their luck placer mining in the Washoe District with scant success, decided to prospect a new piece of ground at the head of a ravine on the upper end of a canyon on Gold Hill, so dubbed by the placer miners of Johnstowns.

About the first of June, 1859, while trying to develop a little water supply for their rockers, they dug a small pit about four feet deep to act as a reservoir. As O'Riley and McLaughlin sweated and dug into the stratum of the decomposed odd-looking blue-black rock, they were raising the lid on a Pandora's box. This was the top of the famous Ophir Mine.

Their little reservoir was nested in the apex of a $20,000,000 bonanza. They tried a charge or two of the decomposed blue-black dirt in their rockers and found the bottoms covered with curious-looking stuff—silver filled with spangles of native gold. This curious stuff was black sulphurite of silver. The gold they recognized; but they thought the black concentrate was a base metal of some sort—"bogus stuff."

As these two Irishmen were weighing the pros and cons of their new find, old "Pancake," a loquacious sharp-eyed opportunist (whose real name was Henry Page Comstock), came by, astride his mustang pony. He stopped, slid down, checked the cleanup from the rockers, "hefting and running his fingers through the gold and picking into and probing the mass of strange looking stuff exposed."[1] He bellowed to the astonished Irishmen, "You're working on my ground!" Rather than have trouble with him they dealt him in. O'Riley and McLaughlin were simple hard-working placer miners, ignorant of geology. They could not conceive that they were in possession of a location that would produce hundreds of millions in silver. In all probability they didn't bother to have the stuff assayed. They sluiced and took out the gold, which because of its alloy with silver was much lighter in color and weighed less. It brought them only eleven to twelve dollars per ounce, while the gold from the California placer mines with which they were familiar had returned them nineteen dollars per ounce. This odd appearance of their ore and the supposed poor grade of their bullion created an uncertainty in their minds. A specimen of this ore came into the hands of Judge James Walsh of Grass Valley, who had it assayed, and it returned a value of several thousand dollars per ton in gold and silver. The good judge loaded his pack mules and left for the Washoe District before morning.

The original discoverers of the Comstock Lode did what simple ignorant men have been known to do from the beginning of time—they sold out for a pittance. Patrick McLaughlin received $3,500. Comstock sold his interest to Judge Walsh for $11,000, while Peter O'Riley held onto his interest for a little while but finally disposed of it for a paltry $40,000. They all died broke.

DISCOVERY OF BODIE

To Terrance Brodigan and Wakeman S. Bodey[2] must go the honor of the original discovery of the first clues of its golden hoard. The former was a typical genial, industrious Irishman who left the old sod as a boy and followed the trail of adventure and the Golden Fleece. He had mined in Tuolumne County with some success and had become one of Sonora's leading businessmen. He was possessed of a probing restlessness. Brodigan was an adventurous spirit. After leaving his Irish home in Donigan on the banks of the Boyne, he first migrated to Australia, where he tried his hand at sheep raising. When stories of gold in California reached his ears, his natural restlessness and independent disposition brought him by sail across the broad Pacific, and then, following in the wake of the Argonauts, he arrived in Sonora in Tuolumne County in 1851, where he eventually became proprietor of the Sonora House and Livery Stable.

A friend and fellow placer miner and sometime guest of Brodigan was Wakeman S. Bodey, whose name has marked the place of discovery for over a hundred years. (On orthographical change of Bodey's name to Bodie, see page 27 below.)

Bodey originated in Poughkeepsie, New York, where he had owned and operated his own business. We find him listed in the Poughkeepsie village directory of 1843. In the issue of 1845 he is listed as a tin manufacturer with a shop at 354 Main Street and a home at the corner of south Hamilton and Montgomery streets. He was well respected in his community—but in his heart burned a consuming lust for adventure. His willingness to gamble his all is now history. When the thrilling news of gold in California hit the Eastern seaboard in 1848, he was among the first to answer its siren call. Joining the first wave of adventurous Argonauts, he closed his shop and bid his wife, Sarah, and children goodbye and sailed for the California gold fields around the Horn on the sloop *Mathew Vasser,* landing in San Francisco in 1849, among the first eager gold seekers to walk the plank sidewalks of that bustling port by the Golden Gate. He soon turned his footsteps to the placer fields, gulches, and gravel bars of the Sierra, where for ten years he tried his luck with modest results. In an interview published in the *Daily Bodie Standard* of October 27, 1879, Joseph Wasson (writer and state senator from the Fourth District, comprising Inyo and Mono counties, regarding his just published *Bodie and Esmeralda Publication*) stated, "Bodey [before joining up with Terrance Brodigan to investigate the new placer discoveries east of the Sierra] had been hovering about Oak Flat, Humbug, and other well-known placer resorts in that famous county of Tuolumne."[3]

As the spring of 1859 warmed the foothills and melted the

snow in the passes of the Sierras to the east, the rumors and whispered stories of rich new placer diggings a few miles south of the Sonora Pass on the eastern side of the Sierra and along the upper reaches of the Walker River fanned the restless hopes of many miners of Tuolumne County.

Sol Carter had pushed across the Sonora Pass over what was to be the Sonora-Mono Trail with pack trains of supplies for placer miners whose rockers were returning them rich wages from the newly discovered diggings of Dogtown (discovered 1858).

Brodigan, as the proprietor of the Sonora House and Livery Stable, was located at a key post to obtain news of the new mining activity, and in dispensing lodging and fodder for Sol Carter and his pack train and others journeying to and from these new placers east of the Sonora Pass, he acquired a wide and friendly acquaintance, thus coming into early possession of stories and news that found its way back over the Sierra.

Ross E. Culcord (later governor of Nevada, 1893) in his *Reminiscences of Life in Territorial Nevada* tells us that when his party crossed the Sonora Pass in the spring of 1859 to prospect at Dogtown, some seventy men had preceded them, Sonora being the jumping-off point and supply base for these parties. So it was that when the news of the discovery of the Monoville placer diggings in July, 1859, reached Sonora, Brodigan and Bodey made plans to cross the Sonora Pass and prospect for new gold fields. In further excerpts from Joseph Wasson's interview in the *Daily Bodie Standard* of October 27, 1879, we read:

> . . . in July 1859 the Diggings of Monoville were discovered. This added fuel to the flame or feeling created in the breast of the Citizens of Tuolumne, and in the fall of 1859 Brodigan came over with one party and Bodey with another. . . . The two parties prospected along the route, coming together at a point on the old trail not far from what is now known as Leavitt Station [Leavitt Meadows] on the present Bodie and Sonora Wagon road.
>
> Bodey and Brodigan were well acquainted at Sonora, the former being a guest of the latter as records show. They came out to Monoville in a company. Here they halted. Brodigan hunted

around Mono Lake awhile with Jess Stewart, once sheriff of Tuolumne County.

[R. E. Culcord relates, we note here, that he remembered Bodey as a camp follower of Brodigan's during his prospecting stay at Monoville, which diggings Culcord and his party left in the fall of 1859.]

Getting restless and desirous of carrying out his original intention he determined to strike out on a prospecting tour. In this he was followed by Pat Garrity, William Boyle, W. S. Bodey from Monoville, 15 miles southwest of Bodie. The Brodigan-Bodey party swung around the foothills next to Mono Lake and brought up first in the canyon where Aurora has since been built. They dug several holes for placer, but owing to the threatening attitude of the Indians, nothing definite was effected, and the party started back toward Monoville, camping and prospecting for a day or two by the way in the ravine alongside of which are now located the works of the Dudley, Defiance, and Red Cloud (all famous Bodie Mines). At this juncture it was resolved that the results of the expedition be kept secret until the spring of 1860, and the party returned to Monoville.

Immediately following this, Bodey, who was doubtless a good prospector, was tempted to break the bargain and in company with others returned and went over the ground again. Brodigan made preparations to return to Sonora for the winter and started for home, notwithstanding, he was quite apprised of Bodey's bad faith. Meeting a new batch of adventurers from Sonora, he turned about then led them into the new diggings. Among them was one Tom McLaughlin, now residing in Los Angeles. In the meantime, Bodey with Black Taylor, half Cherokee, had thrown up a little dugout cabin at the head of Green Street, under the shelter of a point of rocks, about mid-way between what is now known as the Bulwer and Walts Spring. There is left but a trace of this old cabin, having been built over recently by James Congray who owns the whole business. Late in November 1859, Brodigan again started for Sonora. When the party got along about the Dogtown divide, Bodey and Taylor were caught up with. They were equipped with a single animal heavily packaged with provisions. They soon turned in the direction of their new camp and Brodigan dropped back a moment to give Bodey his parting blessing, adding that they would meet in the spring. Bodey and Taylor made a beeline for their new habitation at the head of Green Street. But the former never again got sight of it, as far as this world was concerned. He fell by the wayside, under a point of black palisade rocks about three quarters of a mile southwest of his destination. He and Taylor were not lost, although there was a blinding snowstorm raging at the time.[4]

The winter of 1859-60 came early to the eastern slope of the Sierra and it was one of the severest the country had known. Dan De Quille (William Wright) in his famous history of the Comstock Lode, *The Big Bonanza,* published in 1876, comments on this storm: "The snow fell on the twenty-second of November; it snowed all day and four days later again set in when snow fell to the depth of five or six feet, cutting all communication between Gold Hill and Virginia, though the two towns were but a mile apart."

Continuing from Wasson's interview in the *Standard*: "In that unexpected storm, Brodigan and his party came near losing their lives, having to abandon the Sonora Pass Trail and return home around about by the way of Carson Valley and Placerville. Brodigan was given up for lost and he found the people of Sonora on the eve of organizing a party to search for him. The body of Mr. Bodey was not found until after the snow melted in 1860, and it was buried in the same blanket in which he was rolled and left by Taylor before life became extinct."

Brodigan and Bodey, the discoverers, profited exactly nothing from their find, although Brodigan, some eighteen years later, resided in Bodie during its heyday and for a time operated a successful business delivering pure spring water to the hotels, restaurants, saloons, and private subscribers of the camp.

Poor Bodey! As he floundered and sank exhausted into the white oblivion of the swirling, deepening snow, what were his final thoughts? What were his plans and hopes for his wife and his still living sons, Ogden and George?[5] All his life he had toiled at building a business and security—and he had chucked it for a fling on the golden wheel of chance in the "days of '49." For ten long years he had labored with pick and shovel, rocker and sluice box, on the banks of the Merced, the Mokelumne, the Tuolumne, and countless others. There had been small winnings, modest little cleanups, a generous part of each he had proudly and dutifully sent on to his waiting wife.[6]

But here at last in this high, bleak, but beautiful land—what territory or state could claim it, California or vast Utah Territory, none knew for sure[7]—here within the last fortnight or so, the fickle odds of chance had delivered a sure strike. The heavy yellow ribbons of placer gold in each panning from the new location were certain proof—this he knew for sure—yes, it was almost within his grasp—what a beautiful horizon—or was it a mirage? Snow—numbing cold—exhaustion—oblivion. There would be no days of wine and roses for this Argonaut.

CHAPTER II

Bodie and the Comstock - 1860

As the great Time Machine of the nineteenth century inexorably rolled into 1860, there emerged a "Great Decade" which would leave a stamp of progress unequaled in the history of the United States—a decade of frightful decisions and a bloody and horrible Civil War that would weld and forge a great people into a world power. The people of the industrial East and the cotton- and tobacco-growing South would be linked to the great rich wilderness region of the Far West by the completion of the first transcontinental railroad and telegraph systems. The discovery of mineral wealth in the Far West would give powerful impetus to quick development of what had been a remote region. Indeed, the outpourings of hundreds of millions in silver from the Comstock Lode would endow the Federal Treasury with the enormous credits it needed to win a war and create an army and naval forces so powerful that Louis Napoleon, Emperor of France, would be forced to pull his army out of Mexico and abandon France's military adventure in the Western Hemisphere.

The coming of 1860 saw the West in the grip of mining fever greater than in the days of '49. From the polished tables of the staid countinghouses of the fabled city by the Golden Gate to the placer "diggin's" scattered over the length and breadth of the Sierras, to little cow towns and sturdy growing villages in Brigham Young's "Kingdom of the Saints," a vast maelstrom of gold and silver excitement swept the West in the spring of 1860. It would bring ten thousand frenzied men to the Comstock Lode.

River steamers from San Francisco with smoke-billowing stacks and thrashing paddle wheels edged their way to the Sacramento levees, crammed with eager men, machinery, and freight of all kinds. Hundreds of tons of freight, Virginia City bound, lashed on high-wheeled wagons pulled by horses, mules, and bull teams were strung out over the rutted, muddy roads, from Sacramento to Placerville to Strawberry Flat in the high Sierras. Over the wind-swept passes snaked long lines of freight wagons, carts, pack trains, and men on foot–a surging potpourri of human efforts to get in on the fabulous strike on the Comstock.

The older placer-mining districts of Bidwell's Bar, Grass Valley, and Sonora in Tuolumne County were emptied of miners making for the big strike at Virginia City.

Terrance Brodigan, the surviving leader of the Argonauts who had discovered the new placer diggings fifteen miles northeast of Monoville in October, 1859, was swept up in this Washoe fever, and headed for the Comstock. The find that he and W. S. Bodey had made in the fall a few short months before seemed slight and insignificant indeed alongside the fabulous assays and bonanza tales. Everyone knew that the Ophir shaft was down hardly 200 feet and its rich ore body was assaying in the thousands per ton—that it was 50 feet wide and getting wider. The other mines on the lode—the Savage, the Mexican, the Gould, and the Curry—were likewise disgorging wealth with every shift. Thus in the frenzied excitement of the moment, Brodigan forgot his Bodie. The melancholy news of his partner's tragic end in the November blizzard dampened his spirit and feelings toward their recent find. The very thought of the place now caused his naturally buoyant and adventurous spirit to wear the buskins of tragedy. It is human nature to back away from a frustrating and bruising experience and to detour from what has been unpleasant. And so Brodigan made his choice in 1860 and went to Virginia City. By May, Brodigan and thousands of other eager miners were swarming over the slopes of Mount Davidson and the adjoining hills around Virgina City. While Bodie, his bright hope of a few months before, presented a picture in stark contrast. Scarcely a dozen men would dig and seek for gold beneath the brooding forms of Bodie Bluff and High Peak. However, all it lacked was the uncanny alchemy of $500 rock and the magic of the $1,000 assay of a discernible ore body to light its fuse to fame and its magic hour. This would take almost seventeen years. During these seventeen years there were short periods of excitement followed by longer periods of gloom that caused almost total abandonment of the mining district. It was some eighteen years later, when the mines of Comstock were nearing depletion and Virginia City was on the downgrade, that Terrance Brodigan returned to Bodie, the camp he had helped to discover. In January, 1878, he bought a lot in downtown Bodie from Peter Wolf and ordered lumber to build a hotel. As a businessmen he lived in Bodie during its heyday and was one of its well-liked and most prominent citizens. (His son, many years later, was secretary of state in Nevada.)

What was doing in Bodie in 1860?

I quote from an interview in the *Daily Bodie Standard* with Joshua Kirlew, May 10, 1880, who first came to Bodie in May, 1860, to prospect for gold:

> BODIE TWENTY YEARS AGO. WHAT A PIONEER MINER KNOWS OF THE EARLY HISTORY OF MONO COUNTY, THE DOG CREEK 'DIGGINS,' A FOUL MURDER, THE FIRST TUNNEL IN BODIE, ETC.
>
> A Standard reporter had a pleasant interview with Mr. Kirlew Sunday afternoon and from this old pioneer learned many interesting facts about the early history of Mono County and of the Bodie District.
>
> Mr. Kirlew, John Anderson, a young man named Oliver, and one or two others left Sacramento with a pack train in the spring of 1859, bound for what was then known as Washoe and Virginia City. The party separated, Kirlew and Oliver going to Mono at Dog Creek on the eastern side of Big Meadows, and came upon a man named Marsh living in a sod hut and prospecting the mouth of the creek. They ascended Dog Creek a few miles prospecting, stopped at the house of a white man who had a Chinese wife. There was a small store at Dog Creek kept by a French woman, a widow. The prospectors then went to the mining town of Monoville on the upper side of Mono Lake, the "diggins" having been discovered in July 1859.
>
> Four miles south of Dog Creek, Lee and Dick Vining [Lee Vining Canyon and the present town of Lee Vining at the junction of route 395 and route 120 are named after Lee Vining], Joshia A. Talbot, Dod's Cross, the Cripple, Ramsey, and all the others from Mariposa and Tuolumne Counties were at that time en-

gaged in mining here. Here Kirlew and Oliver engaged in mining for wages; but when their employer cleaned up he skipped the camp carrying all his dust with him. Meantime, the two companions had located a claim which they considered valuable; but young Oliver became discouraged and exchanged his interest in the claim with Kirlew for the latter's interest in their pack animal, the only property they had left. Kirlew, subsequently, sold the whole of the claim for a jackass, and came to Bodie.

While Kirlew was still in the Mono mines, one day a man named Farnsworth came in on horseback showing a bullet mark in his leggins and said that his partner had been killed by the Indians while crossing the Owens River. The miners doubted the story, but did not suspect Farnsworth of murder. Shortly afterwards, some men came in and reported they found a headless body of a man on an island at the crossing of the Owens River; they also reported the Indians, everywhere, peaceably disposed. Lee Vining observed that Farnsworth's leggins was powder burnt, as though, he, Farnsworth, had fired the shot at close range. These circumstances led the miners to call a meeting and place Farnsworth under guard, and send a committee to the Owens River to investigate the matter. The committee of nine went to an Indian Camp near the scene of the murder and explained the matter to the chief. The latter with a squad of warriors accompanied the committee to where the body had been buried, exhumed it and held an inquest. One of the Indians said that two white men had been encamped on the river about two or three miles above where the body was found. The committee repaired to the camp where they found everything spattered with blood, the latter partially covered with ashes. Leading from the camp to a cliff overhanging the river, they found blood spots on the granite, and that an effort had been made to obliterate these by the use of charcoal. The head of the murdered man with a hatchet wound on the right side was found among some roots at the edge of the river. The committee took the head and started back to Monoville, first dispatching two men posthaste to inform the miners of what they had discovered and tell them to put Farnsworth in irons. The night before these two men reached camp, Farnsworth made a dash for liberty at midnight and escaped in the midst of a furious snow storm. He was never recaptured. The young man, thus so foully murdered, was named Hume, age 23 or 24 years, and had come from San Francisco. Farnsworth met him in Virginia City and represented that he, Farnsworth, had a very rich claim on the Owens River which he would sell for a mere song, inducing Hume to accompany him. The murdered man had with him at the time a fine gold watch and chain, $700.00 in gold and other articles, all of which Farnsworth took. . . .

After selling his claim in Mono, Mr. Kirlew struck out alone for Bodie "Diggins" fifteen miles northeast of Mono where he had heard an old Frenchman was working with a rocker. Reaching Cottonwood Creek, he concluded that it must be the stream on which the Frenchman was at work; but after hunting one day in vain, he concluded to cross over the divide. He reached the divide at six o'clock on the morning of May 12th, 1860 and stopped to watch for the smoke from the Frenchman's cabin. At length, he saw the smoke ascending from an underground stone cabin, situated where the Opera Dance House now stands. The old Frenchman could speak but a few words of English; but gave Kirlew to understand that his name was Lunce and that he was born in Paris and, then, was 67 years of age, and that he was a soldier under the great Napoleon, and bore several scars from the bloody field of Waterloo. On his left arm was tattooed a mounted cannon and on his right, a likeness of a Field Marshall of France in full uniform and drawn sword, with the name of the Marshall below the picture.

Lunce had two hand boxes and a rocker in which to wash dirt. Kirlew joined him, the latter packing the dirt, old Lunce doing the rocking. Their claim was 300 yards south of Bodie Bluff and near a low ridge or divide which runs south from the bluff. They made about three dollars per day in gold, rough and fine. After working two weeks Kirlew took the dust and dull picks and went to Mono where he sold the dust to Pat Hickey for fourteen dollars per ounce in trade and had the picks steeled at Van Patten's blacksmith shop. He stopped two days at Von's restaurant in Mono and then returned to Bodie.

Taylor and Burnett soon afterwards came over from Mono and started the first tunnel just across the low rise or divide nearly opposite the claim of Lunce and Kirlew. Taylor was then, as afterwards, known as "Bodey Taylor," from having been a partner with Bodey, and from having been with the latter when he perished. Taylor and Burnett argued that there must be a rich vein in the ridge from which the gold came, and hence the tunnel. They camped on the flat northwest of the tunnel. They worked until the 8th or 9th of August, when two men came up the canyon on their way to Mono to get men to assist in forming laws for a new Quartz District, 10 or 12 miles down the canyon, at Aurora. They had several men in the new camp, but required nine men to organize the district. Taylor and Burnett went down and participated in the organization of the Aurora District.

> Kirlew continued to work with old Lunce for some time, and would occasionally prospect for quartz, finding some rich looking float rock in the gulch near where the Bodie Tunnel now is. Kirlew took the samples to Mono and had it assayed by an Irishman by the name of Gardner. The return was so large in gold and some silver that Kirlew concluded Gardner was joshing him, and soon afterwards took similar samples to Sacramento where Blake and Walter Company gave still larger assays. He subsequently returned to Bodie and located a large number of quartz claims.
>
> On the first of September, Kirlew left Mono on foot and made his way to Virginia City where he worked a month or so packing water on a jackass for workmen on the Ophir Grade and proceeded to Sacramento by the old Placerville Road. In the spring of 1861, he returned to Aurora and Bodie, since which year he has been drifting about, prospecting and mining at various points from Yuma to Kootenii.

After reading this reminiscence, one cannot but feel that old Josh Kirlew was the embodiment of all the tough, indomitable, optimistic, genial, companionable prospectors of the Old West. Men like him were not turned back by heat or cold, wild Indians, hunger, privations, or personal hardships. They, like him, were in on the birth of all of the fabled rich and roaring camps of the "Early West." If they had one fault, it would probably be their abiding faith that richer diggings with new bonanzas could be staked just over the next range. His failure to stay and develop his good claims cost him again and again fame and fortune. These men were not given to poor-mouth stories and sour grapes. The next rainbow was a beautiful and exciting thing and was positive proof that a pot of gold was theirs for the finding, just waiting to be located at its beckoning end. To these rugged, toiling seekers must go the honors of exploring and opening up the remote regions of the American West for men who followed them.

It might be well to note here that according to W. M. Bunker in his 1879 report on the Esmeralda Mining District, Braly, Corey, and Hicks are credited with arriving in Esmeralda Gulch on August 22, 1860, and along with other men organizing the mining district on August 30. Mr. Kirlew, in his reminiscences, places the visit of the two miners from Aurora as some time around the eighth or ninth of August, 1860. There is admittedly here a discrepancy of two weeks or so; but should some fastidious historian resort to hairsplitting on dates in the old prospector's tale, I feel that it should be remembered he probably kept no written diary with date and events all in order and that his going back over a period of twenty years and being able to place the event within the month that it took place should give the reader nothing but respect for the old pioneer's recall.

The two men who trudged twelve miles up the canyon to Bodey's "Diggins" to recruit miners to help organize the just-discovered Esmeralda District were the first harbingers of a new gold strike that for a time almost totally eclipsed Bodey (as it was spelled in 1860). However, the rapid rise of Esmeralda District and Aurora, which became the county seat of Mono County, California (boundaries of California and Utah Territory were but vaguely defined in 1860), brought mining capital, a population of several thousands, and the pulsating economy of a booming mining camp to within a short horseback ride of Bodey's Bluff.

The eye-blinking pace with which the Esmeralda District soared to prominence can best be attested to by the fact that James Braly, J. M. Corey, and E. R. Hicks discovered the district in the late summer of 1860. In March, 1861, S. M. Culiver and Company of San Francisco shipped the first quartz mill to Aurora in the Esmeralda District. This pioneer mill was of 8-stamp capacity and powered by a 14-horsepower steam engine and was erected by Edmond Green; but some ten months later we read in the January 11, 1862, issue of the *Mining and Scientific Press*: "Aurora is the county seat of Mono County . . . there are now ten or twelve fireproof buildings, seven quartz mills in operation, and four more building . . . turning out about $4,000 per day in bullion."

Mr. W. M. Bunker in his 1879 report states: "In the fall of 1862, the Wide West Bonanza ore shute on Last Chance Hill was tapped. This fanned the Esmeralda excitement into a bright flame."

Mark Twain, who was rusticating in Aurora at the time, vividly describes the event:

> Wide West had struck it rich! Everybody went down to see the new developments, and some days there was such a crowd of people about the Wide West shaft that a stranger would have supposed there was a mass meeting in session there. No other topic was discussed but the rich strike. Nobody thought or dreamed about anything else. Every man brought away a specimen, ground it up in a hand-mortar, washed it out in his horn spoon, and glared speechless upon the marvelous result. . . . The Wide West Company put a stop to the carrying away of "specimens," and well they might, for every handful of the ore was worth a sum of some consequence. To show the exceeding value of the ore, I will remark that a sixteen-hundred-pound parcel of it was sold, just as it lay, at the mouth of the shaft, at one dollar a pound; and the man who bought it "packed" it on mules a hundred and fifty or two hundred miles, over the mountains, to San Francisco, satisfied that it would yield at a rate that would richly compensate him for his trouble.

This and many other amusing and vividly told happenings of life in the Esmeralda Mining District as well as Mono Lake are described by Mark Twain in his book *Roughing It.*

The vicissitudes of living in Aurora as this mining camp came bursting out of its swaddling clothes were many. Mark Twain and his cabin chums were long on mirth and hope and speculation but short on capital. There was an agreeable flow of spirits from day to day, but when some of their wildcat mining stock failed to pan out, living was at times precarious and hand to mouth.

Bob Howland, a friend and cabin mate of Mark Twain, said that at one time when they were living on short rations, Mark came home one night with five or six dozen empty cans in a gunny sack which he emptied expansively in studied disarray out the door. When Bob asked him what he was about, he replied that the passers seeing the array of empty oyster and fruit and jelly containers would have eye-filling proof that they were living just as well as anybody else in camp, if the empty cans counted for anything.

Incidentally, it is to Robert M. Howland that history is indebted for adopting the spelling "Bodie," as it has now been for 110 years. Judge J. G. McClinton,[1] who came to Aurora in 1860 on the heels of its discovery and was later a Nevada state senator and presiding judge in the Eighth District, and one of the earliest men to own and develop claims in Bodie and Aurora in the 1860's and well known for his knowledge, his veracity being unquestioned by the pioneers of both camps, described how the spelling was changed: "The way in which the orthography of Bodey's name came to be changed as applied to the district was as follows. In 1860, Professor J. E. Clayton and the Hasslet brothers, Ben and John, located the Bodey Ranch between here [Bodie] and Aurora. They cut the natural growth of grass and packed it to Aurora, then a thriving young place, and built a small log stable. Then they gave a verbal order for a sign, "BODEY STABLE"; but the painter for an eye to the beautiful, which I highly commend, executed it "BODIE STABLE"—and the word looked so much better in that form that the people soon adopted that style of spelling it. I am not now certain to whom we are indebted for the orthographical improvement, but I think it was Robert M. Howland who is now in Bodie, and at any rate, Bob was the first sign painter I remember having seen in Aurora."

In doing research on the early history of Bodie I was privileged one sharp, clear, beautiful spring day in 1937 to have the opportunity to interview two old-timers who had lived in Bodie in its heyday. One was John Parr, whom my father first met in the spring of 1876 when John and Tom Parr, Horace Marden, and others under the direction of Warren Rose and H. M. Yerington, who had bought the 16-stamp brick mill and mines of the defunct Empire Gold and Silver Mining Company, came to Bodie to refit the mill and put it in operation. I visited with Mr. and Mrs. John Parr at their home in Piedmont, California. Both were in their eighties, alert and active. The talk ranged over the early days of Bodie when they lived there, during its heyday. Mr. Parr affirmed that Bob Howland was the man who changed the spelling of Bodey's name in lettering it for a stable in the early days of Aurora.

Later that day it was my good fortune to be with W. H.

Metson at his office in the Balboa Building in San Francisco. "Billy" Metson, as he was known far and wide, from Bodie to Nome, for his sagacious ability in mining law, supplied me with many facts and anecdotes and history of the early days in Bodie. Metson arrived in Bodie on July 10, 1880, a young lad fresh out of high school where he had graduated with honors—to take up his duties as a law clerk for "Pat" Reddy, Bodie's leading attorney. Metson said Pat Reddy knew Bob Howland in Aurora in the early 1860's and often declared that he was the man who publicly changed the spelling of Bodey's name.

By early spring of 1863 we learn the current news of Bodie's development in the *Mining and Scientific Press* of Monday, February 16. The Esmeralda correspondent in a letter of February 9, 1863, writes:

> Bodie District is the greatest excitement of the day, assays from $50.00 to $400.00. . . . A new town has been surveyed and lots are held at high figures. . . . Several new houses are being built. This new mining district which has come into special notice in the last two or three weeks past is located about ten miles south of Aurora City, Esmeralda. . . . The locality was first discovered by some Frenchmen as early, we believe, as the summer of 1858. It was worked as a placer "diggins" until the summer of 1860 when some of the disappointed adventurers to Washoe turned their steps southward and prospected along the base of the eastern slope until they reached Esmeralda where they made a halt. From this place a small party went still further west until they encountered the Frenchmen above with their rockers washing the golden sands from the limited placers of what thereafter was known as the Bodie "Diggins." The newcomers discovered gold and silver bearing rock which led at once to considerable prospecting and some mining machinery was brought in during this early period, although there was an almost total lack of roads. Matters were thus allowed to rest until sometime last fall, when a company made up chiefly of San Francisco and Sacramento capitalists recommenced operations. There were such flattering indications, that a consolidation of some eleven companies was made into one incorporated body in the name and style of the Bodie Bluff Consolidated Mining Company with Governor Stanford as president and F. K. Bechtel, Esq., as secretary. Their operations this far have met with the most encouraging results.

> About the middle of last month, the town of Aurora was all excited with gold stories from Bodie's mines and everybody went out to see the rich strike that had been made, and came back fully satisfied that it was a good thing there for somebody. Favored by the unusual mildness of the winter, the company has been able to push on its operations with an unusual degree of vigor. . . . About two weeks since, Mr. T. J. Hubbard, superintendent of the consolidation of the company, has been able to push on its operation vigorously. According to the Aurora Star of January 31, Mr. T. J. Hubbard came into town with about ten pounds of some very rich ore from the company's New Mexico Shaft. . . . This vein has been opened to a depth of 80 feet and exhibits a character of most unquestioned richness. The vein is six feet wide. The tunnels are being run into the Isabella and others of the company's veins which are most promising in their indications. . . . There are two other consolidation companies in the district in active operation. Mills will, doubtless, be put into operation there. The nearest mills in present operation are nearly six miles distant from Bodie on the road to Aurora.

The Bodie District was visited in the summer of 1864 by one of the most distinguished scientists and respected mining geologists in the world, Benjamin Sillman, professor of general and applied chemistry at Yale. Professor Sillman camped in the vicinity of Bodie Bluff and High Peak. He based his Empire Report on his examination of the Bodie District. On the strength of this report "a group of New York capitalists organized the Empire Gold and Silver Mining Company, with a reported working capital of $1,000,000."[2]

The Mining and Scientific Press of August 27, 1864, reported that the mines of the Bodie Bluff Consolidated had been purchased by a New York company and that they planned to develop the property and erect a mill.

The Empire Gold and Silver Mining Company's head office was in New York City; but the management of their affairs in Bodie was placed in the hands of Howard and Sanchez, bankers of Aurora, and under the management of Dr. J. L. Howard, who awarded the job of planning and constructing Bodie's first stamp mill to B. O. Cutter of San Francisco.

This mill was erected at the base of the northeastern slope of Bodie Bluff, about one mile down Bodie Canyon from where the town of Bodie now stands. In 1876–77, when the camp under the impact of rich ore discoveries began its great resurgence, this mill was renamed the Syndicate Mill. The stone foundations and bricks from its walls can still be seen lying in tumbled disarray at the sage-carpeted base of Bodie Bluff.

At the very time the plans and foundations for this mill were being designed the gold-mining West was but dimly aware that three frightful years had been peeled from the Great Decade. Her citizens, for the most part, reveled in plans that bore a hazy golden hue. Almost everyone had a nodding acquaintance with men who had struck it rich. And so the striving went on. Within the nation, but a broad continent away, a bitter striving of another kind was coming to a crashing finale. The Southern Confederacy was only a shell—three years of cruel war had destroyed thousands of her best men, and the élan of her gallant armies had been tossed on the tide of failure. The closing days of 1864 saw the South split in two by Sherman's ruthless march to the sea, where he outmaneuvered the daredevil and impetuous Hood, smashing his ill-led army and driving it into Atlanta. The backbone of the Confederacy was broken, never to recover. Her armies and her people's hopes were gone with the wind.

With the passing of winter the Empire Company moved as fast as the rutted and bridgeless roads would allow. High-wheeled freight wagons groaning with heavy loads of machinery, boilers, timbers, and thousands of bright-red brick from Aurora geed and hawed up Bodie Canyon to wearily unload their freight at the northern base of Bodie Bluff. Freight charges were ten cents per pound; but to the eager profit-bent New York investors, who had scanned Professor Sillman's report and heard his often-stated opinion, "Outside of the Comstock, there is no mining district in California or Nevada known to me which embraces so many elements of a great future as Bodie,"[3] freight at ten cents per pound and other costs equally high seemed a trivial thing if they were on the trail of another Comstock.

Quick profits they expected, so their mill had to be built and running in the shortest possible time.

By June, 1865, T. Cronin, who held the contract, had his bricklayers and stone setters toiling at putting up a solidly built, imposing brick building with high arch windows and doors in a modified Gothic style. The mill had sixteen stamps, eight wheeler pans, three settlers, shaking tables, and a continuation of riffles and sluices. It was powered with a 35-horsepower steam engine and had a tubular boiler. It was a copy of the Antelope Mill, one of Aurora's finest.

The *Mining and Scientific Press* of September 23, 1865, in describing the completion of the new Empire Mill at Bodie, stated that ". . . the first movement of a quartz mill in the Bodie District was made by this one on the sixth instant by setting the stamps to work, and on the thirteenth instant by moving her entire machinery which now is steadily running."

Besides the Empire Gold and Silver Mining Company, there were several other consolidations active in Bodie in 1865 trying to develop their properties. The Homestake and Cornwall consolidation was situated on the southwest slope on High Peak. The San Antonio claim was just north of the Empire Company, and here Judge F. K. Bechtel had a horse whim, one of the few crude hoisting machines in the camp. Most of the shafts were a hand-windlass and bucket-hoisting operation. The Bunker Hill Company, whose shaft was down 180 feet, was located on the southeastern side of Bodie Bluff and High Peak (later the Standard Mine). The High Peak and Tunnel Company was located on the west side of the Hill.

John W. Biedeman (for whom Mount Biedeman, located about five miles southwest of Bodie, is named) was one of the principal owners of the Homestake Company. The second mill in Bodie was built by Homestake. It was a 12-stamp plant, powered with a 30-horsepower steam engine and was located near the base of the southwest slope of High Peak, almost adjoining the present site of the Standard Mill. This mill first began crushing ore on December 27, 1865.

In September, 1864, Bodie was visited by a famous traveler and journalist, J. Ross Browne. He spent three days touring the Bodie mines and then journeyed on to investigate the "Dead Sea of the West" (Mono Lake). His experiences and adventures on this trip appeared in the *Harper's New Monthly Magazine* (Vol. XXXI) in 1865. He made the trip to Bodie in company with Judge F. K. Bechtel, and his vivid description of the road leading up the canyon from Aurora would do justice to any travelogue:

> On a fine morning in September, we set forth on our expedition. The rugged cliffs along the road cropped out at every turn like grim old castles of feudal times; and there were frowning fortresses of solid rock that seemed ready to belch forth murderous streams of fire on any enemy that might approach. . . . Some eight or nine miles from Aurora, we reached the base of the conical hill surmounted by a range of reddish colored cliffs, very rough, jagged, and picturesque, a capital-looking place for a den of robbers, or a gold mine. This was the famous Bodie Bluff. The entire hill as well as the surrounding country is destitute of vegetation with the exception of sage brush and bunch grass. . . . In the undeveloped conditions of the mines which are yet but partially opened, much is left to conjecture. . . . One of these was the San Antonio, a mine in which the Judge held an interest in connection with a worthy Norwegian by the name of Jensen. As I had traveled in Norway, Jensen was enthusiastic in his devotion to my enjoyment, declaring he would go down himself with me and show me everything worth seeing, even to the lower levels, just opened. While I was attempting to frame an excuse, the honest Norwegian had lit a couple of candles and given direction to one of the boys to look out for the old blind horse attached to the whim, and now stood ready at the mouth of the shaft to guide me into the subterranean regions.
>
> I descended several of these shafts rather to oblige my friend, the Judge, than to satisfy my own curiosity. This thing of being brought down 200 feet into the bowels of the earth in a wooden bucket and hoisted out by blind horses attached to whims may be amusing to read about; but I have enjoyed pleasanter modes of transportation. I am astonished that every hair of my head is not quite gray. I penetrated more shafts in the earth, was dragged through more dangerous pits and holes in wooden buckets, was forced to creep over more slippery ledges rich

in mineral deposits, and to climb upon a greater number of rickety ladders than I would not like to undertake again for less than a 1000 shares in the Empire Gold and Silver Mining Company. Mining was crude and primitive in those beginning days of Bodie; but, nevertheless, hope and enthusiasm were high, and real estate was "boomin'."

Bodie had some 15 or 20 frame and adobe houses, and a boarding house. Lots and streets were laid out by means of stakes, and new houses were springing up in every direction. Speculation in real estate was quite the fashion. It was amusing to witness the enthusiasm with which the citizens went into the business of trading in lots. Groups of speculators were constantly engaged in examining choice locations and descanting upon the brilliant future of the embryo city. A pair of boots, I suppose, would have secured the right to a tolerably good lot; but having only one pair and that pretty well worn, I did not venture upon an investment. . . . Some of the city's dignitaries, however, duly impressed with the importance of having a view of their town appear in the illuminating pages of Harpers, paid me the compliment to attach my name to the principal street and thus in future ages I confidently expect my memory will be rescued from oblivion.

Alas, for the transitory memory and short-lived enthusiasm of the early city fathers of Bodie! I, who am a second-generation Bodieite, must sadly admit that no street map of Bodie bears the name of that illustrious journalist.

The last day of Mr. Browne's stay in Bodie was a Sunday on which he attended the prime spectator sport of the day—a badger fight.

In the beginning of 1866 the Empire Mill found that their crushing capacity was limited to about ten tons per day, just about all the 8-wheeler pans could accumulate; and plans were made to put in more pans to try and increase the tonnage to 30 tons per day. In January of 1866, John S. Mayhugh, an Aurora correspondent of the *Mining and Scientific Press,* gave the bullion shipments of the Empire Mill at about $12,000 to $15,000 per month, all of their ore being mined from the company's Osceola ledge. By April of that year the superintendent of the Empire had gone on record that new and better milling practices had been put into effect and that he expected to be able to double the amount of bullion shipped to the New York office by May. It is a known fact that he was unable to make good on this commitment. The Empire Gold and Silver Mining Company failed in 1867. It is not difficult to understand that ten tons per day of $40 rock, with mining and milling costs of $10 per ton, would produce sour stomachs for New York investors who expected a quick return with big dividends. In the spring of '65 some very rich streaks of ore had been found in the company's New Mexico claim—just enough to give the investors gold fever; but no substantial tonnage of rich ore was developed in the Bodie mines during this early period, and for the most part, both the Empire and Homestake, Bodie's only two stamp mills, had to subsist on a steady diet of poor rock. As a consequence both these early enterprises ended in failure. The Empire Company shut down all their operations and retained only a watchman where in the spring of 1865 as many as seventy men had been employed.

On June 10, 1868, the *Aurora Union* reported that Governor Blasdel of Nevada was in Aurora on business and that he had purchased the Homestake Mill and Mine at Bodie. He put his son in charge of refitting the mill and carrying out plans to sink the mine shaft 100 feet to develop additional ore; but this effort fizzled out and the Governor subsequently, in disgust, moved his mill out of Bodie.

And so Bodie, for a time, faded into the limbo of forgotten mining camps. For the most part, the place after 1869 was looked upon by most mining men as a dud—a firecracker that didn't go off. Mining capital that once eagerly poured in hard cash for brick mills and the latest in mining machinery abandoned the place as a blotched abortion, their plans for fortune gone like fleecy vapor.

CHAPTER III

Rags to Riches

Mining reached a low ebb in Mono County by 1868. Hardly more than a score of miners were to be found in Bodie. The Esmeralda District's boom had run its course. The rich surface diggings of 200 to 300 feet had been exhausted, and some of the deeper mines had encountered a heavy flow of water which the pumps of that day were unable to handle. The once bustling town of Aurora presented a gloomy spectacle of disappointment and failure. Most of its mines were closed and its mills silent. The *Mining and Scientific Press* of October 17, 1868, stated that the *Aurora Union* in a self-obituary had discontinued publication, its editors sadly announcing, "for the present and, perhaps, forever."

In Bodie three or four little die-hard partnerships struggled on for two or three years. Mooney and Company, who included a working partnership of Walker, Peter Essington, and Lewis Lockberg, mined ore from their claims and hauled it with bull teams over a road that was not much more than a glorified trail to a big water-powered Mexican arastra on Rough Creek. This crude, primitive stone attrition-mill was simple to construct and operate but possessed the drawback of limited capacity. About 1½ to 3 tons a day was its maximum production and the efficiency of its recovery left much to be desired. On rich ore it could be made to pay, but on low-grade ore it was a losing proposition. Another severe limitation on the Rough Creek arastras was their location. The long, hard winters made their milling season short. Abundant proof of this is stated by Dan Olson, who reported in mid-May of 1868 that he and his partner had about eight tons of rich ore mined from their claim at Bodie, "but, owing to the deep snow and mud on the road leading to the company's Arastra on Rough Creek, they have not had a crushing yet."[1] Besides the long winter, the milling season was frequently curtailed by the water supply falling off badly by the middle of September, ending the supply of turning power to the arastra's grinding stones. In addition to Mooney and Company, and Dan Olson and his partner, Kernohan, there were the Swenson brothers, another bunch of hard-rock Swedes who had also put together a water-powered arastra in Rough Creek. This outfit stubbornly dug on in Bodie for a few years before calling it quits. As time went on, Mooney and Walker decided that they had had enough of lean years and hard work, so they pulled out and left the struggle to Essington and Lockberg.

When the Empire Gold and Silver Mining Company closed all their Bodie operations, they installed "Uncle Billy" O'Hara as the caretaker of their mill and mines. O'Hara was a fabulous character, an American Negro who as a boy and then as a young man worked in various capacities on steamboats that plied the Mississippi River, "when New Orleans was the liveliest, gayest, and wickedest city in the U.S. . . . Those flush days when the American public travelled, drank, gambled, talked politics, and traded 'niggers' in the brilliantly lighted and gorgeously furnished salons that floated on the bosom of the 'Father of Waters.' "[2] It was during this time that Uncle Billy fell in with William C. Ralston, the energetic captain of a cotton boat, and became his steward. When the news of the discovery of gold in California swept through New Orleans, enchanting the high and the low of Dixieland adventurers, many of her solid citizens saw a dazzling opportunity to reap a golden harvest out of the California trade. Among them was William C. Ralston. He left New Orleans and river boating, and with his devoted and resourceful factotum, Uncle Billy, set sail for Panama. After an uneventful voyage they landed at Chagres on the isthmus and then took the jungle trail overland to Panama. On arriving in Panama, Ralston found that two of his old friends, Garrison and Fretz (both former riverboat skippers), had started a banking business and were setting up a transportation company. Knowing Ralston's energy and ability, they persuaded him to join them for a time. But when the captain of their newly acquired steamer, the

New Orleans, died of cholera just before sailing time on September 1, 1851, Garrison and Fretz installed their youthful junior partner, Ralston, as the master. He came aboard with his steward, Uncle Billy. Much to the relief of the impatient passengers, the departure was made on time.

Nineteen days later, about midday, a lazy plume of smoke crawled over the horizon, and soon the San Francisco waterfront people learned that the *New Orleans* was coming through the Golden Gate. Of the 204 passengers aboard the stubby little paddle-wheel steamer, none would have greater impact upon the history of California and the West than her captain, Billy Ralston. He would become president of the Bank of California, for a time the most powerful banking institution of the West, and one of the "king-makers" of the Comstock, and the builder of San Francisco's $6,000,000 Palace Hotel. Standing by his side was his genial dusky steward, Billy O'Hara, who would one day figure mightily in Bodie's early development.

Twelve days later, on October 1, Billy O'Hara made his big decision—Ralston sailed for Panama with the *New Orleans,* but his faithful friend and steward of many years struck out on his own, and headed for Columbia in Tuolumne County to try his luck. For a time he tried placer mining, but finally turned to the restaurant business.

"The oldtimers of that section remembered 'Uncle Billy' and his wife for their kindness to the sick."[3] After his wife died he came across the mountains to Aurora in 1863. This mining camp was then in the height of its glory, with an estimated population of more than 10,000 and fourteen busy stamp mills. On arriving in Aurora, Uncle Billy took over the management of the dining room of the Exchange Hotel, an imposing new brick hostelry. He stayed in Aurora in this capacity until the Empire Gold and Silver Mining Company hired him to go to Bodie in 1865 to take charge of their boardinghouse. Here he soon developed a fervent belief in the camp's destiny. That faith burned with an unflickering flame. When the camp was virtually abandoned as a mining district in the gloomy years of 1869 to 1876, Uncle Billy stayed on and gave assistance and encouragement to all who would try. He lived to see the camp at the peak of its glory. When he died in 1880, he was eulogized in Bodie's papers as the "Foster Father" of Bodie.[4]

After Governor Blasdel moved his mill out of Bodie, the camp was almost depopulated. Hope and confidence had all but disappeared; even the hard-rock Swedes left for Virginia City and other camps; however, Uncle Billy's faith in Bodie remained unshakable, and so this doughty African stayed on through the gloomy, lonesome years. He had lent some money to the owners of the Bunker Hill claim (the Standard Mine), and when they pulled out and left without paying, he was forced to take the property for the debt. He refused to give up even when the New York experts pronounced the property worthless. Finally Peter Essington and Lewis Lockberg (former partners in Mooney and Company's operations in 1868) returned to Bodie.

Uncle Billy persuaded them, once again, to try their fortunes in the Bodie Bluff mines. He sold them the Bunker Hill claim for $8,000, the money to be paid when taken out. "The new purchasers went to work and sunk a shaft, 120 feet deep, without striking anything. They were about ready to give up in disgust when one night a cave-in in the shaft exposed the rich ore body that has since made the Standard Mine famous."[5] In the next two years they paid Uncle Billy, and then mined and milled about $35,000 in their reconstructed Rough Creek arastra.

George Storey, who had heard of the new find of rich ore in the Bodie district, arrived in 1876. He persuaded Essington and Lockberg to sell out to the San Francisco capitalists he represented, namely Seth and Dan Cook, Colonel J. F. Boyd, William M. Lent, and Colonel Charles W. Tozer. Storey obtained a $10,000 commission for swinging the deal. Essington and Lockberg were paid something in excess of $65,000 for their interest.

In consummating the deal, the Cook brothers and William Lent dispatched John F. Boyd in September, 1876, to Bodie to double-check the glowing report on the Bunker Hill riches that George Storey had painted. (They all had melancholy memories of the great diamond-mine hoax that four short years before fooled some of San Francisco's sharpest speculators. None other than William C. Ralston, along with William Lent, and John Boyd, and a score of other prominent businessmen had been taken in by a glittering tale and forty acres of western desert liberally salted with worthless South African reject "niggerhead" diamonds. Lent had the unpleasant memories of being president of this fiasco.)[6] However, Boyd's thorough and painstaking examination confirmed the fact that they had in the Bunker Hill a good mine with a rich ore body. The Cook brothers, Boyd, Lent, and associates incorporated the Standard Mining Company and began operations immediately. Work was pushed forward on timbering and installing steam hoisting machinery. To Malter Linde and Company of San Francisco was entrusted the construction of their new 20-stamp mill, which began crushing Standard ore in July 1877. Prior to this, from fall of 1876 until July 1877, the Standard Company milled all their ore in the Syndicate Mill on the north side of Bodie Bluff.[7] Almost 10,000 tons of rich ore was handled during this period, and from the profit of this milling, the Standard Company equipped their mine and built their mill.[8] Exactly twelve months after purchasing the Bunker Hill claim, the Standard Company paid their first dividend of $50,000. This amount was paid every month for thirty consecutive months until March, 1880, when it was raised to $75,000 per month.

The year 1876 saw California's centennial celebration of the founding of the city by the Golden Gate, and the beginning of Bodie's resurgence. One hundred years had passed since a detachment of Spanish soldiers under Lieutenant Don Jose Joaquin Moraga and Father Palou had founded the Presidio and Mission of San Francisco, and only seven short years since the historic final rail was laid and the golden spike driven at Promontory Point linking with shining ribbons of steel an overland railroad from California's Golden Gate to the great cities on the Atlantic seaboard. In just one century thirteen small colonies clinging to the Atlantic shore and a tiny outpost of a Spanish king had soared to the estate of a great nation. In the summer of the centennial year of 1876, of the original founding party of Lieutenant Moraga and Father Palou, none remained; but of the historic enterprise, so dramatically completed at Promontory Point only seven years before, hundreds were to be found scattered throughout the length and breadth of the West. These hardy pioneer construction men, made of whalebone and catgut, had entered into the surging western economy of mining, business, and agriculture which was rolling on with bustling vigor.

In that summer of 1876, Ed Loose came to Bodie to be with his older brother, Warren. Ed was one of those rugged young knights of hardship, sweat, and toil. He and Warren, along with their brother, Will, had won their spurs to manhood in the historic project that culminated at Promontory Point.

Bodie at that time was a tiny camp of hardly more than twoscore persons, but it was a seething little hamlet of excitement and rumor. It was bandied about that the Bunker Hill, the only claim in camp with a known substantial body of rich ore, had been sold to San Francisco capitalists; that they were making arrangement with H. M. Yerington to refit the old Empire Mill (renamed the Syndicate) to crush their ore; and that they planned to build a new 20-stamp mill. Rumor followed on rumor.

So it was that young Ed Loose, all six feet and two hundred pounds of ambition fired with the camp's enthusiasm, proceeded to locate a claim adjoining the Bunker Hill on its southwestern line. He called it The Bodie.

The new owners of the Bunker Hill, after organizing the Standard Company, pushed the underground development of their new property by sinking a shaft and running several drifts and crosscuts to explore the valuable veins of rich gold-bearing quartz that every shift was exposing. They uncovered riches so great in one part of the mine that it was named the "treasure house." Samples from this section assayed $6,000 per ton. It didn't take the Standard management long, after analyzing the dip and strike of their rich ore bodies, to reach a firm conclusion that these riches would extend into Ed Loose's claim, which adjoined their southwest line. Their first move was to question the validity of his location, and then to scare him into giving up his ground; but Ed didn't scare easy. His answer was to call for reinforcements. He took in his brother, Warren, as a partner. Warren wrote to their athletically renowned brother, William, in Utah. Will arrived in Bodie in May, 1877, to round out a tough, determined triumvirate.

For the story of how it was in Bodie in that summer, and of the early beginning of the famous Bodie Mine, and of the typical power plays launched to somehow gain control of this valuable ground, I quote from the colorful diary of Eliza de Luce (Mrs. William A. Loose):

> Will's arrival was heralded with great joy. He went, with the welcoming party, the rounds of the saloons and was greeted in true Western fashion, glass in hand. This greeting was not by his brothers or by their intimate friends but by a certain froth floating on the surface of the fortune hunting and amusement hunting population. They had heard that Will could outrun, out-wrestle, out-ride any athlete; and could out-shoot for accuracy and quickness any of the crack shots. So, they thought they were due to see sport . . . in its most deadly aspect; for all had heard that Bill Lent, a part owner of the Standard Mine, was sending some San Francisco "Badmen" up to Bodie to run the three brothers out of town. So, the fun-loving population wanted to be in on the show. Applause and drinks were plentiful. . . .
>
> Warren and Edwin rescued Will from the admiring mob, as soon as possible, and took him out of the bright lights of the saloons, 500 feet up the hill above the town to their mine. . . . On arriving, Warren lit a lantern which disclosed their layout. Then he explained to Will, "I knew that you couldn't understand it. It's this way: Everybody knew that Ed located The Bodie and that the Standard Company was mad about it, and that they ordered us off, and sent up a gunman named Burkhart to make us go. He brought several bums with him and told us that he would give us 24 hours to leave camp. Then the boys in the saloons organized and sent word to Burkhart that he'd better leave camp himself. That night, they went around in a crowd shouting, 'Where is Burkhart? We want Burkhart!' So, Burkhart did leave camp and went to San Francisco and reported his failure. Burkhart reported that he had left Bodie because he was only one against a thousand; but that he would go back and give that mob all they wanted, if the Standard Company would give

him five men and deputy sheriff's badges. . . . A disgusted Lent cut short the bully's whining report with, 'Well, Mr. Burkhart, we thought you said that you wouldn't need any help, that you would have the situation well in hand in 24 hours. We don't care to go into a real war or pay an army. . . .' Burkhart was shown the door. . . .

"We were anxious to get a good depth to our shaft, so, we worked several shifts for a while. We sent for you to come and help us. That news was seized upon to indicate that you were a fighter. Just today we heard that the company was sending up three well-known gunmen from San Francisco who had contracted for the sum of $15,000 to run us out of Bodie. When you came in on the stage, the news spread like wildfire that you were our answer to the company's threat. We were going to bring you here on the hill when you first came in; but, O'Shaughnessy and others who were helping us said, 'No! Let the lads have a look at him.' So–O'Shaughnessy passed out some cards with your records. Everything you did pleased them, even to throwing your whiskey over your shoulder. He told them that you had saved 20 lives in the floods in Eureka last year. They saw that you wouldn't get drunk with any man when you tossed off your whiskey. The card read that you were 6′2″ in your stocking feet, weight–175 lbs., had put 90 out of 100 shots in the bullseye consecutively. . . . O'Shaughnessy had the word passed along that you didn't know anything about the card." . . . At this point Will asked, "What is that pile of lumber for out there on the dump?" "Oh, that's to build a fort with. It's all planned and worked out here on this drawing, and we had hoped to get started on it by tomorrow." . . . Will urged, "Why not build it tonight?"

So with the comfortable allies of darkness and a small storm lantern, three determined young men dug, hammered, and hustled together a frontier-type defensive works—a crudely built parapet that bristled around their windlass, shaft, and one-room shelter.

And, when morning dawned, the inside walls of the fort were complete. The outer wall was breast high and three men were shoveling rock and soil into the space between the walls. This space was two feet wide and was planned to turn bullets by being filled with rock and gravel . . . the getting of this shaft down to find the ore in place was a difficult task. It was well known, mostly by the reports of miners, that the Standard Company was working and taking out rich ore on the 200-foot level which was on the ground located by brother Edwin, as The Bodie Mine. Of course, if and when Edwin proved all of his points legal, then he could sue the Standard for the amount of ore taken out of the Bodie ground.

My husband, Will, was far from explaining to me all the difficulties that they faced in the effort to protect their location and to get some of the wealth from the earth on Bodie Hill and in The Bodie ground, the wealth that they knew was there.

As the long summer days wore on, the brothers toiled determinedly inside the walls of their little redoubt, sinking their shaft and at the same time keeping a wary eye peeled for "Kanky" Jim, "Bat" Murphy, and "Smokey" Jones, the San Francisco thugs who had arrived in Bodie openly boasting of how they would dispose of the Loose boys.

In July the brothers were sinking their shaft. Will was sixty feet down, mucking out a round. Warren was on the surface manning the windlass. His attention was momentarily distracted by the arrival of the friendly O'Connor family from Aurora. Somehow the windlass bar slipped, sending the loaded bucket of rock crashing back down the shaft as it unreeled. To save his brother from being crushed in the shaft, Warren threw himself head and shoulders under the flagellating iron of the windlass handle, stopping the bucket. The rain of blows on his head and shoulders knocked him senseless, probably causing a severe concussion. The O'Connors took him back to Aurora with them, where he could be treated by the skillful hands of old "Doc" Sinclair.

This accident curtailed the mining operations in the Bodie claim; but the struggle to hold the ground went on, and it had its humorous moments as chronicled by Eliza de Luce.

Will was getting his breakfast when he noticed three men about halfway up the hill. . . . They were in plain sight, and they had some kind of a contraption that they were carrying around. They were not near the tracks of the wagon road, but off to the south of the road. Will decided to see just what those men were doing carrying that thing around. He took his field glasses first; but he didn't bring up either man or contraption so that he could recognize them. . . . "A light cannon might be mounted on a wooden frame, and might be more accurate than a heavy piece held in a man's hand." So, Will decided to take a shot at the contraption. He raised the rifle, and sighted carefully a little inside of a sure hit, and pulled the trigger. He saw a cloud of dust. The contraption was thrown down the hill several yards and landed broadside. Three men were scattering wide apart and rolling and scrambling on hands and knees down the hill. . . . Nothing more happened, so he ate his breakfast and ruminated on what might happen if it was a real war. For his part he did not like it. "Why did he shoot at a contraption? The bullet might have ricocheted and hurt somebody whose name didn't happen to be 'Kanky' Jim, 'Bat,' or 'Smokey.' " . . . What had he shot at? A contraption of some ignorant, stupid person? Of course, no culprit would get in the way. "What would people think of his indiscriminate shooting? Of course, it might be only a ruse to get close to The Bodie ground, and then overwhelm the watcher." No matter, Will was immensely dissatisfied over the outlook. Then up drove a buggy. Edwin and O'Shaughnessy were there to say, "Howdy do," and console him for so much solitude and tell him the news. Bill Lent had arrived in Bodie to look over the Standard Mine and its machinery . . . and he didn't mention the three brothers with The Bodie claim, or the set of hoodlum bullies that he had sent up from San Francisco to drive out any adverse claimants. . . . O'Shaughnessy and Edwin seemed to think that Lent had come from San Francisco on purpose to settle the issue of The Bodie Mine. . . .

Then Will told them of taking a shot at some queer looking chaps that were wandering around the side of the hill, and that he did not shoot at them, only short of them; that they had a contraption with them, and that they knocked it over and fell down three or four times before getting on their feet to run. Ed and O'Shaughnessy laughed and said, "They'd heard about it, and 'Kanky' Jim was one of the three. . . . The contraption was a surveyor's tripod and transit that he had shot at. . . . Someone, who wanted to locate a claim on the side of The Bodie, offered $500 to a surveyor to locate the corners. Those men with the transit had started up the hill to survey out another claim, when Will espied them and took a shot at the contraption, causing an ignominious stampede. There were a lot of people well concealed, watching the results. If it had been safe for that bunch of men to advance on to the forbidden ground, then a swarm of men and claim hunters would have been there." Will said, "I was doubtful of the wisdom in shooting at a contraption not knowing who backed it and what business they had in coming; but now I see it was all right." Edwin said, "All right? I should say it was. It was the wisest thing you ever did. This hill would be swarming with men and they would be locating all over The Bodie, crossways, cornerways, and every which way. We heard that Lent called 'Kanky' Jim and his two fellow outlaws into his office and said to them, 'I thought that when I saw you fellows in San Francisco you weren't afraid of a "buzzsaw." There's just one man up at that claim on the hill. I'll give you fellows $5,000 if you'll just walk up there now in broad daylight. That man on the hill don't know you, don't know you're coming; but I'll just bet $5,000 that you dare not go up there.' 'Kanky' said, 'I don't know that I want to be sent up against a dead shot in broad daylight. I wouldn't mind going up tonight.' 'Tonight, nothing,' said Lent. 'It's now or never. Get out! I don't want no truck with assassins nor cowards. Get out of my sight.' "

O'Shaughnessy said, "In fifteen minutes we heard all about the interview; so, we feel sure a settlement is in the making. We came up on purpose to tell you what a fine thing you had done, driving those petty pirates off the ground. It'll be hard to hire surveyors now for a job of locating corners. The price is too high." Then the three laughed–a shouting laugh–"and I hope it will stay high 'til this thing is settled. You are the boy that will keep the price up." Then they shook hands, and congratulated each other and Will on the end that they said was now in sight. . . .

Lent walked around the Standard, was taken down a shaft by his own engineers and shift bosses. Then he had a meeting with O'Shaughnessy and Edwin. Finally the lawyer was called in, to draw up a very tight paper, to sell all of their right, title, and interest in The Bodie mine, and any other ground claimed by them in the Bodie Mining District. They were to remove their fort at once and all of their personal belongings. This paper awaited only the signing and the payment of money.

Word of the settlement was sent to Warren who came in the next day on the stage from Aurora. He arrived looking a little pale and a little thin. But, he said, "Sound and well." So he and each of the brothers and all who had any interest in their affairs were well pleased at the culmination whereby everything was settled satisfactorily. They received the congratulations of everybody. Edwin "set 'em up" at O'Shaughnessy's besides making a tour of all the saloons in the camp. Warren pleaded illness, Will –lack of time, he must go home.

The fort was torn down by a miner who needed the lumber to build a lean-to at the back of his house for a woodshed.

> The money was paid in gold in twentys, and was paid in the Wells Fargo office backroom and was divided there. O'Shaughnessy received a large interest, Edwin and Warren divided with Will. Will took a receipt for his share from the Wells Fargo Express Company and cashed it in Sacramento. After buying presents, he brought home the remainder to me. It was carried in belts about his body and in valises among some clothing in coin bags made out of canvas, so that they could be distributed and not be too heavy in one valise. When he got home, he stacked the twentys upon a table by my bedside so I could see them—count them, if I chose. . . . I told Will that it didn't concern me half as much as my three day old baby boy. And I didn't think that Bodie had paid us enough for the many things it had cost us. . . . Will received $9,000 for his share, and was well satisfied. Said that it was fine for three months' work. I was unsatisfied and called the price a measly speck. Will had risked his life and was a subject for assassination at any time for three months. It gave him an after-reputation as a fighter, and he didn't like that, and I didn't like that. But, Women are hard to please.

William Lent and his associates, after acquiring the Bodie Mine, lost no time in pushing ahead with the sinking of the shaft. They installed a horse whim and put on a full complement of miners, and the work was stepped up to a round-the-clock operation.

In the realm of human affairs, nothing succeeds like success. About a month after acquiring the Bodie, Lent and fellow investors were happily enjoying the first $50,000 dividend of the Standard Company.

As the news of the camp's riches spread with tales of new mines opening, it brought a quick reaction in places like Virginia City, Eureka, Nevada, Sonora, and San Francisco. It drew ambitious prospectors, miners, businessmen, saloonkeepers, and calculating hard-eyed madams, whose unerring business perception sensed a new market for their sure-fire merchandise. They lost no time in cramming many a Bodie-bound stage with bevies of perfumed and plumed sporting girls to equip new *mansions de joie*.

On October 10, 1877, Bodie's first newspaper hit its feverish bustling streets. The *Bodie Standard News* came out as a weekly paper and was launched by the famous western pioneer newspaperman Frank Kenyon. Back in 1862 and '65, as a young man, he was the editor and publisher of the first newspaper in Idaho—the *Golden Age,* published in Lewiston. The *Bodie Standard News* proudly carried, under the banner of its name on its front page, the bold sentence: "OUR STANDARD, MONO COUNTY, HAS THE RICHEST GOLD MINE IN THE WORLD."

On November 7, 1877, the *Bodie Standard News* gleefully printed an item from the Standard Mining Company's letter of October 25: "Shipped today, two bars of bullion, $40,162.33. Everything is running well. . . . I am raising most of the ore this month from the 450 foot level where the ledge is from 8 to 10 feet wide."

In the same issue an observant reporter chronicled: "Building in Bodie for the past week had been going on very rapidly. . . . Everyone seems anxious to get their lumber, as fast as possible, from Bridgeport. Vaims & McVarish have commenced the erection of a two-story building 26′ x 40′ on the corner of King and Main Streets. It is to be used as a lodging house. . . . Thomas Williams has received part of the lumber for a building, 26′ x 50′. . . . We are glad to hear the hammer and the buzzsaw in Bodie from morning 'til night."

And it was with real zest that Frank Kenyon, in the issue of November 14, so eloquently editorialized the most important subject in Bodie:

GOLD—GOLD

But a few short months ago, Bodie was an insignificant little place. Now, she is rapidly growing in size and importance; and the people are crowding in upon her from far and near, and Why? Because of the rich discoveries in GOLD, yellow glittering precious Gold. The baseness of man, and yet his antidote, his blessing and his curse. His happiness and his misery. His solace and his affliction. The forger of change, and manumitter. The pastor and the prison, and the releaser. The richman's strength. The poorman's weakness. One is strong because he possesses, the other weak because he wants like the Sybarite. One has a bed of roses on which to recline, the other like Proteus, a barren rock. One has a palace over his head, the other a lofty dome, the blue vault of the heavens. One dyes his clothes in purple, and has fine linen, and dines sumptuously; and the other like Lazarus is covered with rags and subsists on crumbs. All mankind thirsts for Gold, from dimpled childhood to wrinkled age. . . . Hardships and privation are suffered for its acquirement. Friends are given up. Homes forsaken. Country abandoned. The genial warmth of our own fireside replaced by the chilling wintry blast or by the burning sun, under which death holds carnival and revels among the malignant diseases. Gold is the panacea for all diseases, the universal dissolvent sought by Paracelsus of old. . . . Gold gravitates to Gold. . . .

The *Standard News* of November 14, 1877, proudly printed the account of the visit of a San Francisco stockbroker, who wrote:

I feel no hesitation in saying, I'm glad I went. For some time past, I've been hearing people talk about it. I noticed that William M. Lent's countenance was illuminated by a genial glow whenever the name of Bodie was mentioned in his hearing; and that "Johnny" Boyd's cheery voice had a happy ring, whenever he answered your inquiries about The Standard Mine; and that the Bodie and Bechtel stockholders stood on the steps of Nevada Block and chewed their toothpicks with the air of men who had $200,000 in the bank; and no Chinese laundrymen or Montgomery Street tailors to molest and make them afraid. . . . I invested a twenty in a ticket for Carson City via the "Lightning Express." The next morning found me at Carson City, where at 10 o'clock I heard the driver cry, "All aboard for Bodie!" We rolled into Aurora the next morning and soon started up the canyon for Bodie, twelve miles east. The road carried us past abandoned shafts and tunnels, and past the wrecks of the Real Del Monte and other dismantled mills. Sad monuments of big assessments and blasted hopes. . . . The whistle of the Syndicate Mill was sounding as we drove into Bodie. The populace turned out in mass to receive the stage and get the mail. The first familiar face I saw was that of my old friend, George Storey, interested in the Standard and other mines; and his cordial greeting soon made me feel at home. Storey was the first to call the attention of capitalists to the Standard Mine; and when that mine was incorporated, he earned as a commission a big block of the stock. . . . I made the grand rounds of Bodie Bluff and saw enough to satisfy me that Seth and Dan Cook and John Boyd and William M. Lent and other stockholders will be our next "bonanza kings." . . . The Standard is extracting ore above the 450 foot level and has a shaft down 800 feet in good ore. There is millions in it. Careful figures say that there are 40 months' dividends of $2,000,000 in sight. The ledge holds out all the way down, and, in fact, is growing wider. . . . The Mill is now working what they call over here "poor ore," that is, $40 rock. It would make a Grass Valley man's eyes pop out of his head to hear $40 rock referred to as poor ore. The Bodie is next door to The Standard on the south; and they are now cross cutting to find the continuation of the Standard ledge. It is the big gamble of the camp; and if that ledge is cut, in my opinion, you will see Bodie's stock soar up among the twenties. . . .

The Bechtel is yielding large quantities of $10 rock, and is a second Standard. The Bulwer, to the west of The Standard, is looking well. In fact, all the claims on Bodie Bluff look well. . . . As Gasper would say, "Bullion talks." The Standard ships about $5,000 per day, soon to be followed by the Bechtel, which is incontestable evidence that the precious stuff is there.

The town of Bodie is lively, and things are booming. I left with a regret. And, as the stage rolled down the Main Street, I could hear the boys singing to the tune of "The Mulligan Guards,"

Oh, talk about your silver lodes,
And dips and spur and angles.
We've got the stuff on Bodie Bluff,
The yellow gold and spangles.

We'll take it out, you bet your life,
And coin it into twenties.
And if you ask us, who's our boss?
We'll answer you, Bill Lent is.

The last of November the *Standard News* carried an item that points up the early beginning of civic interest: "The Free Public Well which Hank Rogers and Harry Williamson and two assistants had constructed was receiving the installation of a patented non-freezing force pump and would soon be ready for the general use of the town's people."

The same issue, of the twenty-eighth, mirthfully printed a short parody served up as a typical Bodie ditty:

If a Bodie meet a Bodie,
And a Bodie cry,
Then a Bodie ask a Bodie,
If he will have some Rye?

The Bodie loves his toddy,
Just as well as pie.
And, if Bodie wants his toddy
He'll get it on the sly.

As the year came to a close the camp was treated to a lot-jumping and shooting affray. A bearded chap by the name of Clethens tried to jump a lot owned by John Wheeler. He brought in a load of lumber and started to erect a fence around the property. Wheeler appeared and proceeded to throw the lumber out in the street. Clethens tried to ambush him from the cover of a wagon, with a double-barreled shotgun, but failed to do any harm. Wheeler whipped out his revolver and returned the fire, with equally bad aim. At this point Clethens lost his nerve and ran across the street to the safety of Bob Foute's house. This noisy affair ended with both parties in the pokey.

In that last week of 1877 the *Standard* reporter came up with the cheering news that Bodie would have a triweekly mail service. C. N. Novacovich, Wells Fargo agent in Aurora, stated that F. Cluggage, owner of the Carson and Aurora stage line, had been given the contract and it was expected that by July it would be changed to a daily mail delivery.

How 1878 came to Bodie is graphically described by E. S. Williams in a letter published in the *Mining and Scientific Press* in January:

> It is storming fearfully and people are flocking here that have neither friends or money. Tonight, a woman came into town and could hardly find a place to go. No room for anything or anybody. I cannot for the life of me see what is bringing people here. There are ten for every job. This is a hard place.

The thermometer is sitting on the table, four feet from a red hot stove, and registers 62 degrees. The wind is howling. The snow falling and drifting. Making all together a very dismal picture; and prompts one in comfortable quarters to pity the houseless and homeless. Every space large enough to contain a human being is filled. Saloons and lodging houses are full, and lots of all-night stove warmers up at the mill where they stand in the furnace room to keep from being frozen.

In spite of this typical Bodie weather, life in the camp was varied and surprising. Tempers were volatile and lead was hot. On January 15, in a blazing street duel, "U. P. Jack" paid the full price for a slow draw. He went down kicking in a hail of bullets. However, as he lay dying on the frozen street, he managed one last shot that winged his antagonist, James Blair, in the left arm near the shoulder. Dr. Blackwood operated on Blair, removing the shattered humerus bone from its socket, but the patient died a few days later.

The above incident set the pace and instituted a typical act of brawling violence that would, by frequent repetition, create the national image of "The Bad Man From Bodie."

Human nature wasn't much different a century ago from what it is today, as witnessed by the calculated stimulant to circulation flung to the gaze of the eager readers by the public laundering of a juicy mystery in the *Bodie Weekly Standard* of February 20, under the intriguing headline "The Latest Sensation":

For several days past rumors have been flying through our midst relating to the sudden mysterious disappearance of one of our well known citizens. Many fear foul play. [A local reporter sifted the details and boiled them down and evolved the following facts.] The missing . . . only a short time before vanishing into thin air, was seen to have in his possession checks and other money aggregating $1,700. Of course, the possession of so much money only strengthened the belief that he had been murdered. . . . But, there is another side to the story which may throw more light on the whereabouts of the missing man.

Last Thanksgiving Day, two loving hearts were joined in Hayman's Bond at Aurora. The bride and groom were from Bodie,

> and when the nuptial knot was finally tied, the happy couple returned to their home. Matters progressed smoothly and love seemed to make all sunshine and rose water in the humble domicile of the newly wedded pair. The biblical injunction, "Go forth and multiply," was even rigidly carried out. But, there is where the first cloud over the matrimonial horizon arose. The young wife allowed her religious fervor to go too far in carrying the above holy injunction. At the end of the first two and a half months of her married life, she presented her lord and master with an heir. Being an old-timer he knew, of course, that many things in conjunction with high altitudes and pure mountain air are conducive to early vigorous production, not only of plants, but also of children. Therefore, at first, he was well pleased with the efforts of his better half. But, upon mature deliberation and second thought, he soured a little on the first exuberance of his joy, and finally concluded that his two and a half months' acquaintance with his wife hardly warranted her in making him average his four and a half months which he would have been willing to do provided she had waited two months longer. In other words, he was willing to shoulder the responsibility of four and a half months, if she would do likewise with the other four and a half months, and thereby split the difference. But women are proverbially perverse, and this was not an instance where one was otherwise. She had her own way, and hence the moody brow and downcast eye of her liege lord. However, he bethought him of the story of the "son-of-a-gun" from White Pine who gathered about himself his portable valuables and silently folded his greatcoat about him and lit out.

The sequel: Shortly thereafter the *Bodie Standard News* and its enterprising editor, Frank Kenyon, were sued for libel. Mary Kigbaum of Bodie claimed malicious injury to her good name and asked $25,000 in damages. On March 6, the newspaper proudly stated: "Although the 'Standard' is a young journal, yet having been in existence only 5½ months, it now has a libel suit on its hands, which in the amount of damages asked will compare favorably with any interior newspaper on the Pacific coast."

The cry of "Fire! Fire!" rang through the frozen wind-swept streets one Tuesday night in mid-February, 1878, and the citizens rushed from their beds and valiantly fought to save their embryo city from destruction in Bodie's first fire. The restaurant and lodging house on King Street, owned by Sam Chung, the camp's leading Chinese businessman, was enveloped in a raging fire that brought total destruction to a new two-story building valued at $10,000. With no water pressure and no organized fire department, it was only through the volunteer efforts of the hardy Bodieites the town was saved. They contained the fire by quickly razing two or three buildings between Chung's restaurant and Gilson's and Barbor's store, the largest mercantile establishment in town. A defective stovepipe in the roof of the kitchen had apparently caused the conflagration.

A reporter for the *Reno Gazette* who visited Bodie that February recorded the following facts about the town:

> Bodie has a population of 1,500, about 600 of whom are out of employment, and of which of the latter number, not 250 would work if they could find work to do. There are in town 17 saloons, 5 stores, 2 livery stables, 6 restaurants, 1 newspaper, 4 barbershops, 2 butchershops, 1 fruit store, 4 lodging houses, 2 boot shops, 1 tin shop, 1 jewelry store, 1 saddle shop, 2 drug stores, 3 doctors, 4 lawyers, a post office, Express Office, 15 houses of ill fame, 1 bakery, 2 blacksmith shops, 2 lumber yards, 2 stage lines, the usual secret societies, and a Miners' Union. Lots are worth from $100 to $1,000. Lumber sells at $70 to $100 per 1,000. There are six good mines and about 700 locations. . . . There are two 20 stamp mills which turn out about $40,000 per month. The average new arrivals per day is 10, and in the spring everybody looks for lively times in Bodie.[9]

The diligent reporter who so meticulously listed Bodie's population, professional cards, and merchants who catered to the camp's needs and appetites, from food, raiment, and thirst to sex, could find nary a single organization or exhorter for those who were spiritually inclined. In fact, a few weeks later, when the *Nevada Tribune* carried a short, snide utterance by a Reno churchman to the effect that, "Out in Bodie they have a preacher who talks it so fine that on one occasion, in speaking of the crucifixion of Christ, he grew quite eloquent in describing the manner in which they took the deceased down from the cross . . . ," the *Bodie Standard News* rushed into print to put the record straight with the sarcastic retort: "Hold it, Deacon, Hold on Deacon. There is some mistake about this. If Bodie had ever been favored with the service of a preacher, he might have used the language described; but, unfortunately the interests of our people have been neglected. We cannot but indulge in the dark suspicion that the good Deacon himself caused the remarkable sentence quoted in one of those discourses for which he is so eminent. With characteristic modesty, he thus asks to place his fame upon the shoulders of the imaginary preacher of Bodie."

John Peters wasn't the wealthiest man in camp, but he considered himself the luckiest. John was a God-fearing Irish patriot who loved his whiskey and his many friends. On the last night in February, after a rollicking night on the town, John bade his friends good night and started for the Standard's lodging house on the hill. It was there that the bottled lightning he had consumed so freely struck his guidance system, and zig-zagging up the hill, he missed his quarters completely. Wandering a little beyond the Blackhawk Mine, he stumbled and fell 110 feet down a shaft, where his worried friends found him two days later, stone sober, no bones broken, and very few bruises.

In mid-March an inquiring reporter paid a visit to Bodie's first school. Miss Nelly Donnally was the teacher of some fourteen bright-eyed pupils, who were attending classes in the new Cary Building on South Main Street. Miss Donnally expressed a hope that more of the parents in Bodie would take an interest and send their children to school. There seemed to be more children at home than were in attendance.

On May 8, 1878, the *Bodie Standard* boastingly informed its readers that the first dispatch over the wires of the new telegraph line had been sent through to Genoa, Nevada, the previous night: "Mr. Samuel Kimber, a fine operator, will have charge of the Bodie office. The completion of the telegraph line will enable us to place before our readers the stock reports, and the latest intelligence from abroad, one full day in advance of the outside papers." The *Press* announced that later in the month the paper would come out as a triweekly and that Henry Z. Osborne—a talented pioneer journalist connected for many years with the press of New Orleans—would be the new managing editor. (Osborne, who later distinguished himself in the halls of Congress, founded the *Los Angeles Evening Express* in 1887. Subsequently he sold out to Hearst, who published it as the *Los Angeles Evening Herald*.)

In the same issue the Mexican celebration of Cinco de Mayo (Fifth of May) was described as a great success. Mexicans and their friends from near and far gathered to celebrate the sixteenth anniversary of the defeat of the French at Puebla. "A salute of 21 guns was fired at sunrise; and a liberal display of flags and the firing of guns was the marked feature of the day. At night a grand Masquerade Ball was given by some of our Mexican friends. . . . The dance went on and joy was unconfined until the break of dawn Monday. The entire celebration was marked by good order, and was altogether a very pleasant affair."

The pulse and tempo of the camp was increasing from day to day. Every freighter and stage brought new arrivals. An editor of a Nevada paper who visited Bodie wrote: "It is impossible for anyone who has lived for any length of time in California or Nevada to visit Bodie now, without finding many old friends. . . . They have gathered from the four quarters, apparently; and men who have long been lost to memory and sight in the swiftly fleeing years here greet you with a cheery welcome and an invitation to take something."

In May the whole town was pleasantly stirred with a strange and romantic incident. Alex Marden, a newcomer to Bodie, was making his way past burly groups of roughly dressed miners, being careful to avoid the dashing duty carts and light rigs that seemed to be forever weaving in and out of the way of high-wheeled freighters and 18-mule teams. His eye chanced on a restaurant sign which proclaimed M. Y. Stewart the proprietor. His thoughts braked to a halt. These initials were the same as those of his boyhood friend, Mike Stewart, back in Saint Stephen, New Brunswick. Eagerly turning in at the door, he made the inquiry that happily united two old friends who hadn't seen each other for over a quarter century. In 1850, as young lads, they had left home for California and the gold fields, sailing on the

Vannelia. She was wrecked in a terrific gale. The passengers and crew were picked up by a passing vessel and young Mike and Alex, along with the others, deposited in the Western Islands. After about six weeks the American consul sent them back to Boston in his own barque with the other stranded passengers. The boys finally made their way back to Saint Stephen. However, Mike Stewart, determined as ever, again struck out for the gold fields. He sailed from New York on the *Cortez* via the Isthmus of Panama. Alex Marden stayed in New Brunswick for seven or eight years before finally coming on to the American West. Marden imparted to Stewart the news (he had received a recent letter from his wife, who still resided in Saint Stephen) that Michael's wealthy uncle, Cummings Robensen, had died and willed his fortune, valued at $75,000, to his favorite nephew. Stewart knew of his uncle's death, but not of the fortune left to him.

Exciting rumors swept the camp. On June 5, 1878, the *Bodie Standard News* headlined a story "BIG STRIKE IN THE BODIE MINE—A Remarkable Rich Ledge." Bodie's stock had for several days been steadily advancing in price—from one dollar per share a week before to $3.50 the previous afternoon. There had been plenty of rumor and speculation on the cause of the advance, but now it was out: "On the main west cross-cut on the 250-foot level, a rich ledge of ore has been cut." Superintendent Irwin in his report stated: "The ledge is about 2½ feet wide. . . . Along the hanging wall, there is a strip about 2″ wide, of extremely rich ore which will assay as high as $1,000 per ton and which will up the entire ledge to $100 per ton."

In that first week in June these events occurred to enrich the local intelligence:

Captain John, chief of the Piutes, was celebrating the arrival of a son, a papoose whom he promptly named Colonel Blasdel, in honor of the well-known superintendent of the Red Cloud Mine, who had so gratuitously provided "Heap Hog Die" (Indian for good grub).

The telegraph link to Aurora, Nevada, was completed. "Mr. Fred Bunch is the Aurora operator."[10]

View of Bodie. Pencil sketch by J. Ross Browne, 1864. *(Sutro Library)*

Off for the Bodie Mines. J. Ross Browne whimsically sketched his departure from Aurora accompanied by Judge Bechtel. *(Sutro Library)*

Mining at Bodie Bluff *(north side)*. J. Ross Browne and Judge Bechtel visit the crude horse whim at the San Antonio Mine, 1864. *(Sutro Library)*

J. Ross Browne. A self-caricature. *(Sutro Library)*

INCORPORATED JANUARY 26, 1863.

Capital Stock,
$1,110,000.

No.

Shares

Bodie Bluff Consolidation Mining Co.

CUMBERLAND 600 FT.
BUNKER HILL 1000 "
NORTH AMERICA 1000 "
ST. CHARLES 1000 "
NEW MEXICO 1000 "
MAIN TOP 1000 "
OSEEOLA 1000 "
MIZZEN-TOP 1000 "
FORE TOP 1000 "
ONEIDA 1000 "
IZABELLA 1500 "

Aurora, Mono Co., Cal.,

This Certifies, 186

That is the owner of Shares

in the Capital Stock of the Bodie Bluff Consolidation Mining Company.

Transferable on the Books of the Company, by endorsement hereon, and surrender of this Certificate.

11,100 Shares,
$100 Each.

Agnew & Deffebach print, S. F.

Secretary.

Leland Stanford

President.

Stock Certificate of the Bodie Bluff Consolidation Mining Company held by Leland Stanford. *(Stanford Library)*

The Empire Mill. Bodie's first stamp mill, built in 1865.

Governor Henry G. Blasdel of Nevada. Disappointed with Bodie, he moved his Homestake Mill away in the early 1870s. *(Nevada Historical Society)*

Earliest known photo of the Standard Mill in 1877. The picture was taken before the installation of the tramway, the construction of which was begun on November 7, 1877. *(California Historical Society)*

William M. Lent. *(California Historical Society)*

John F. Boyd *(extreme left)* and the William M. Lent family, on a holiday in Yosemite, 1879, pictured in front of the valley's first church. Spooner *(extreme right)*, the guide. *(California Historical Society)*

The three Loose Brothers: Warren, William, Edwin. Edwin was the original locator of The Bodie Mine. William served as a Mono County Supervisor in the "rip-roaring" years of 1879—'80—'81.

Eliza de Luce. *(Dona de Luce Abt Collection)*

The Camp in its "Heyday," 1879. A rare panoramic photo by R. E. Wood. The Standard Mill is in the foreground. The Miner's Union Hall and The Bodie House to its right stand out prominently on Main Street. *(Raymond G. Osborne Collection)*

"Heyday" 1879 further north. Photographer Wood shows Bodie's Main Street, a solid concentration of stores, saloons and business houses. Note the large, tall white house on West Green Street *(upper center)*. Years later it was acquired by J. S. Cain and moved two blocks east to its present location. *(Raymond G. Osborne Collection)*

Captain John. The last chief of the Piutes in the Bodie, Mono Lake and Aurora areas, he was the son-in-law of Captain Truckee, who was one of Colonel John C. Fremont's trusted Piute scouts. The Truckee River was named in his honor. *(Los Angeles County Museum of Natural History, by permission of J. McLaren Forbes)*

Bodie Indian girl and papoose. The continuous and unbroken zigzag pattern woven into the hood of the wicker pack cradle indicates a baby girl. *(Grace P. Crocker Collection)*

Patrick "Pat" Reddy. A fighting, redheaded, one-armed counselor of law who became one of the best-known trial lawyers in the West. *(California Historical Society)*

A party of enterprising Mexicans drove a band of mustangs to Bodie, and a big crowd watched the sale. The little plugs went from $10 to $40 per head. There was considerable sport in lassoing the ponies.

Bodie had a distinguished visitor in Dr. B. M. Geiger, who built the famous Geiger Grade into Virginia City. He came to visit his son-in-law, C. L. Anderson, the local surveyor. Geiger opined: "The outlook here is much better than the Comstock, when the same amount of work was done."[11]

R. M. Briggs, registrar of the U.S. Land Office, arrived in Bodie Wednesday morning after a long dusty ride from Independence. He had announced that the new land office would be opened in Bodie on July first.

A Mexican, Jesus Revis, was in jail for the killing of Antone Valencia. Valencia made a pass at Revis with a knife on the sidewalk in front of the Summers and Williams butcher shop. Revis promptly drew his pistol and shot Valencia. He died a few hours later, but, though conscious, refused to say anything about the affair.

Hank Blanchard, of the Southern Transportation Company, was in Bodie. "He proposes to run his teams into Bodie every other day after Saturday next."[12]

A few days later it was officially announced by Constable J. F. Kiergan that Teddy Brodigan was appointed a special constable for Bodie.

As the tempo of the camp increased, so did the violence and tragedy. The *Standard News* of June 19, 1878, carried two stories of the quick demise of a couple of Bodie's best-liked and prominent Irishmen.

It was after midnight when Alex Nixon, president of the Miners' Union, shouldered his way through the swinging doors of Gallagher and O'Brien's Saloon and bellied his way up to the bar. Alex was known as an aggressive and resourceful leader although inclined to act at times in a cock-o'-the-walk manner. After an evening of making the rounds to slack his thirst and chat with his friends, he was more than a little muddle-headed. At the bar he set 'em up for friends, among whom was Tom

McDonald. Thereupon, "McDonald asked O'Brien to loan him $1.00, as he desired to treat. Nixon objected to McDonald receiving the money from O'Brien and handed him a dollar himself. While O'Brien was fixing their drinks, a dispute arose" over who was the best man. Nixon let fly with a haymaker which floored McDonald. Deputy Constable Brodigan rushed in and temporarily restrained Nixon; however, when McDonald had picked himself up from the floor, he started to draw. Nixon countered by pulling his "Whistler" from his hip pocket. Both men fired simultaneously. Nixon went down, mortally wounded, crying out as he staggered and fell, "My Gawd, boys, I'm shot; run for a doctor." With the raw obstinate courage of the Irish, as he lay helpless on the floor he ripped off two last wild shots at McDonald, both going wide of their mark. In spite of the ministrations of Dr. Berry, he died two hours later. When the wild shooting started, the saloon emptied as miners, barkeepers, and barflies alike burst their way out the doors and windows into the street. None of Nixon's shots hit anything, although one ball splintered through the partition and was found imbedded in a head of cabbage in Wagner's restaurant the next day.

The whistling echoes of the gunfight in Gallagher and O'Brien's Saloon had barely faded away, when James Doyle became a mine-accident fatality. What was thought to be the final round of holes in a connecting tunnel between the Bodie and Standard mines was blasted out at 2 A.M. Doyle hoped to be the first man through the opening between the two mines; but instead he fell a victim to his own ambitions. He was found, a corpse, a short time later, lying near the head of the drift, suffocated from the poisonous fumes of the "giant" powder.

The profound sorrow that touched Bodie with the tragic exit of Nixon and Doyle passed quickly. The sporting fraternity rapidly revived with the happy news in mid-June that the town was to have a race track.

A group of prominent businessmen that included M. Y. Stewart, Silas B. Smith, B. E. Butler, James Pollock, and William Whitrow subscribed $250 to get the project started. The *Bodie*

Standard News boasted that there were several good horses in this section and others would be brought in.

Also spotlighted was the announcement of the first organized baseball club in town. They met the second Sunday in June at the Miners' Union Hall and elected G. C. Gorman president, with W. D. Hayes secretary and Frank Hurlbuth treasurer.

Another step in the camp's rapid progress was noted with a headline story in the *Press* on June 19: "PIONEER STAGELINE—About 2 o'clock Sunday, the first stagecoach of this line arrived in Bodie from Sonora. . . . The fair through is $30 by rail; but if passengers prefer taking the steamer at Stockton, it is only $26.50. The stage leaves Bodie, Sunday, Tuesday, and Thursday at 4 o'clock in the morning, and arrives at San Francisco at 5 P.M. the next day."[13]

The first organized celebration of its kind was that of July 4, '78, and the committee of arrangements announced in advance that they had interviewed Captain John, chief of the Piutes, and arranged for a genuine old-fashioned war dance. The chief promised to have "heap Indians," four or five hundred. They were to gather on the "hills north of town, and paint themselves in the fashion of Wild Tribes and ride up and down over the hills, and, at the same time, giving vent to the old time 'War Whoops' familiar to ears of many an old prospector in Bodie when in days past he heard it with fear and trembling."[14]

The committee promised Captain John they would provide a nice fat barbecued bullock and plenty of bread and cake. "Heap Hog Die"—it was a deal!

July Fourth of 1878 was a noisy celebration. "As the sun rose from behind the hills, beautiful and bright, the people of Bodie were aroused from their peaceful slumber by the firing of 13 guns."[15] The younger generation were soon out in force, firing crackers and torpedoes by the hundreds. "Nearly every house in town had a display of American colors. . . . Main Street from one end to the other was resplendent in patriotic holiday attire. By mid-morning, the sidewalks were crowded with citizens and strangers and porches and windows along the line of march were adorned with an array of beauty which would hardly be expected to exist in the sagebrush country. A high altitude must be favorable to female beauty, and how. . . . At 10:30 A.M. the procession formed near the Miners' Union Hall and marched down the Main Street. The spectacle was, indeed, a beautiful one as the flags flying, the band playing, and horses prancing."[16] After the Carson City Brass Band and heading the procession was Colonel S. W. Blasdel, the grand marshal, mounted on a coal-black horse, beautifully caparisoned, and carrying in his hand the baton of authority. He was attended by his staff, all mounted on splendid mettlesome horses; then followed the Mexican War Veterans under the command of Major John F. Kirgan, assisted by Captain Jim Dyke. Next came the car of state, occupied by thirty-eight little girls representing the then number of states, all surrounding the Goddess of Liberty, personified by Miss Rosa McAlpin. The car of state was arrayed with excellent taste and festooned with American flags. Next came the carriage containing the officers of the day; Colonel S. B. Ferguson; the chaplain, the Reverend Mr. Fletcher; and the reader, Mr. John J. Welsh. Prodding this carriage of notables along marched the Bodie Miners' Union, 150 strong, all wearing blue silk badges on which were printed the words "Bodie Miners' Union" and a picture of a miner with a pick and shovel. Close to the Miners' Union came Bodie Masonic and Odd Fellows associations, then the Bodie and Red Cloud baseball clubs, nattily attired in their new uniforms, "followed by the Junta Patriotica Mexica de Bodie, well mounted and wearing the sashes of silk in which were blended the colors of their native country. They were very picturesque, and added greatly to the handsome appearance of the procession."[17] Last but not least came the young men of the B. S. S. mounted on their fine horses with new silk badges bearing the initials of their order.

"The different features of the day were well carried out. The baseball match was short and decisive."[18] The Bodie club walloped the Red Cloud, 20 to 5. "The turnout of the festive crew [the Horribles] was too funny for anything and the war dance of the Piutes, together with the previous subsequent consumption of 'Hog Die' at the Bar-be-cue, was grand and gloomy and peculiar."[19]

The dust from the war dance of the Piutes and Bodie's first organized baseball game had barely settled before the exuberant citizens of this throbbing outpost of civilization elbowed their way into the mahogany bars to quench their thirst—Blue Blazers, Whiskey Straight, and Tarantula Juice for all tastes sluiced down hundreds of parched patriotic throats.

One scribe exulted that the camp now had 27 saloons dispensing 1,700 drinks a day; but old-timers, who long afterwards remembered this Fourth, chuckled with disbelief at such a pygmy-size figure. Vigorous, proud, and confident men tossed off many a toast that day to old friends, new friends, and to the golden wonder of Bodie Bluff and High Peak, that in eighteen short months had raised a tiny hamlet to a roaring mining camp, whose Main Street was over a mile long. They raised their glasses to GOLD. GOLD, its magic had brought them here, had created their city. The very ground under their feet shook and throbbed as the muffled distant thunder of the stamp mills crushed the rock and produced the bullion. Toasts were in order to the mighty Standard that had just paid its eleventh consecutive monthly dividend of $50,000.

Scattered among the joyous celebrating citizens in the streets and saloons were fifty miners from the Bodie Mine. Their bosses had asked for no disclosures on what was doing in the mine; but their secret was impossible to cloak with silence. Many a group marveled and strangers were stunned into silence as small pieces of sugary quartz chock-full of the precious yellow metal was passed from hand to hand. The rock was literally laced and wired together with gold. There were many guarded questions. "Whence the rock? What level? How wide the ledge?" Much was told in boastful secrecy, and it was a glittering and fabulous tale. And so backs were slapped, and confidences exchanged, and many a citizen who held Bodie stock found it increasingly hard to sleep following that Fourth.

As the sun sank behind the towering granite wall of the Sierras, the velvet darkness of a July night closed in upon the celebrating citizens of the new El Dorado, where the *pièce de résistance* of the day's program was announced by the melodious music of Professor Porter's string band playing for Bodie's first Grand Ball in the new Miners' Union Hall. It was the swankiest affair in Bodie's brief history, and the elite and bon ton of all Mono County were in attendance.

That first week of July witnessed the initial expression of civic effort in the celebration of the Fourth, the first Grand Ball, and the first organized baseball. The last of the month brought the disclosure to the *Press* of a dazzling golden treasure, the mining of which in the next five months would vault The Bodie Mine into first place among all the Drift Mines in California in the year 1878. The shattering impact of this would in one year skyrocket the camp's fame into the Western firmament as the nation's newest El Dorado, where it would become forever synonymous with "Bullion and Bad Men."

On July 28, a visiting scribe from the *Virginia Enterprise* was allowed to descend into the Bodie Mine and view the ledges which the main crosscut west had exposed. His breathless account follows:

> At a distance of 528 feet from the shaft the Bruce ledge was cut. . . . The face of the drift in this ledge shows ore of almost fabulous richness. The quartz sparkles with coarse gold, and when pulverized in a mortar and honed out, a single handful of the rock will show a return calculated to stagger an ordinary prospector and make him doubtful of his own eyes. . . . This ore is now sacked before hoisting from the mine. If it keeps on for awhile as it is now going, the gold can be winnowed from the quartz. . . . About 125 feet still further west of the Bruce ledge, the Burgess vein was cut by the main drift. Though but a few inches wide at this point, its great riches made it equal to a ledge of corresponding width. A drift south was started on it, and about 30 feet from the main west drift. It widened to 4 feet wide, the ore being simply a conglomeration of coarse gold, decomposed quartz, and clay. Even the clay is full of small nuggets of gold. The gold found in this ledge is the coarsest yet discovered in the district. A friend of mine took from the face of this south drift in the ledge an average sample. I know it to be average, for I picked the rock down myself. Twenty-six

ounces of this rock pulverized in a mortar and honed out, the result was about 20 ounces in gold. How high is that?[20]

Finally on Wednesday, July 31, 1878, a feverish and rumor-ridden Bodie was electrified by a headline story in the *Bodie Tri-Weekly Standard* written by a reporter whose brain and pen alike were whirling with excitement and intoxication, as he dashed off the following eyewitness story;

In company with Mr. A. C. Burgess, President of The Bodie Company, and Superintendent Mohler, the Standard reporter visited The Bodie Mine this morning and was cheerfully shown all the information which he desired. In fact, the whole mine was thrown open to him, and every courtesy extended. For thoroughly reviewing this immense hidden bonanza which up to a few days since was beyond the gaze of man. After months of incessant toil and perseverance, encountering obstacles at every turn, their labors have been crowned with success, by opening up of ore bodies which almost dazzled the eyes with shining metal. Gold was plainly discernible in many places, without even the aid of glasses, as we viewed the veins which are being uncovered from 15″ to 4 feet in width. . . . When the main shaft had reached a depth of 260 feet, the west crosscut was started, and is being driven ahead as rapidly as possible. . . . The ledges tapped by this crosscut are the Burgess, Bruce, Molly, Bodie, Gilda, and Granger. The drift on the Burgess is about 60 feet, and all the way across between the walls, high assays are obtained. When the vein was first struck, it was not nearly so rich as now; but has since widened out and improved in quality, until now the 15-inch ledge is 4 feet wide in the face of the drift. And, from hanging wall to foot wall, it assays $3,000 per ton, while choice samples will go over $4,000 per ton. The walls are well defined —the rich gold can be plainly seen as the ore is knocked down by pick or blast. . . . This is one of the grandest bodies of ore which has ever been uncovered, not even excepting the Comstock. For in richness, it compares more favorably than with any of them. The mines, indeed, are few in number which can show a 4-foot ledge with every prospect of being much wider which will assay across the face of the drift the enormous sum of $3,000 per ton. The Bruce ledge is also a bonanza within itself. This vein was 2 feet wide when first struck, and rather low grade, but has widened out as the drift advanced till nearly a 4-foot ledge is open to view. The "Pay Streak" is from wall to

> wall, and is, without doubt, as rich ore as ever was struck in the camp. It will probably average from the vein $2,000 per ton. . . . The ore is sacked and hoisted up ready to be shipped to the Syndicate Mill. The result of Friday's run at that mill was 287 pounds of amalgam.

One day's crushing produced $16,000 in gold bullion. *The mantle of gold had replaced the raiment of rags.*

CHAPTER IV

The Bodie Strike and Stampede

"It was like a blinding flash—Many people would not believe it!"
—JOHN PARR.[1]

The fantastic gold-wallowing tale is colorfully told by D. M. Riordan, superintendent of the Syndicate Mill from August 1878 to 1880, and John Parr's immediate superior.

> The Burgess vein showed some value and on this vein a drift was run which in going south. . . . developed a chamber of ore over nine feet in width and which ran up to nearly $100,000 per ton. [I wish to qualify this statement by Mr. Riordan and point out that this represented the top assay. However, mill foreman Parr puts the average on the first 1,000 tons of this milling at $600 per ton.] The Bodie folks made arrangements with the Standard people to change our mill from Standard ore to Bodie Mine ore; and, from that chamber of ore, we milled and shipped over $1,000,000 in gold bullion in six weeks. During the crushing of this ore, so rich was it, we ordinarily could not run more than five stamps or one battery, though the mill was a 20 stamp mill with pan capacity to correspond. We have had the amalgam accumulate in the pans, not once, but frequently, so that it would stop the engine. In one day's run that I remember, we got about 900 lbs. of gold amalgam. I have had the gold accumulate in the battery until, recognizing by the sound that the stamps were no longer crushing rock, that they were not striking iron, I would take off the screen to find that the gold had accumulated in the bottom of the mortar until it was flush with the die and, I have taken out of a single mortar with an ordinary iron fire shovel, such as we used in cleaning up, free gold enough to fill a Wells Fargo express box. 80 lbs. of amalgam from one charge in the pans was a very usual thing during that run of ore. And, we were obliged to retort during the whole time as rapidly as the retort could be cooled and a fresh charge of amalgam put into it. During the run of this ore,

> Peter Holmes, Bob Pixley, and myself, one day went into the mine, and, before going, stopped at one of the stores and got an ordinary 5 lb. shot bag to take with us, as a sample sack. We filled this shot bag with the loose dirt scraped off the face of the drift with our own hands. From this we panned out in Peter Holmes' office after coming down, gold enough to make four match boxes. Any miner will understand what this means. It is a fact that this run unfitted some of our best men for ordinary mines or ordinary ore thereafter.[2]

The town was agog over the mercurial surge in the stock of the Bodie Mine, which had slowly inched up to $1 per share by June 1, 1878, and had then shot up to $18 per share by August 7. This jetlike escalation had almost overnight made giddy-headed rich out of hundreds of Bodieites. Many had bought the stock for less than 40 cents per share a few months before as a wildcat speculation. As the days of August wore on, the excitement in the camp grew with feverish intensity, day by day, as the big black matched six-horse teams of Horace Marden wheeled overloaded creaking ore wagons all day long from the Bodie Mine through the streets and down the canyon, one mile, to the Syndicate Mill. Accompanying each load were two well-mounted hard-eyed guards whose ready Winchesters were eloquent evidence of the high-grade gold-studded quartz in each load. This eye-filling spectacle was reaffirmed each night with new rumors and treasure tales from the miners who dug the ore and from the mill hands who labored under the watchful supervision of Riordan and Parr.

The sensational yield of 1,209 pounds of amalgam from the first four days' milling of Bodie Mine ore produced four bars of gold bullion worth $47,023.19.[3] The dazzling impact of the first week's production run on this ore and how the news was delivered to the San Francisco Stock Exchange is described in a reprint of the account in the *San Francisco Exchange* on the occasion of the advancement of Bodie Mine stock from $10 to $18 per share: "Mr. William M. Lent, the well known and popular operator, waltzed into the lobby of the stock exchange yesterday morning. . . . It was evident that there was something up in Bodie—He wore salmon-colored kid gloves, and his mustache was elegantly waxed; and he had a telegram in his vest pocket from Col. Boyd. And, the result was that Bodie bounced. . . . Lent was happy when he saw the 'Bears' take the water at $18.00 per share."[4]

The company officials, stockholders, Bodieites, and everybody who had ever heard of the mine were totally unprepared for the haul made from the milling of the first 1,000 tons of this treasure horde. Mill foreman Parr in his reminiscences puts the cleanup from this run at $601,000.

This dramatic golden harvest blurred the senses of the majority who beheld it, and for months to come, thousands of the sane, practical and hardheaded citizens of the mining West fell a prey to its golden fantasy. Their thoughts, hopes, and actions were held in the meshes of a dream. This fantastic cleanup ushered in the wild days of August, and no pioneer Bodieite who lived there through those days ever forgot its exhilarating impact on their lives.

By early September, '78, the residents of Bodie were in a frenzy. The big cleanup sent the stock zooming above $50 per share. The streets of Bodie were overflowing day and night with feverish, sleepless stockholders and citizens who wished they were stockholders. The camp was swept up in a gold-fever hypnosis.

How it was during that curious fall was related to me by an old-timer who was a young toddler then. He recalls his slightly older playmates tell that "kids were put to bed early while their parents, their heads stuffed with grandiose dreams, dashed out into the streets to gossip, and, if possible, gather more news on the latest sensation at the mine, or what the latest stock quotation was. The wild upsurge of Bodie Consolidated stock carried many of the other stocks on the board to new heights, and almost everybody in the camp held stock in some Bodie mining venture. Knots of miners gathered on the board sidewalks all night or toasted the rosy future in the saloons. The whole town suffered from insomnia that fall."[5]

Tuesday, August 13, '78, was a typical wild day, and the

tempo of that day is colorfully profiled in the *Bodie Tri-Weekly Standard* of that week: "The excitement regarding stocks commenced late Tuesday evening when it was generally known that the Bechtel was quoted at $5.00 per share, and the Tioga at $6.00 per share. Tuesday, from early morning until 3:30 in the afternoon, the excitement was intense and one could not walk in the streets without being buttonholed and asked, 'If you have any Belvedere, Tioga, or Bechtel?' Several thousand shares changed hands during the day, and as the time drew near for the stock report to reach here, all were on the 'qua de vive,' whether owners of stock or not, to learn how they stood."

And so it went on day after day that fall. It was indeed a time of foolish venture for many otherwise calm, levelheaded citizens. The papers of the day were full of stories about common everyday people who made big winnings on Bodie stock. The *Virginia Enterprise* in an August issue stated: "A miner at the C & C shaft some time ago bought 400 shares of Bodie Consolidated stock for 40¢ per share and recently sold it out for $17.00 per share—a net profit of $6,640.00. Had he held it till yesterday, he might have sold it for $24.00 per share."[6]

A big winner was a well-known Bodie storekeeper. During the cold bone-chilling days of that past winter, a gloomy Bodie gambler, whose luck had run out, as well as his stake, decided that he had enough of a frozen isolated little camp where the surrounding peaks seemed eternally shrouded in freezing "Pogo Nip" and the restless chilling wind never ceased to drift the snow on its bleak hills. Calling on the storekeeper, whose $60 bill he could not pay, he announced that he had enough of a camp with only one paying mine and the rest just a bad gamble. Being down on his luck and broke, he tendered in payment 600 shares of wildcat stock his cards had won. The sad and disgusted merchant took the seemingly worthless shares of Bodie Mine stock in payment, and tossed them into his wife's old trunk where, along with other bad debts, they were mercifully forgotten. Six months later, in the wild days of August, '78, his wife's memory rushingly came alive with an almost forgotten incident and she quizzed her husband, "Say–haven't we got some Bodie stock?"

They suddenly remembered—the down-and out gambler—last winter—a sheaf of "wildcat" stock—the old trunk. Rushing into the back storage room, they popped open the ancient portmanteau and feverishly pawed through its many forgotten contents, until at last they found it. Eureka—600 shares of Bodie Consolidated! A hurried perusal of the latest telegraphic stock report disclosed that it had just hit $50 per share. Halleluiah!

The second week in August the Bodie Consolidated declared a $3 per share cash dividend, and the local press boasted that the Bodie Mine was producing $20,000 per day and confidently predicted, ". . . six months more will prove the Bodie to be the richest gold mine on the Pacific coast."

Rumors were flying through the camp that there had been a big strike in the Black Hawk. By the third week of August the stock of this rather lightly regarded mine had jumped from 25 cents per share to $1.75. The *Bodie Tri-Weekly Standard* of the twenty-first carried a story of a rich three-foot ledge cut in a west crosscut on the 300-foot level. Colonel Sam Ferguson, superintendent of the mine, took several important mining men —who included Judge F. K. Bechtel; Porter Holmes, superintendent of Belvedere and Aurora Tunnel; and Colonel S. W. Blasdel, superintendent of the Red Cloud Mine; and the *Standard News* reporter—on a conducted tour, during which they viewed the new find, which assayed $60 per ton. It was opined that the ore in this ledge resembled that of the Standard Mine at that depth, and that very probably it was a northerly continuation of that famous ore body.

Gold fever, greed, and Bodie whiskey produced gun-fever with fatal results for the instigator. As dawn broke on August 27 the citizens of Bodie were erupted from their beds by the sound of heavy rifle fire. Ex-soldiers among them recognized a wildfire fight as the staccato reports of fast-shooting .44-caliber Henry rifles echoed over the town from the direction of the Black Hawk shaft on the high shoulder of Bodie Bluff to the north. Deputy sheriff John Kirgan, Bodie's famous peace officer, and his deputies urged their horses to their utmost and covered the short mile uphill ride in record time. On arriving they found

Jack O'Hara gut-shot and dying. He and his partner, Phil Riley, and two other whiskey-brave Irishmen had tried to jump the Black Hawk Mine. They opened up on the hoisting works from behind a breastwork of rocks, about seventy-five yards beyond the Black Hawk shaft, riddling the hoisting works with bullets. They got their answer, quick and decisive, as Colonel Sam Ferguson and his miners coolly returned the fire. When O'Hara bit the dust, Riley and the two remaining gunmen sobered rapidly as their courage evaporated. They scattered and fled back down the sage-covered bluff. This ended the proceedings so far as the citizens of Bodie were concerned.

The following week, early in the evening of Tuesday, September 3, the *Bodie Standard News* hit the streets with its first extra, whose headlines screamed, "KILLED": "This evening at about half past six o'clock, John Enright was shot and killed in Teague's saloon by James Harrington." Enright, a former express messenger, and Harrington fell to arguing over the ownership of some mining claims. Violence erupted when Enright called his adversary an "S.O.B." This got him a poke in the eye. His rage rising out of control, he whipped out his British "Bulldog" and fired, missing. Harrington countered with his pistol and deadly accuracy. The first shot ripped through Enright's left side, about six inches below the nipple, and the other just below the shoulder of the left arm. He fell to the floor, dead.

Deputy Sheriff Kirgan came on the scene and in his firm Texas manner took charge. He arrested Harrington and promptly installed him for the night in Bodie's well-known Crossbar Hotel, unlovingly known among lawbreakers of the time as Hotel de Kirgan. The case came to trial before Judge D. B. Goodsen. Harrington pleaded self-defense. After hearing both sides, the court promptly discharged the prisoner. Attorneys were White for the prosecution and Briggs and Gorom for the defense.

On September 4, 1878, the *Bodie Standard* carried pulse-quickening news: "Bullion shipments during August have amounted to over $700,000. Those from The Bodie Mine alone to aggregate over $600,000. There is no camp on the Pacific coast which presents such an enticing field for investment. . . .

New Bodie stocks are finding their way to the boards daily. New incorporations are coming on the market, and new locations are being made daily; and, there is no abatement of the excitement, nor is there likely to be any so long as Bodie continues to send down one half million or more per month and continues to roll out its princely dividends. The Standard, the pioneer mine of the district, just paid its twelfth consecutive dividend of $50,000, aggregating $600,000; and The Bodie Mine has just distributed $400,000 cash out of one month's work . . . but these are not the only mines that have great promise. There are at least half a dozen others whose owners and managers claim for them already surprising value."

This tale of sudden riches that seemingly stretched endlessly into a golden future was heady stuff—part fact and part fantasy. It had something for everyone: the calculating men of the counting houses, capitalists, sharp operators, prospectors, miners, businessmen, whores, deadbeats.

Its roaring impact on the West broke swiftly like a mighty avalanche crashing the glacial blue of a Sierra lake and ramming mountains of wild water to violent impact upon every concentric point of the startled shore.

In the restless gold-feverish, rumor-racked camp itself the "Bodie Strike" and the soul-tingling possibility that any day, anywhere along better than two and one-half miles of lode, bigger and better bonanzas were impending became practically the only topic of discussion. A century ago there was little diversion. There was no radio, no TV, no movies. The nearest railhead was over 120 miles away, better than twenty-four hours by the fastest stagecoach, over a rutted ribbon of dust cluttered with lava rock and sagebrush that passed for a road; a primitive highway through a trackless wilderness, bridgeless and innocent of grading.

Over these tortuous, lonesome tracks they came in wild eager confusion, hardy eager men, all pioneers—many among them, veteran Argonauts of the days of '49 and hundreds who were sons and daughters of those of '49; ex-soldiers, veterans of the Indian campaigns, Union army, and hundreds who had worn the field gray of the Confederacy; emigrants, Irishmen, Swedes, "Cousin Jacks," Italians, Frenchmen, and Chinese, and others who had come to this new land of freedom and hope from across the sea, upon whom the impact of the news of Bodie's riches was like a golden promise—at least a chance to be in on the opening of another treasure house of the Golden West. There were silver miners from the fading Comstock, gold miners from the Coeur d'Alene, hard-rock men from the mines of Eureka and Pioche, and the Panamints, businessmen, saloonkeepers, madams, and gamblers from every place east and west of the continental divide.

And so by the end of August the stampede to Bodie was on. They came in a great variety of transportation—horseback, muleback, shank's mare, and the more affluent ones in their own four-in-hand outfits, sturdy plodding bull-teams (oxen) pulling wagons piled high with lumber and household goods. Merchants-to-be carted their store goods and fixtures as they jolted along. Those who were fortunate enough to get tickets, and traveling light, scrambled aboard the fast-moving six-horse stagecoaches and temporarily trusted their lives and fortunes to the firm, gauntleted grip of those revered knights of the whip who were the undisputed bosses of the road.

In early September a scribe witnessing the stages arriving in Bodie recounted: "Two lines of six-horse coaches with an 'extra daily' on the Carson route came in filled with passengers from deck to keel. Sixteen is an average load; but, as a stagecoach or streetcar is like a can of sardines, there is always room for just one more." Peering into his rather murky crystal ball, he expansively opined, "We shall soon have our railroad which will obviate the discomfort now experienced in traveling thitherward."[7]

The trials of the rutted road to Bodie in September, '78, are amusingly given by a businessman who piloted his own four-in-hand outfit in the stampede:

> Eleven months' residence in the Panamints and three years in Darwin has been pretty rough on yours truly; but, a ride over the road from Darwin to Bodie through the famous Owens Valley and over the hills is quite enough to make one feel like

engaging in something else more exhilarating. If there ever was a country cursed with bad roads and "toll gatherers," we certainly believe that Inyo and Mono counties could carry off the palm. It would seem that the $2.00 per head poll tax collected from everybody that is old enough to vote and a good many more who never ought to vote has been expanded in packing large sized rocks and placing them in the wheel tracks where it is absolutely impossible for the best "Jehue" in the country to miss them in passing over these roads; and, if anybody thinks Inyo county is a coward, we can assure him or her that she has more sand than any "Jayhawker" ever traveled. . . . We reached Bishop Creek (third day), and although it is the paradise of Owens Valley, we are sorry to say, it has the poorest accommodations of any town in the county. It is sadly in need of a good hotel and butcher shop or at least someone who has spirit enough to kill a chicken or calf when no other meat is in the house except poor bacon. . . . Pete Gealhard's Station at Black Lake is one of the very best to be found on the route (fifth day). He is an honest German, and he and his better half give you more than your money's worth. Our next station was Adobe Meadows kept by Frank Shaw who had some fifteen hundred acres fenced in, but raises little else than good hay and fine stock. We got a good dinner there; and then came on to Dexter Wells, 23 miles from Aurora, where an old "batch" has it all his own way. Gets you up an excellent meal for "six bits" and charges you 10¢ per lb. for grain, 25¢ per head for hay, nothing for looking at the upper end of Mono Lake, ten miles distant from his place; and talks Danish to you 'til you fall asleep, like a Chinaman smoking opium, when you are packed out to the barn to sleep on hay over which numerous chickens have ranged for several months. Our next place is Aurora where we stopped only long enough to feed our animals. . . . We came on to Bodie, arriving at six o'clock P.M. on the 30th (seven days from Darwin). We met here hundreds of old friends.[8]

The rush to Bodie in the fall of '78 virtually depopulated many other camps. The *Alpine Chronicle,* published in Silver Mountain, graphically described the exodus: "The stampede for Bodie has commenced. Monitor will soon be a town of windows."[9] On September 21 the same sheet reported: "County Supervisor, R. B. Love, is making arrangements to remove to Bodie, having purchased a lot there. He will supply people with the best of beef, mutton, and pork, cheap for cash . . . it having been stated that he has taken down buildings in this town for removal to Bodie." In the "Local Intelligence" column of the same paper we read: "Good bye. On Wednesday last, Bob Love's hogs, good fat four-legged ones, took their departure for Bodie. Bodie has drawn heavily on Alpine County, and if Markleeville, Monitor, and Woodfords are being depopulated of their leading citizens, Silver Mountain will not hold on to her four-legged hogs. We presume, however, the latter will prove as acceptable to the Bodieites as the former."

In the short time between August, 1878, and December of that year, Bodie gained twenty saloons, 3,000 people, and a newspaper. The two Folger brothers, acting on the old proverb "If you can't whip 'em, join 'em," loaded up their *Alpine Chronicle,* press, type, and all, and joined the Bodie stampede. In December, '78, laboring at the handle of their little press, they cranked out Bodie's second newspaper, the *Mono Alpine Chronicle,* which they later renamed the *Bodie Chronicle.*

The cry "Lumber—lumber!" in Bodie that fall "went up from hundreds of people waiting to commence or finish their respective houses and stores." Hank Blanchard of the Southern Transportation Company informed an inquiring reporter, ". . . there is now nearly 50,000 feet of clear lumber on the way here from Carson City."[10] The same scribe noted in the local press that "the champion single-line teamster arrived in town today from Carson with a load of lumber etc., weighing upward of 40,000 lbs. This immense load was hauled by 16 fine looking mules, all of which made a display such as is seldom seen in any camp."[11]

Locally, N. B. Hunnewill of the Eagle Sawmill out of Bridgeport pushed his facilities to the utmost to supply his eager Bodie customers, who were desperately trying to get a roof over their heads before winter arrived. His mill, along with other Mono County mills, provided much of the lumber for the mushrooming new camp.

The *Bodie Standard News* of September 4, '78, observed with unrestrained conceit:

. . . there are half a dozen new hoisting works on the road. . . . The whole mineral belt from the Black Hawk on the north to the Seigniory on the south is being advanced as never before since the camp struck. . . . The new hoisting works for the Summit, Bodie and Champion mines are now on the grounds and those for the Richter, South Bulwer, Old Dan, Maybell, and Concordia will reach here in a few days. . . . The hoisting works for the Champion are complete and have been in first class running order for a week. The shaft will now be driven down as rapidly as possible. The South Bulwer, recently incorporated . . . shows up a fine 2½ foot ledge which is improving in quality and, from its location, being south of the Bulwer and Belvedere, and only a short distance from the Bodie Mine, makes it a valuable claim. . . . J. M. Dawley and John Turner paid $20,000 in cash besides considerable stock and, one hour after the purchase, $40,000 couldn't have bought the mine.

On September 16 the Mexican population of Bodie held their Hidalgo Day celebration. The *Standard News* of the eighteenth reported that possibly two hundred members of the Junta Patriotica Mexica de Bodie took part:

It began with the firing of guns at twelve o'clock midnight, and at six o'clock A.M., and another at noon, and again at midnight. Daybreak found both American and Mexican flags flying from different parts of the town; and the streets presented a holiday appearance. The principle feature of the day, at least there was more fun in it for outsiders, was a game called "Correr El Gallo," which offers an opportunity for horsemanship for which the people of the country are justly celebrated. A smooth place was chosen in the south part of town where the horses would have a good chance to run. A live rooster was buried in the ground—its head only appearing above the surface. The riders took their stations, about 50 yards from the rooster, and one by one they dashed their horses toward it, and sought to catch it by the head while passing. It is by no means an easy thing to do, to reach over and touch the ground while the horse is running at full speed; but to catch a rooster's head, which dodges like lightning, is a good deal harder. A great many touched it and took up handfuls of dirt and feathers; but, it was some time before it was pulled entirely out of the ground—Ed Loose finally caught the fowl and swung it above his head; but he had but one minute, however, as another man seized it and dashed up the street as fast as his horse could run. And then, there were lively

> scrambles on horseback, one taking it from the other. This lasted for some time and gave a great deal of excitement. In the evening there were literary exercises in the Miners' Union Hall. Mr. Royce Carrsco delivered an eloquent oration, and G. Noble made a speech which was received with enthusiasm, after which a very enjoyable social entertainment was given. The day passed off without mishap of any kind and was enjoyed by all.

Meanwhile, in the shafts and tunnels of the various mines on the hill above the town, the sinking and drifting operations were driven ahead as fast as the machinery of the time would allow. At least a dozen well-financed mines with new steam hoisting works drove their workings downward to reach the hidden bonanzas that the Standard and the Bodie mines were extracting by the hundreds of thousands of dollars each month and that each new company was positive lay hidden in the quartz veins within their boundaries. The old saying that haste makes waste is doubly true in mining, which operation inherently entails many hazardous jobs. Some of the companies and even the miners themselves many times played fast and loose with safety precautions. So in the rush to "find it," four lives were snuffed out that fall.

In the first week of October, Thomas Dorsey was killed in a cave-in in the Ajax Mine. One week later Frank Higgens, a miner in the Richter shaft, fell out of a bucket as it was being hoisted and dropped seventy feet to his death.

On October 4 a sturdy thirty-five-year-old Irish miner by the name of Andy Hagerday never knew what hit him as he labored at the bottom of the Champion shaft. A timber crashed eighty feet down the shaft, striking him on the shoulder, and breaking his collarbone in pieces which were driven into his lungs, killing him.

Probably the most spectacular tragedy occurred in the Mono shaft. The *Standard News* of December 17 headlined the story "The Killing of Lawrence Sheridan." He and J. M. Cody and another miner were working in the bottom of the Mono shaft when the brakes failed to hold the cage and it dropped with a car of tools on it, crushing Sheridan and killing him. Cody and the other miner managed to jump to safety in the adjoining compartment of the shaft before the cage struck the bottom. Cody testified at the coroner's inquest that he "thought" the accident was caused by carelessness of some person or persons who had the management of the cage at the time.

The camp of Bodie was the mining focal point of the West in 1878 and '79, and an enthusiastic observer who threaded his way through a traffic jam on Main Street on October 16, '78, made the observation that "each day our streets are absolutely blocked up with teams which come from all directions, loaded with every variety of freight. . . . The scene on the Main Street during the day is exceedingly lively and makes all feel more and more confident of the future of Bodie. The amount of goods already here only represents the advancing guard of more to come, all of which will be needed before spring comes. Not a merchant seems to want to be behind the times and will soon be ready to supply everyone with everything necessary."[12]

With the approach of winter, the sport enthusiasts throughout the camp, headed by Colonel Blasdel, superintendent of the Red Cloud Mine, were promoting the organization of a snowshoe (ski) club. A reporter quoted the sports-minded superintendent as saying: "The sliding here is magnificent, and the pleasure attending the exercise, unexcelled. There are a large number of experts among us; and a club formed here would be productive of much pleasure and amusement during the long winter months through which we must pass. . . . Last winter, a man came from the Red Cloud Mine to the Village, a distance of two miles, in five minutes. At times, going so fast that an observer could see but a faint outline." The incredulous reporter added: "We must have more practical experience of the truth of the same before swallowing the whole yarn. Anyhow, the boys will have a chance this winter to show their respective qualities as snowshoe artists."[13]

It was on November 6 that the local press, in a florid self-benediction, headlined a story "Something Definite":

The Standard News takes to itself the credit of having been the first to awaken among our people a true realization of the danger of fire in which we are placed. . . . We are proud to say that our efforts have resulted in success. . . . At a meeting held Tuesday evening a committee was appointed with power to send below and purchase a Babcock Fire Engine, and have it delivered at once. For the information for those unacquainted with properties of this engine, we have penned a description of this apparatus. Weight of the engine when ready for action is 2,200 lbs. And, the cylinders contain 120 gallons of water. There are 200 feet of hose reeled up on the carriage, all of which is mounted upon a strong truck with drag ropes. The apparatus costs $2,250.00 at San Francisco. . . . The engine will arrive in Bodie within ten or twelve days. It is to be hoped that there will be a full meeting of the company tonight to carry out the measure now in contemplation.[14]

In 1878, Bodie was enjoying magical success. The weather, which at best in the Sierras at elevations of 8,000 or 9,000 feet can become suddenly bitter and hostile to man and beast after September, put on a magnificent show of glad-handedness and warmth that lasted into December and confounded the dire prophecies of the old-timers. On November 27 a reporter genially informed that "no reasonable person could ask for anything finer in the way of weather than that which we are now enjoying. Clear and bracing atmosphere with the thermometer about 60 degrees during the day, and probably as low as 30 degrees during the night. It is good enough for anybody. We have now had almost continuous good weather since July."[15]

As the delirious days of late fall hurried to a close Bodie's stand on the threshold of greatness was never doubted by her citizens. And so it was with chest-thumping pride that the editor of the *Standard News* on November 27 printed a letter from an eminent San Francisco mining reporter under the headline "Bodie Vs. The Comstock Etc.":

Editor of the Standard:

It is the opinion of our shrewdest operators that next spring will witness a furor in Bodie Stock. The magnificent dividends dispersed by the Standard and Bodie mines has given the stock speculating community the most satisfactory and convincing evidence of the great mineral wealth of Bodie. . . .

A contrast between the Bodie mines and the Comstock presents a striking advantage in favor of Bodie. At present time there is not a single dividend paying mine on the whole length of the Comstock while assessments are steadily increasing. . . . When we turn to look at Bodie, a brighter picture meets our gaze. We see the Standard and The Bodie Mines making regular disbursements and we will soon see the Bulwer wheeling into line and know that with the opening of the coming spring, at least six mines will be on the dividend basis.

It is not extravagant to put the production of the Bodie district for 1879 at $10,000,000 equal to one half of the gold production of California for 1878. . . .

With this prognostication for a golden future, how could they miss! And so the stampede surged into a magic 1879.

CHAPTER V

The Cauldron of Gold Fever and Hope - 1879

As destiny swept the electric year of 1878 to a close it plunged Bodie into the turbulent golden cauldron of its heyday.

How it was in the beginning of that flush magic time is vividly described by a well-known Grass Valley businessman who in the closing weeks of the year visited the exciting new lode and glowingly assessed the camp and its future:

> Bodie has a population of about 5,000, including the suburb on the hill. The main street is nearly one mile in length, and lots are staked off in all directions on the hillside. Buildings grow as if by magic, and the resident of Bodie who absents himself for a week or two on a trip to the Bay Area returns and views, with surprise, the buildings erected in his absence. The growth of the town has no parallel in the history of mining. The average arrivals are about thirty per day, and all departures intend to return. Society has not assimilated; but the elements exist in a state of chaos. There are 47 whiskey saloons, 10 faro tables; and this is not in disparagement of the district, but evidence of its prosperity. There are, however, 2 banking houses, 5 wholesale stores, an excellent daily paper, and all the accessories of civilization, and refinement will soon follow.[1]

A local scribe, who ran with the sporting crowd and inked the pulse and the flavor of the time, reported that at least fifteen of Bodie's saloons had gambling rooms

> in which are dealt Faro, Roulette, Vingt-et-un (21), and all the other games known to the profession. Most of the games are well patronized by a truly cosmopolitan crowd of customers from all the walks of life. And at the tables may be frequently seen representatives of nearly every portion of our country, as well as those of Europe. The man with a rich brogue from the Emerald

> Isles, the descendant of the noble ancestors, who in kilted skirt and tartan "we Wallace bled," and the natives of the great Empire on whose soil the sun never sets, the one who was born in Veterland, the Swede, the Norwegian; the child of sunny Italy, the son of La Belle France, the African, and even the almond eyed Chinaman frequently takes his chance copping the ace.
>
> The professions "Bless you" are all represented. Hardy miners are elbowed by their own superintendent, and the faded Cyprian with tawdry finery and lack-luster eyes flanked on the right by a disciple of Blackstone while on the left by him of the Caduceus. We have no church, but Miners' Union Hall answers that, and a variety of other purposes. On Saturday evening, for an instance, the hall was occupied for a grand testimonial complimentary benefit to "Billy" Costello, the champion lightweight of the Pacific Coast, matched to fight Harry Maynard for $1,000 aside. . . . At ten o'clock Sunday morning, Reverend Father Cassin of the Roman Catholic Church said mass in the same place; but dismissed his congregation in time to allow Reverend G. B. Hinkle of the Methodist Episcopal Church to preach to his little flock at 2 P.M., in the evening the platform of the same hall was occupied by an amateur minstrel performance on which occasion were recreated not a few of the dead and buried jokes of the past generation. . . . Bodie is a lively place and, as we have endeavored to show, contains all kinds of people. Everybody coming here can find what they want–if they are looking for a fight, they can drop into it and get gloriously whipped in three minutes of entering town. If they wish to behave themselves, they will be safe and as little interfered with as they would be in streets of New York or Boston.[2]

As the camp eagerly raced into the new year of 1879, its citizens were enjoying an almost open winter. Wheel traffic continued unabated. In January the local press complained that "our peace officers report, 'Everything quiet about the town.' In fact, no arrests have been made for several nights, and unless some fighter from foreign parts makes an adventure here shortly, our winter is likely to roll around with disgusting sameness as regards matters riotous. However, we do not despair as any day may bring forth some new cause for grievance which will convey the cheerful sound of pistols to reverberating through our present quiet streets."[3]

Truly the pace of living in the new El Dorado had been a

glorious hectic one during the last half year. Bodieites who read San Francisco and eastern papers were well apprised that their district was now the focal point of the "mining West." From this wonderful plateau they savored the life of a winner, and took time to enjoy the antics of their neighbors. A high percentage of the camp's inhabitants were old-time Nevadans. Hundreds had lived and worked on the Comstock. So the local press took special pains to provide its readers with coverage on the doings in the Silver State.

The *Bodie Standard News* headlined the story "Governor Kinkaid's Levee." The Carson correspondent of the *Esmeralda Herald,* a real bluenose, who covered the soirée, filed a story with his paper which the *Bodie Press* eagerly reprinted for their free-wheeling subscribers and the other itching readers who after gulping the lines would faintly belch, "Ain't it awful":

> The initial levee of Governor and Mrs. Kinkaid held at the new opera house was a magnificent affair, and the attendance was very large, in fact, so great was the attendance that the dancing resolved itself into a scientific pastime. The struggles of the gentlemen to avoid trampling and mangling the elegant robes of their partners, reminded me of the gathering of exceedingly bad skaters whose gyrations are so well known to all. And right here let me snarl a few words about the costumes of the ladies, which were, in not a few cases, simply outrageous. The décolletté cut of their dresses were exceedingly indecent. Nearly every woman on the floor who wore a low neck dress did not have a chemise, and their attempts to conceal their charm behind fans were as wretched as the exposure of the capillary substance under their arms. In many instances, their bodices were cut so as to expose to the public eye the lower extremities of their shoulder blades while in front, the opening extended to the "Rose of Anacreon." The styles of the British blonde burlesquers were not half as calculating to entrap the unwary and aesthetic as those of a portion of the respectable ladies who attended the Governor's reception.[4]

Early that February the camp was stirred emotionally. The souls of her citizens filled to overflowing with waves of sadness while bringing to a bright luster a new and shining faith in the dignity and worth of man. Under the caption "A Hero's Death" the *Daily Bodie Standard* of February 6, 1879, poignantly recounted:

> Elrod Ryan fell 450 feet and was instantly killed. Another of those terrible accidents occurred this morning which seemed to be the penalty which is incurred in the pursuit of mining precious metals. . . . This morning about 2 o'clock Elrod Ryan was attending the bucket at the surface of the new Bodie shaft. Water had been taken out from the bottom of the bucket and was slopped over ice that had frozen about the mouth, rendering the footing very uncertain. Ryan, it is said, had been handling the cable at the time of the accident, and, slipping, he fell down the shaft, which is about 450 feet deep. The poor fellow, when about 50 feet from the surface with thoughtfulness which entitles him to a place in the ranks of heroes, sang out to men who were working at the bottom—"Look out below, I'm coming." He was plainly heard on the surface and in the mine below; and the men in the shaft had time to get into the adjoining compartment and save their lives. When he struck bottom, he must have been killed instantly as there did not appear to be a bone in his body that was not broken.

As the weeks of the new year rolled by, the rush to Bodie quickened its pace. By February the ground and roads were almost free from snow, as Mother Nature conspired with the whims of capricious fate to speed an early spring development. During the second week of February an incredulous ink slinger for the *Virginia Chronicle* filed a story on "The Rush to Bodie. —The departure of the stage was witnessed by a crowd of about 500 men, most of whom wish to go also but could not find room. . . . About 1½ tons of baggage was left behind."[5]

An alert Bodie observer, seeing the droves of newcomers that arrived each day, pounced on the problem: "The question now is, What shall we do with the boys? And girls, too, for that matter? . . . The question ought to be considered at once by lumbermen and house builders. Buy lots, and put up tenement houses. There are not half enough of them. . . . The roads to Bridgeport have been open all winter, and it is not likely, that they will be at all impeded by snow or mud. Put your teams and men to work at once. The rush is bound to come, and it cannot be stopped."[6]

To keep pace with the population explosion, there was a rash of new saloon openings, and popular "mixyologists" like Pat Leggette, who had forsaken Virginia City, opened the Capitol Saloon and found his highly polished Spanish-mahogany bar crammed with thirsty miners and old friends and patrons from the borrasca-ridden mines of the tobogganing Comstock. Many of the new saloons were nobby joints, where thirsty patrons with snooty tastes could lubricate under dazzling chandeliers and receive a beaming welcome like that of Jack Wilson and Billy Dolan and John Kiley, proprietors of the Palace Club Rooms who opened their oasis with a brass band.

A parched and impressed reporter who was free-loading on the opening night describes the proprietors and their place expansively as the most exquisite caterers on the coast. "Who will not say that a drink in The Palace Club Rooms is not worth 25¢?"[7] (Bar whiskey was 12½ cents per drink in '79.)

A Bodie reporter with plenty of high carnival in his spirit came forth in the issue of February 12 with a breezy story headed "Adelphi Free and Easy": "Messrs. Butler, Larkin, and Love made the necessary arrangements for opening a first class variety entertainment building formerly known as the 'Spanish Hurdy House.' The proprietors are well known artists and have taken great pains and trouble to make the new variety hall a success. Among the company are five lady artists who are the best in their profession."[8]

And so it was that on February 13, 1879, the Bodie Standard News took up its cudgels against a Nevada sheet that had just printed the stinging effusion: " 'Goodbye God, we are going to Bodie in the morning.' was the suggestive termination of a sweet little three year old's prayer the other evening at San Jose, just prior to the departure of the family for the wicked mining camp mentioned." "Not bad that; but rather severe on Bodie. All right partner; but we have no particular use for a God that confines himself to the limits of San Jose; and we don't wonder that even a little three year old was willing to say, 'Goodbye,' when she thought she had a chance to get outside of that detestable place in order to come to Bodie."

In the second week in February the camp had its big labor strike. All 125 members of the Mechanics Union filed out of the Miners' Union Hall into Main Street. After forming an orderly group, they marched down Main, swung right at Standard Avenue and tramped in a body to the mines on the hill. Their first call was at the Champion, next the South Standard, from there the bargaining column marched to the Addenda and the other mines at the south end of the lode.

Their demands were for an eight-hour shift and five-dollar pay. Strange as it may seem to us living in the last half of the twentieth century, this was indeed considered a radical demand at the time. All trades—miners, muckers, mechanics, and engineers—worked a twelve-hour day ninety-two years ago.

The superintendents of the south-end mines, confronted with a bargaining army of hoisting engineers and mechanics, did very little talking on their own to the milling band of strikers. However, "at all of these mines, some understanding was arrived at, by which they continued running. At some of the mines, the superintendents asked for time to confer with their respective companies; which was granted."

On arriving at the Goodshaw and Queen Bee, the strikers found that Superintendent Buckely "had anticipated their threatening action and closed down earlier in the day."[9]

The strikers then countermarched back to the north, stopping first at the Mono shaft, where a defiant Superintendent George Daly rejected their demands, locked the doors to the hoisting works, and unfurled the American flag on the staff high above the works. The column milled around. There was wild talk of storming the works and forcibly carrying away the engineers. The cool heads of leadership prevailed, and the marchers proceeded on to "The Bodie Mine which refused to accede to their demands, and shut down."

That evening the "Mechanics Union met in the Miners' Union Hall and discussed the events of the day and their future movements."

The next day the streets were jammed with restless citizens, as all Bodie awoke to full realization of the situation, that the entire economy of the whole town was based on mining. With hoisting engineers on strike, the shaft mines would be unable to lower and raise miners and ore from their underground workings. Most of the mines being a shaft operation, this strike would mean the secession of pay days in Bodie if it continued for any length of time. The impact of this generated a real fireball of excitement among the miners and businessmen of the camp.

"The superintendents had a meeting during the morning, and, it is understood that they had agreed on some plan of action." By the morning of the fourteenth it was rumored that the Miners' Union had stepped in and appointed a committee of fifteen to meet with the superintendents and Mechanics Union to try and work out a settlement. However, the streets were choked with idle miners, and there was tension and excitement aplenty. The flag was still flying from the staff of the Mono works; and "it is a singular fact that the flying of that flag has given more umbrage than any other thing since the commencement of the strike."[10]

As George Daly, superintendent of the Mono, finished his breakfast and stepped through the door of the Palace Restaurant, he was stopped by a group of men. Daly himself related what happened: "Phil Mahar tapped me on the shoulder and said that he wished to speak to me. He said, 'We wish you to go up to the meeting at the Hall.' I said, 'What meeting? Miners or Mechanics?' He replied, 'Mechanics Union.' And I told him that I had nothing to say to the Mechanics, and that what I had to say had been said at the Mono Hoisting Works on Wednesday. . . . And that I would not go. The spokesman of the party then said: 'Men do your duty!' Two seized me, one on each side and rushed me up to the Hall!" At this point Daly suddenly wrenched free, whipping out his revolver, he sprang with catlike agility from the high board sidewalk into the street. Covering Mahar with his gun, he rasped in a hard voice, "I'll kill the first man that attempts to lay a hand on me!" At this demonstration, most of the men ran. In recounting further details, Daly said: "I moved across and up Gilson and Barber's steps, and as I was going in, one of them said, 'All right young man, you're heading for it. You'll get plugged yet.' "[11]

The following day, headlines announced: "THE WAR ENDED.—The Miners' Union stepped in as arbitrators and sustained the superintendents. They agreed to defend the mines with resumption of work along the lead. . . . The general tenor of the decision in the Miners' Union was to the effect that the Mechanics Union had acted ill advisedly, and, that they had not given the superintendents proper notice of their intentions, and that there were 50 engineers and nearly 1000 miners, and the latter were taking the brunt of the fight in which they had no hand. . . . On the part of the superintendents, it was decided to recommence work today, and before we go to press, every mine on the lead will be working as usual."[12] And so the twelve-hour shift would remain the yardstick for a day's work in Bodie for years to come.

On February 26 the *Daily Bodie Standard* shamefully acknowledged: "Bodie, in her boasting progress and improvements, has evidently forgotten what she needs most—that is a church—a good one with a spire high over her expectations of spring developments. It ought to make the very boulders blush that Mono County never had even a semblance of a church building. Our neighbors, Inyo County, are not much better off in Grace. They have but one building at this time. . . . And it did our soul good to witness the peculiar manner in which the young pumpkin raisers done their sparking while the old folks enjoyed it."

That same week a San Francisco paper printed a scurrilous attack on Bodie whiskey, "containing the following case libel on our local beverage—The barkeeper in a Market Street saloon was mixing some alcohol, kept for cleaning the mirror, with some spirits of turpentine, Jamaica ginger, and Perry Davis Pain Killer, when a Bodie man said 'yes' in reply to his question 'whether he'd like some bitters in it?' He shook ½ a gill of pepper sauce into the tumbler and pushed the bottle toward him. The Bodie man filled a heaping tumbler full, and passed it off and when he had recovered his breath he said to the barkeeper, 'Young man, that's whiskey. I ain't tasted nothin' like it since I left Bodie two weeks ago today. That's real genuine licker, kinder a cross 'tween a circular saw and a wildcat, that takes holt quick, en hols on long. Jus' you go to Bodie and open a saloon. And with that whiskey you might charge 4 bits a glass for it and the boys 'ud never kick!"[13]

By early March the editor of Bodie's newest sheet, the *Mono Alpine Chronicle,* found himself overwhelmed with four months of exposure to the frenzied day-to-day mining excitement; and after getting an eyeful of a new ore body being opened on the 200-foot level of the Noonday Mine, he was in a joyous ink-splattering dither over this latest horn of plenty. He chronicled a piece that pretty well summed up the tenor and rosy glow that pervaded the camp during the heyday: "WHERE WILL LIGHTNING STRIKE NEXT?—A score of claims are open to such an extent that but a few feet of drifting here and there is likely to expose a bonanza that will set all hands as wild as in August last. It will not require so extensive a find as that in The Bodie claim to set off a perfect bonfire of speculation. For, the district has acquired almost a solid history for rich ore discoveries over as wide a field as the Comstock country. This is a view for all to bear in mind. . . . There is nothing on the line of that great lode today that shows itself as favorable as some of the Bodie's we could name. . . . A few weeks in one case, and a month or six weeks in another, will better tell the story as to its extent; but, there is enough in sight to warrant the most sanguine prediction."[14]

Meantime, on Thursday, March 13, a *Standard* scribe on the prowl along Main Street reported that Marden's teams had commenced hauling ore from the Noonday Mine to the Syndicate Mill. "The first load, which stopped on Main Street a few minutes while the team was resting, attracted considerable attention. People crowded around to look at the rock. The universal opinion was that the ore will work well. Many expressed surprise to see such fine rock from a point 1½ miles south of the main bluff. The inclined shaft has been sunk on a ledge to the depth of 200 feet, and drifts are now being run. . . . We have it from good authorities that the ore taken from any place in the ledge in the face of the drift will assay from $60 to $100 per ton and higher. This certainly is very encouraging to the south end mines. We expect soon to chronicle some startling developments from that section. The Noonday is owned by private parties." R. D. Brown was the superintendent and Senator Stewart one of the leading stockholders.

On Friday, June 13, at 8:30 P.M. at McAlpin and Crans' new Bodie theater, the curtain rose for the first time bringing a professional theatrical production to the culture-parched citizens. Some of the stars of that long-forgotten first night in Bodie were John Martell, James Fletcher, Henry Stewart, Miss Terry Wheeler, Miss Louise Summers, and Miss Marsten, "a rare combination of talent."[15] The evening edition of the *Standard* carried the following comforting assurance: "The entertainment tonight will be chaste in every particular, and nothing permitted which shall offend the most fastidious. A special officer is engaged to preserve order. Any person committing any breach of decorum will be expelled from the theater. Bodieites need some place of amusement to relieve the ennui incidental to a mining camp, and, also, to relieve the anxiety experienced by the stockholders; and they are legion. We can assure our best families that the entertainment to be given tonight will be worthy of their patronage."

On the last day of the month an imaginative news hawk, hearing of a minor insurrection against Captain John, chief of the Piutes, reported that

> no mining camp would amount to much were it not to have had at some time in its history a veritable Indian War. Our Indians, at least a couple of them, appreciating this fact, inaugurated this business Thursday. We could not ascertain the names of the distinguished gentlemen; but they opened the war by attempting to shoot or kill or maim Captain John, the high "muckey muck," our Chief of the Piutes here and at Mono Lake.
>
> The first dispatch from the front came to Chief Kirgan by an intelligent counterband Indian. Two braves had gotten drunk and revolted with malicious intent, and with a six shooter and an old Yaeger rifle, had shot at Captain John with the intention of terminating his chiefship. The report was that in addition to the above, the two braves had burned down Captain John's

Wickup. . . . Chief Kirgan, at once, held a council of war all by himself, and issued orders for his aides, Fealan and Grant, to sound "Boots and Saddles" and go to the front—On arriving at the battleground, just this side of the Noonday Mine, they found that they were not at the front, but at the rear; as the two Indians had stolen Captain John's horses and lit out for Yankee Fork, or, perhaps, Benton where, it is believed, they had obtained the pure Kentucky Bourbon upon which they had gotten drunk. Thus has our first Indian War ended, and Bodie's reputation as a live mining camp is vindicated."[16]

With the Fourth of July just around the corner, the camp enjoyed fine weather and remarkably dull times in the justice court. The *Daily Bodie Standard* of Monday, June 30, 1879, under court matters, had only two cases on the docket: T. H. Treloar for assaulting his wife, stood trial and was convicted; and Frank Mendoza was arrested for larceny. He pleaded guilty, and Justice Peterson fined him $40 or 40 days.

The same issue of the *Standard* carried a story that severely dampened the plans and enthusiasm of the small boys of Bodie for the coming Fourth of July. Deputy Sheriff Kirgan called on all the stores where firecrackers, bombs, and Roman candles might be sold and requested them not to put in any stock of fireworks or sell them in the camp, because of the extremely dry year and the complete lack of a water system. There was not a fire hydrant in the town.

The Fourth of July, '79, was grittily remembered long afterward for a fierce windstorm which generated irritating clouds of dust that sanded the barbecue, producing much profanity, and for impressive literary exercises which begot reams of profound oratory. Heading the parade was Grand Marshal C. A. Richardson, with the Bodie Brass Band trooping behind and oom-pahing bravely against the wind and swirling dust. The literary exercises were held at the Miners' Union Hall, where General Kittrell, the president of the day, was interrupted many times by thunderous applause. The General's glowing eloquence transported the patriotic Bodieites as he spoke:

"My fellow citizens, ladies, and gentlemen, we have been called together, on this 103rd anniversary of our country's Independence, to commemorate the most important event which has marked the history of the human race since the birth of the Savior of Mankind; hailing, as we do, from every state of the Union, and representing every brand of nationality of the earth. It is fitting that we enter into this celebration with that degree of ardor and enthusiasm so characteristic of the men of the mountains whose avocation it is to burst asunder the rocky ribs of the adamantine hills, and unfold the hidden and buried treasure which nature's God has so lavishly dispensed through the gulches and ravines of these desert wastes and western wilds."[17]

Following the eloquent General to the platform was the orator of the day, Judge R. M. Briggs, who, likewise, "delivered a splendid oration," for which the *Daily Standard* offered apologies for not having room to print.

People who attended the horse races at Brooker Flat in the afternoon were hard put to see anything of the flying nags through the billowing dust clouds as spectators and horses alike blinked and sneezed through the program. Visibility was so bad that two horses collided, breaking the neck of one.

A comment was made, on a redeeming feature of the day, by the local press: ". . . a feature of the Fourth was the general good order which prevailed. There being only two arrests made during the day. This can largely be attributed to the efficiency of our police officers. Chief Kirgan fully understands what is wanted, and evil doers have no desire to fall into his hands."[18]

As the camp settled back into its daily routine, the readers of the *Standard* were pleasantly lifted to a romantic mood by the "following original poem from the pen of Miss Molly Reynor, Bodie's favorite actress":

REVERIES

Why is it
That I think of thee
In every fleeting hour?
As daylight wanes,
As morning breaks,
I feel thy magic power.
Why is it?

Why is it
My heart beats high
At the thought of seeing you?
And I ask myself the question,
Will he play false or true?

Why is it
That I do not care
What fate the Gods may weave?
Since it brings me love and happiness,
Heaven grant me a reprieve.[19]

The evening of Thursday, July 10, was pleasant and warm; and Mrs. Shay, holding her infant son, was strolling slowly up the hill on her way to spend the early part of the evening visiting her husband. He was on duty, as the hoist engineer, at the Summit Mine. She mused on how fortunate things had been for them in Bodie. Suddenly there was a mighty quivering in the ground, which all Bodie felt. Mrs. Shay's shocked and startled gaze beheld a ghastly orange and red sheet of thundering flames hurl a stone building into fragments as its leaping tongues of horror seared the sky. A holocaust of flying debris knocked her senseless and flung her baby safely into the brush.

This was the powder magazine of the Summit Mine. Five miners, working near, were killed instantly. Not even the slightest trace was ever found of Charles Mallory or W. J. O'Brien; but the torn and mangled bodies of Thomas Flaven, Frank Files, and Hugh H. McMillan were picked up and taken to the morgue. Two other men were fatally injured in the explosion. John McCarthy died the following day, and Hugh McMillan II hung onto life until the morning of the sixteenth, making the seventh victim of this horrible accident. Over six hundred grieving citizens paid their last respects to Files, Flaven, and McMillan as their remains were laid to rest on July 12.

In the minds of many men the man of the hour was M. B. Shay, the hoist engineer of the Summit Mine, who earned the sobriquet of "Lucky" in that fatal moment of the magazine disaster. The four miners who rode his cage never forgot the warm glow of Dame Fortune's smile in that miraculous descent. The *Daily Standard* describes the amazing incident: "Shay was at his post and was in the act of lowering the cage down the main shaft of the Summit with the miners in it for the purpose of landing them at the 200 foot station level. The mark on the cable, which indicated that the cage and men had reached within a few feet of the stopping place, rolled slowly around when Shay, with his hand on the throttle and foot on the brake, felt a sort of a forewarning—or, as he expressed it, 'a sort of a rush of air,' and, with lightning rapidity, he stopped the cage at the point stated, a few feet above the 200-foot station. That act saved the lives of four miners who would have been dashed to pieces 100 feet down to the bottom of the shaft. In the very second in which he felt the warning, came the explosion. Where the engineers stood is a huge mass of slivers; the end of the building being blown to pieces, and the engine stripped of its minor parts." But Lucky Shay came through the horrible ordeal with only "a few bruises and cuts." William Irwin, superintendent of the Standard and Summit mines, paid Shay his highest accolade for the "clear cool presence of mind he exhibited in immediately extinguishing the fires which broke out at the furnace and blacksmith shop."[20]

The pulse of the camp is well recorded by the press of Monday, July 14: "The sad occurrence of Thursday evening has only temporarily suspended the work of the Standard incline shaft and the Summit. The engines are rapidly being put in order and a temporary gallows frame at the former will be ready by the fifteenth. In the midst of life, and death, and dire casualties, devastation, and sorrow, work in a mine must go on all the same. Fresh men supply the places of the exhausted miners, and life and strength immediately fill the vacancies caused by death. Shifts mark the time of the little world in the regions below; and nothing can impede the systematic work except when the Mineral God lets the bottom fall out."[21]

The camp had more than its share of shock, tragedy, and disaster in the first part of July, so it was a welcome relief for its citizens to read the following bit of municipal trivia in a morning yelp of the eighteenth: "BODIE CALABOOSE SOLD.—On account of our county 'Dads' not making an appropriation for liquidating an insignificant debt of $138 hanging over the Bodie Calaboose, the property was yesterday sold at a sheriff's sale to Harvey Boone for $150. Boone transferred the same to Chief Kirgan, in whom the title now rests. If the people want the calaboose they will have to raise about a $1000 or pay a good rent to Kirgan."[22]

In the same issue one of the better jotter-downers with a rather keen appreciation of the nuances of the dramatic arts recounted: "One of the most fashionable audiences that had ever been seen at a Bodie Opera House, attended a farewell benefit of Miss Reynor last night. The seats were pretty well taken and everyone seemed to enjoy the entertainment. Mr. C. A. Thornton, a favorite of the San Francisco theater, as 'Felix O'Callahan' kept the audience in a constant roar of laughter.

"Miss Reynor sustained the part of Julia well and her recitation was greeted with applause. . . .

"The violinist of the evening, Bobby McGlincey, was well received. . . .

"The Bodie Glee Club rendered some very fine quartets and were brought out three times. . . .

"Mrs. Brierely, as Miss Montague, was the charming widow; and the singing of 'Annie Laurie' and 'Coming Through the Rye' was greeted with deafening applause. . . . Everyone pronounced it the best entertainment that has been given in Bodie."[23]

By August the downtown area was beginning to take on a more permanent appearance. Many of the smaller clapboard buildings that had been so hastily thrown together when Bodie first came into existence were being torn down. Twenty-five to thirty new, permanent, solid and substantial buildings were replacing them, many commercial in character.

O'Day and Frasier had developed a clay deposit on upper Main Street, near the Brooker Mine, where their new kiln was turning out brick for their Bodie brickyard.

One of the partners had built a new brick residence. Another imposing brick building was being constructed by Harvey Boone; and there were plans for several more "fire proofs," as they were called.[24]

An inquiring observer learned from Little and Wilkenson, one of the camp's busiest contractors, that they had on hand a big backlog of commercial building contracts, that every inch of ground below Green Street was occupied by business firms and that by November the business houses on Main Street would extend well up toward the old slaughterhouse.

After a night of rumor, sporadic shooting, and wild excitement, the *Daily Bodie Standard* of Tuesday, August 12, 1879, hit the streets with an edition that sold like hotcakes. Its screaming headlines proclaimed:

BODIE, THE SEAT OF A CELESTIAL WAR
BANG! BANG!

FOUR BELIEVED TO HAVE FALLEN VICTIMS
TO THE BULLETS
OUR POLICE OFFICERS TARGETS FOR THE CHINAMEN

THE CALABOOSE PACKED LIKE A SARDINE BOX

SEVERAL OF THE MONGOLIAN FIGHTERS WOUNDED

The shooting on King Street in Chinatown began shortly after 8.30 P.M. on Monday, just after officers, Taylor and Kirgan, acting on a tip from a "denizy" of the district that there was trouble afoot, had stepped back into the street after an inspection of several opium dens. Suddenly a ragged barrage of pistol shots split the quiet of the evening. Officers Grant and Fielen rushed the front door of a house and found a crazy bedlam of shooting inside. Chinese men were lying under bunks and benches, firing in the darkness. The lights had been shot out with the first volley. Crouching in the darkness, the two officers were unable to distinguish any gunmen. They had only the flashes of the pistols as targets. Luckily neither officer was hit by the wild shooting. Finally Grant managed to collar several Celestials. He passed his squirming prisoners to Fielen who by then had stationed himself just outside the door, where other minions of the law dragged them up the street to the lockup.

While this ruckus was going on at the front of the joint, Sheriff Taylor and Deputy Kirgan were having a fair-sized riot of their own out back. About twenty Chinese were holding a position on a small hill and "keeping up a constant fire at the officers. Kirgan dropped one man and Taylor dropped two; but whether they were killed or wounded, no one knows.

> In a very short time, nearly all the male inhabitants of Bodie were in the vicinity of the shooting. . . . The shooting was kept up for all of an hour; and then Kirgan's Boarding House began to overflow with arrivals. Both cells were literally packed. As each one was brought in, his person was searched for concealed weapons.
>
> Our reporter had the pleasure of looking over the variety this morning, and pronounced it, "far ahead of any collection of relics that he has ever looked upon. There were no less than 18 knives, of all shapes and sizes, and of the most unique designs, and 15 guns that could completely demoralize any eastern man." . . . As yet but one body has been found, that of the informer. It is stated, though, by good authority that four are known to be killed; but they were immediately packed off by friends. Such being the case, the citizens of Bodie may never know their whereabouts.[25]

During the height of the riot "Tex" Hitchell, another Bodie peace officer, had a hair-raising experience. Arriving on the scene when the shooting first started, he charged around to the back of the opium den, plunged through the rear door and in the darkness fell through a trap door into the cellar. As he landed he became a target for the concealed "heathens." They fired three shots at him; but fortunately for Tex, the cellar dwellers were lousy shots.

From the testimony taken before the coroner's jury at the inquest over the body of George, the informer, it appeared that the shooting occurred when a group of Chinese conspired to liquidate a secret order to which several King Street Orientals belonged. George, who tipped off Deputy Sheriff Kirgan of the impending trouble, was rubbed out by one of the factions.

The findings of the coroner's jury stated: "We believe that

Lung Wa King, Charlie Fe Lung, Sam Sung, Wing Go Wing, Ah Sow, Charlie Sing Joe, and two other Chinamen were connected in the murder of the deceased. The jury further finds that the Chinese settlement, in the heart of Bodie on King Street, is a public nuisance; that their continual shooting affrays endangered the lives of citizens; that the filth, engendered in their hovels, threatens a pestilence. And the jury earnestly recommends that such steps be taken as will enforce the abatement of the nuisance, and removal of the pesthole elements outside of the town limits."[26]

George Daly, who was now superintendent of the Jupiter Mining Company, returned to his quarters tired and hungry. August 11 had been a busy day for him in Aurora. He had driven his light buggy back to Bodie over the dusty rough toll road as darkness came on, and he was as weary and dragged out as an unwound clock. On pushing open his door, he found a note, in the handwriting of his foreman, Joseph McDonald, whose contents instantly played tag with his blood pressure. Daly himself recounts the message and his subsequent action:

> Some parties had gone and commenced work on the south end of the Jupiter ground. I got up early in the morning . . . rode over to this place and saw some men that I had never seen before. Patrick Reynolds was on the ground. I got off my horse, and said, "Well boys, what are you doin'?" They replied, "We're sinking a shaft." I said, "What do you call this?" They said, "The Owyhee." That was the first I had ever heard of the Owyhee Claim. I said, "We call this the Jupiter." Reynolds said, "You do, heh? The Jupiter ain't got any ground here." I said, "Well, I am playing this for the Jupiter, and all within this post," which I then and there pointed out. One word led to another, and I told them that I was the agent for the Jupiter and its Superintendent, and ordered them to cease work, and they refused. Reynolds then (I think it was) made a remark, the gist of which was, that I could buy anything they had, but I couldn't drive them off. They would hold the ground, and that I would not put them off as long as shot guns would hold it. I made an answer in a laughing way. "Maybe the Jupiter could get some shot guns." Nothing further was said and I rode to the Jupiter Mine, and asked McDonald if he knew any of those men. He said that

> he knew most of them. I asked him to see them and explain the right of the matter, as they wouldn't listen to me. A day or so afterwards, I sent for the surveyor, Anderson [Deputy U.S. Mineral Surveyor], and requested him to go on the ground and run my lines over very carefully, that I wished to be sure there was no mistake, and that they were working inside the lines of the Savage and East Savage (now known as Jupiter). We went on the ground together and ascertained this shaft to be about on the line between the Savage and East Savage.
>
> I accused these men of removing the Jupiter stakes, which they denied. Whereupon, I remarked, that it seemed very strange that the only stakes that were removed were those that came on the Owyhee line. I then said that it was a felony to remove the stakes put there by the U.S. Mineral Surveyor, and that I would have them replaced and keep them there, if it would take a shot gun at each post. I learned that Goff, one of the owners of the Owyhee, was working at the Bodie Mine. . . . I had a conversation with Goff and endeavored to explain our rights to him and settle the matter amicably.[27]

Verbal threats and jawbone squabble went on for almost two weeks; but on August 22, George Daly brought the combustible situation to a head, when he had his miners from the Jupiter partly fill up the shallow Owyhee shaft and put up a small wooden cabin over it. That night he instructed his foreman, McDonald, to detail four miners to stand guard and see that no one attempted to take over the newly erected building.

About 1 A.M. the quiet of a summer night was ripped asunder by the crash of rifle fire; and the celebrated Jupiter-Owyhee battle was on as the six Owyhee partners, who had appropriated a hillside dugout from Peter Burke, opened up on the Daly cabin and at rifle flashes that followed from the Silas B. Smith shaft, about fifty feet beyond their hillside redoubt. After a period of sporadic firing the battle died down.

The second and final phase of the fight broke out about six o'clock in the morning. At the trial Patrick Lowney, one of the owners of the Owyhee claim who took part in the battle, gave this eyewitness account of how it ended: "About a quarter of an hour before the firing began, Goff and myself were sitting outside between the barrel and door with our guns in our hands. I came in before the first firing commenced. Goff stayed out alone. One shot was first fired and then several others. Goff came in after the first shot and said, 'They are on us.' I only fired two shots during the whole night. I was looking through one of the portholes all night. Goff was inside the cabin near the door when killed. Think he had a gun in his hand. After we surrendered and were delivered to the officer, Markey, he released us and we knocked around town all day in different saloons."[28]

For the Jupiter version of the battle, at this point, we pick up the testimony of John Andrews at the trial: "We were all standing there talking about the occurrences of the night, when we were opened fire upon again from the dugout. We scattered, and someone said—'Let's charge the dugout.' It was no sooner said, than we started. We got to the top of the dugout and fired once on the top. I then hollered out and said, 'There is no use of shooting any more.' They were hollering inside, and the firing was stopped. They were ordered to come out unarmed. Five came out and were surrounded, and were surrendered to the police, and the wounded men attended to. And, a very large gun stood near where Goff fell."[29] And so ended the shooting war over the Owyhee claim.

In mid-September, George Daly, Joseph McDonald, John Andrews, and the other Jupiter miners who had taken part in the fight were tried for the killing of John Goff of the Owyhee crowd.

U.S. Deputy Mineral Surveyor C. L. Anderson testified that "665 feet of the Owyhee comes on ground claimed by the Jupiter,"[30] and that a large 4-by-4-inch southwest corner stake he had erected during his June 19, 1879, survey was missing when he rechecked the lines in company with George Daly. And according to his survey, the Owyhee people were sinking their new shaft within the Jupiter lines.

George McArtney, Mining Recorder of the Bodie Mining District, was called for the defense and produced records of the district which showed that the Savage (Jupiter) was located June 18, 1877, the East Savage on November 27, 1877, and the Owyhee claim on April 18, 1878.[31]

The *Virginia Enterprise* of September 17, 1879, made the following summation of the case: "We learned that the testimony, given in the examination of George Daly and his associates at Bridgeport, California, establishes, beyond any possibility of dispute, the fact that the man Goff, who was killed, and his associates were doing their work on Jupiter ground, and that, it was their intention, either to steal the property of the Jupiter Co., or, to blackmail the company, or, to provoke a quarrel in which Daly was to be killed."

Daly and his associates were acquitted, and so far as the laws of the land were concerned, the case was closed. But in Bodie, Goff's friends, in the Miners' Union, stirred up a storm of mob bitterness and hate against George Daly, Joseph McDonald, and the other five miners of the Jupiter.

On Saturday afternoon, September 20, the Bodie Miners' Union met, in secret session, in what was at best a star-chamber conclave, and in utter disregard for constitutional rights and law of the land, issued a manifesto, which they had inserted in the Sunday morning paper.

NOTICE

Hall of the Bodie Miners' Union, September 20, 1879, 10 P.M.

The following resolution was adopted, that George Daly, Joseph McDonald, Barney McDonald, George Harbor, Joseph Burnelle, James Murphy, and John Andrews be ordered outside the limits of the Bodie Mining District within a period of 12 hours from the date of this notice.

Signed, J. P. SHAUGHNESSY, *President*
M. COHEN, *Recording Secretary*[32]

Daly's answer appeared in the same paper, and read:

TO ALL GOOD CITIZENS

The lawless element of the Miners' Union has passed a resolution ordering me and several men in the employ of the Jupiter Company to leave the camp within 12 hours.

We have been by the laws of our country declared innocent of any crime or wrong doing. We are American citizens, and, as such, are entitled to pursue our respective vocations, free from molestation; and, this right we propose to maintain. . . .

Signed, GEORGE DALY

"All parties named proceeded to the Jupiter Hoisting Works . . . and prepared themselves for a siege. Barricades were erected around the building, and portholes cut out to allow fire in every direction; and, arms and ammunition laid in and everything put in readiness for a vigorous defense. As 10 A.M. Sunday morning was fixed for the departure of Daly and his party and nothing exciting having occurred during the night . . . the citizens of the town, the few who were aware of what had occurred on the previous night, were very much excited and called a meeting for 11 A.M. to take council as to what was best to be done."[33]

The secretary of that meeting reported the proceedings as follows: "A number of merchants, bankers, lawyers, and other residents called on the citizens, requesting them to meet at the Engine House, and take the situation under advisement. At 11 A.M. the Engine House was completely filled with people, comprising the better portion of our citizens."[34]

On a proposal by Pat Reddy a citizens' committee was chosen, consisting of John Wagner, Harvey Boone, A. F. Bryant, A. J. Welch, Joseph McDermott, Charles Finley, Patrick Fahaey, C. H. West, and R. D. Ferguson.

The citizens' committee conferred with the Miners' Union and George Daly at the Jupiter Mine.

The members of the Miners' Union were found to be inflexible in their demands, while Daly was fully determined to fight it out.

The Union was in almost continuous session from one o'clock P.M. to eleven o'clock at night, while the citizens' committee passed back and forth attempting to make some compromise. The efforts of the committee appeared to have been directed more to a peaceable solution of the difficulty at a price, rather than to find out the absolute right of the matter and stand by it. Members of the committee urged Mr. Daly to recede from his position on the grounds that bloodshed would be liable to ensue, were he to remain. He, finally, concluded to leave the

> matter, so far as his own actions were concerned, to a committee of his friends consisting of Messrs. William Irwin, Captain Hayne, and Patrick Reddy. These gentlemen advised Daly against keeping up the fight because it would lead to open battle and to private assignations and reprisals. His friends would become involved and great detriment would result to the Camp. Upon these representations, it was decided to capitulate. They allowed Mr. Daly 48 hours to attend to his business affairs, and 24 hours in town once a month. The Union also guaranteed him and his friends freedom from molestation and insults during the remainder of his stay.[35]

The general feeling among the thoughtful tax-paying citizens of the camp was one of nauseated anger and disgust, that a power had risen, entirely unknown to the law, which assumed to say who could and could not live in Bodie. The *Daily Standard* editorial on September 23 pretty clearly wrapped up the whole situation in a blast of sarcastic ink:

> PEACE
>
> Grim Visage War has smoothed its wrinkled front, and peaceful gentle white-robed Peace now hovers over the Bodie Bluff. Our devoted people, devoted to the business of money making, and the sale of Pots and Pans, Whiskey, Flour, Vegetables, Newspapers, and the other necessities of life, can, once more, regulate the entire attention of their minds and bodies to their several pursuits. It is true that half a dozen men have been compelled to leave town. Some of them have families here, wives and children. When we contemplate how easily peace is obtained by simple sacrifice of the honor and manhood of the community, we can but think of the Revolutionary Fathers as an absurd lot of stubborn old fools—They fought eight years to establish American Liberty. How more sensible the conduct of the citizens of Bodie who would see American Liberty to the devil before they would fight eight minutes for it.
>
> The editorial ended with a resounding:
>
> LET US HAVE PEACE

The last week in September, to the lip-smacking delight of the boys in the press room and the news hawks of the *Daily Standard,* Ike Philips held the grand opening of his Parlor

Saloon, which took over the entire ground floor of the paper's new office building. And a drooling reporter, who counted himself fortunate to cover the event, extolled:

> Last evening one of the finest openings that ever took place occurred at the Standard Building. . . . Mr. Philips has truly earned a name for having The Parlor, for it resembles that part of the house more than any of its kind in Bodie. We have not space to describe its beauties in full. We were about to tear ourselves away when Ike threw open the door, and our first impression was that Mr. Philips had received a private dispatch from General Grant that he was about to visit Bodie, and Mr. Philips was preparing the repast. There was a little roast pig, decorated in fine style, several platters of salad, cold meats, and a huge pan of pork and beans, and several other favorite dishes. And, at 9 P.M., they commenced to serve up the feast. The Parlor was a continual jam until a late hour; and Mr. Philips may feel proud of having the most successful opening that ever occurred in Bodie.[36]

October 9, 1879, was a black day in Bodie's mining history. At the change of shift, nine men with their tools boarded the cage to descend the Tioga shaft. The lax and butter-fingered hoist engineer failed to clutch the cage reel to the engine. As the cage left the surface station, on its downward flight, the fumbling engineer was unable to hold it as the brakes faded away, and it dropped like a plummet 520 feet to the bottom, flipping into eternity J. R. Cassidy, H. Richards, Sam Martin, Manual Garcia, and Joseph Brodrier. Their five broken bodies were brought to the surface, along with four badly injured miners who somehow survived the camp's worst underground mine accident.

Later in the month a hard-working miner by the name of Almond Parks left a widow and two children to mourn his untimely fate. After mucking out a round in the bottom of a winze in the Black Hawk, known for the bad air that prevailed, Parks started up the ladder to take a rest and get a lungful of fresh air. Fifty feet up the ladder, overcome by the fumes, he lost his grip and fell to his death.

Bodie was the roaringest camp in the West that fall. The

stampede had brought thousands of people to the district. The streets of the town were full of hustle and bustle, from dawn to dusk. Hundreds of teams, pulling everything from freighters to light buggies, choked the streets, and runaways were frequent.

J. R. Ritchey, a well-known businessman, stirred up plenty of excitement in the crowded downtown area, just after lunch on October 9. He was driving his big powerful gray down Main Street, when the horse became frightened and bolted.

> When opposite Robinson's Blacksmith Shop, the wagon struck against a derrick standing in the street and was thrown against the sidewalk in front of Kemp & Coleman's Occidental. It struck with such force that Mr. Ritchey was bounced into the air. Still clinging to the reins, he came down, struck the lamp on top of the post, bending it completely over, and fell with terrible force against the sidewalk. The horse broke free from the wagon, and with the traces dangling, dashed down the street. In an open carriage in front of Sun and Company's store sat Miss Addie Kennedy. The runaway horse struck the carriage in which the young lady was sitting. Her horse became frightened and took off. It had not gone far, when she was thrown out, and for a time it was feared Miss Kennedy had sustained a serious injury. The two horses broke free and dashed down Main Street. Miss Kennedy's horse was stopped at the post office, the carriage badly smashed.
>
> Mr. Ritchey's horse raced down King Street, and came upon a crowd of Chinamen who were holding a festival over a dead Chinaman. They scattered like sheep, leaving the corpse to take care of itself.[37]

Miss Kennedy was taken into the store of Sun and Company and revived with smelling salts. Helping hands carried merchant Ritchey to his store. The doctor who was called could find no broken bones, only a few bruises. The whole affair was pronounced a miracle.

Judge J. G. McClinton,[38] superintendent of the Consolidated Pacific Mining Company, took great delight in the bird's-eye view of the camp that the high eminence of the company's hoisting works afforded. He swelled with pride as his gaze leveled south across almost two miles of beehive activity that was Bodie in late October, 1879. His eye took in the long line of puffing hoisting works and pounding stamp mills. All along the great new lode, men could be seen mining, hoisting, hauling. Far to the south end he could make out the buildings of the new 30-stamp Noonday Mill, the largest in the camp and scheduled to start crushing any day now; while over the far horizon the friendly glittering Sierra giants of Castle Peak, Dana, Ritter, and Banner held sway. What a change had been wrought in this place since 1861, when in that little ravine coursing west from the Mono shaft, he found a placer location notice written on the leaf of a memorandum book, tightly folded and stuck in the protective fork of a large brush, bearing the signature of W. S. Bodey! Yes, the thought of this old prospector, whose name this booming metropolis proudly carried, conjured up a feeling of bitterness and disgust at some of the lying impostors that he had encountered, who claimed friendship and partnership with Bodey. Lately some of these brazen liars had pushed themselves into print with yarns spun out of whole cloth. The Judge was well acquainted with Terrance Brodigan and Pat Garrity, the still living members of the district's discovery party. From them he had many times heard the factual account of that first prospecting trip to the district. From Johnson King and Black Taylor, long since departed, he had learned the facts of the discovery and burial of Bodey's remains, after the winter snows of 1859-60 had melted.

As he beheld the stimulating panorama the recesses of his mind suddenly zeroed in on a long-forgotten incident. Yes, there it was behind that low hill and not far from the eastern face of that dark vaulting ridge of black palisade rocks. McClinton's suddenly triggered mental recall brought it all back now in sharp focus. About eight years ago, on a hot July day, he had ridden over from Aurora to visit the then dead and desolate camp of Bodie, to check on some mining claims. "His horse wandered off into the hills west of the present town. While hunting for the animal, he came across a pile or ridge of loose stones, that attracted his attention in a general way. The stones left a flat but not a special impression."[39] Yes, he remembered now! It certainly tallied with Taylor and King's account of Bodey's resting place. He could almost see the area—a little over a mile southwesterly from where he stood. A day or so later he discussed the long-forgotten incident with Joseph Wasson, who had just compiled a revised edition of his *Bodie and Esmeralda Publication.*

And so it was that on Saturday, October 25, 1879, they made a tour of the area on horseback, and in

> . . . less than an hour's time McClinton came upon the identical old stone pile. They decided to prospect the new find thoroughly. [The following morning they returned with] a pick and shovel and Indian Tom to the scene. The Judge, being under the weather, Wasson took the pick and went at the work prospector fashion, the Indian following in the wake with a shovel. The work commenced about half past eleven A.M. In about three quarters of an hour, a much decomposed silk necktie was uncovered. Soon followed a rather well preserved shoe attached to the right foot of all that was left of W. S. Bodey. The heel of the shoe was worn and broken down to the upper leather as if it had been used more as a slipper. The bones of the foot were found quite disjointed. The shoe of the left foot was missing entirely, that foot apparently being wrapped in some sort of cloth. The work of exhuming was continued by Wasson, McClinton, and Indian Tom until the skeleton was laid bare above the hip joints. Then it was concluded to leave it, until inspected in place, as the miners say, by the leading citizens of the district. . . .
>
> This morning, October 27th, a party of gentlemen, consisting of Honorable F. K. Bechtel, Honorable Joseph Wasson, William Irwin, H. V. Davidson, Sheriff Elect James Showers, George Gilson, J. C. Turner, Col. S. W. Blasdel, Warren Loose, Sam Martin, J. T. Baker of "The Morning News," E. R. Cleveland of the "Free Press' and a representative of the "Standard News" went out to the half open grave. The party took turns in shoveling out the dirt, and soon the entire skeleton was exposed. The skull was well preserved, the teeth being in a perfect state of preservation. About the waist was found a belt with a leather scabbard and knife attached. When this relic was found Warren Loose was digging and exclaimed, "There's his knife, I've heard Brodigan say he always wore it." The hilt of the knife was marked with a medallion of a woman's head on one side and a

lion on the other. The scabbard is, evidently, a home-made affair, fastened with bullet rivets.

The remains were brought downtown and left at Dr. Davidson's office, together with other relics.

Brodigan saw Bodey a day or two before his death and will probably be able to identify the knife and other effects.[40]

On the first Sunday in November the whole camp turned out to honor the tenacious old Argonaut whose name it bore. The *Daily Bodie Standard* of November 3 recorded that

> . . . the genuine remains of "Old Man Bodey" were given a very respectful funeral yesterday. The afternoon was delightful, and the good people of Bodie turned out and gave what was left of the Old Pioneer a square shake down. His last little bed being quite an improvement upon the old horseblanket fare accorded him in the loose rock and sagebrush soil of 20 years ago. Mr. Ferguson's pithy and poignant address at the new grave was a fitting tribute worthy of the living and the dead. He was not the less impressive because of the presences of the score of graybeards numbered among the pallbearers and spectators who entered into the spirit of the scene as it deserved. It is now in order to provide a substantial monument over the consecrated spot in the new cemetery; and, also, some mark of respect at the spot where the body was found. However much more we are all now given to money-getting and bread-winning, the occasion is one that should not be lost sight of with the burial of this well-known Pioneer's remains–Let us have no halfway measures; but stand in and complete the work at once.

The same sheet announced that H. Z. Osborne, who had been managing editor of the *Standard* since May, 1878, was leaving the paper. He had acquired a commanding interest in the town's newest publication by buying the interest of John M. Dormer and Harry Fontecilla and joining up with that organ's remaining partner, E. R. Cleveland. The result became the spectacularly successful *Daily Free Press.*

As the busy days of late fall arrived the camp was subjected to a siege of pneumonia, or typhoid pneumonia as it was sometimes called. Many of its citizens were laid low with this malady. Although some did not survive the plague (as the *Virginia En-*

terprise called it), the number of deaths was grossly exaggerated. One writer in the same paper dashed off a well-varnished account that claimed the people in Bodie were "dying like sheep, without medical attention; and are not given a decent burial; and, he expected, that men will be rolled up in blankets and dumped into some old mine shaft soon."[41]

No less an authority than Bodie undertaker H. Ward was called upon to refute the rash of absurd stories making the pages of the outside press. This worthy statistician of the marble orchard penned a hasty last-minute census of citizens who had recently answered the toot of Gabriel's horn: "Permit me, through your paper, to correct some misrepresentations which I read in the 'Enterprise' of Sunday, November 13th, headed 'A SHOCKING CONDITION OF THINGS IN BODIE.' In the first place, there never have been 12 dead bodies buried in Bodie at one time since I have been here the last two years. The most at any time was seven. The last month, October, there were 29 deaths. I buried them all myself, except one. That one was sent below for interment. In the present month, November, up to the 17th, there have been 20 deaths all told, of which I will give you the names and dates for publication if you desire."[42]

However, the *Daily Standard* of the eighteenth, which published embalmer Ward's tally sheet, came forth with, "The boys don't swing the 'Hurdies' to any great extent in these funeral times of Pneumonia,"[43] and followed with another flip literary jab: "A dog was run over in the Main Street by a wagon the other day, and killed. We mention this fact for fear that some of the outside papers might get hold of it and say that the dogs of Bodie were dying of the Pneumonia, and that the papers are keeping it a secret."[44]

It was almost a year later that a thoughtful scribe, after considerable meditation on the real cause of the outbreak of sickness that fall, hit the nail on the head with the sage observation that "it is a well known fact that the wells of Bodie are simply receptacles of the drainage of surrounding outhouses and surface filth. The water is so obnoxious as to be unfit for any use and is a certain source of dissemination of disease."[45]

As time marched swiftly through the last half of November the camp needed something to take its mind off its troubles. The diversion arrived with a bang in the person of a torrid Spanish whore, named Rosa, whose fading shopworn beauty still quickened the glances of lonely miners. A press hound, conveniently on the scene, recorded that "a fracas occurred about 12 o'clock last evening between a Spanish woman, one of the demi-monde, known as Rosa, and a man named Green, in the Can-Can Restaurant, in which the latter man received a frightful cut across the face." Rosa and the man had some angry words. She flashed a wicked little two-edged stiletto and proceeded to perform some painful surgery, one slash of which extended from an eye diagonally over the cheek and mouth to the chin. "Special officer Farnsworth arrested the woman and locked her up for the night. Green made a complaint today before Judge Peterson of an assault and an attempt to commit murder, and Rosa is now rustling for a bond in the sum of $1,000."[46]

Four days later she had her day in court. The pad-and-pencil boys joyfully jotted down the spectacle. "The examination of Rosa, the Castilian Cyprian who cut Green last week, was going on before Judge Peterson today. It was anticipated that there would be a spice of wickedness in the evidence. In consequence, the court room was crowded with eager onlookers. The defendant, a rather petite good looking if somewhat haggard brunette, gave the court and crowd and prosecuting witnesses a reckless devil-may-care look of defiance. She was dressed in black with a light scarf around her neck, and was the cynosure of all eyes. One fellow, while elbowing his way in, was heard to remark, 'She's a wicked lookin' cat, ain't she.' "[47]

About a week later Rosa was free from her first entanglement. Enjoying the publicity and its business advantages, she decided to eliminate certain competitors. The *Daily Standard* of the twenty-eighth tersely records the action: "A Cyprian on the rampage—Rosa, the same Spanish maid who slashed Green across the cheek, got full of fighting whiskey, and donned her war-paint, and started to clean out the soiled Dovecotes on Bonanza

Street, Thanksgiving evening. The officers put her in a little bed in the jail, where she now remains."[48]

Another grisly mining accident occurred, this time at the Jupiter Mine: "A carpenter by the name of Smith Russel was caught between the cage and the shaft timbers and absolutely crushed, breaking nearly every bone in his body."[49]

Nothing produced a crowd on the streets of Bodie quicker than the arrival in town of matched perfection in horseflesh—just as today's display of Detroit's latest chrome power package brings them on the run.

A keen-eyed observer noted that "General Kittrell has returned from Independence, where he purchased a magnificent pair of buggy horses. . . . They are a beautiful sorrel, and about 16 hands high, clean limbed, proud spirited 'high steppers,' but gentle and kindly natured. The price paid was $900, and they are worth it, for they are known as the best pair of horses in Inyo County; and the General is justly proud of his purchase."[50]

"Wells and Kilpatrick of the Bodie Foundry offered to furnish a cast iron monument to be erected to the memory of W. S. Bodey. The Pioneer Society will act upon the offer next Tuesday evening."[51]

A stabbing affray drew the attention of the town during the last of November. A prominent counselor at law and a masonry contractor had it out on Main Street, while a sporting saloon crowd looked on. "The unfortunate affray occurred in front of the Mammoth Saloon in which John A. McQuaide stabbed Thomas Muckle. . . . McQuaide had just gotten out of the buggy when stonecutter, Muckle, approached him in a slightly 'oiled' condition and began berating him over a money matter with negligible results. Thereupon, the impatient Thomas bounced a haymaker smack dab on the counselor's left optic. The legal beagle retaliated with a lightning thrust of an abbreviated Bowie—stabbing Muckle wickedly, but not fatally, under the left rib cage. McQuaide was immediately arrested."[52] Later he stood trial and was acquitted on a plea of self-defense.

The fun-loving sporting crowd of the camp were not above

pulling off a practical joke. A day or so after the McQuaide-Muckle blood-letting affray,

> Ed Jackson ran into the Rosedale Saloon, exclaiming that he had been cut. His shirt bosom was all bloody, and he showed two frightful gashes on each side of his throat. Officer Kirgan was quickly called and on seeing the wounded man exclaimed—"Great God, who's done this?"—and at the same time pulling out a pistol from one pocket and a pair of handcuffs from another, and was just going to rush out to capture the perpetrator. Then he thought that he would take a good look at the cut. He lifted up Jackson's hat and tried to wipe the blood off his neck with a handkerchief to get a fair view of the wound, but the blood was so thick that it wouldn't wipe off worth a cent. Jackson, meanwhile, kept staggering about, as if going to fall. The bystanders didn't seem to be the least bit excited—"Damn you fellows," ripped out Kirgan, "Some of you go and get a doctor. You'd stand around like knots on a pine log, and let a man bleed to death." The flinty-hearted fellows showed never a sign of sympathy, and nary a one stirred, and some of them began to laugh—Kirgan began to scent a very extensive mouse and taking a good look at the blood, found it to be paint. With an exclamation more forcible than polite, he swore that he would put Jackson in jail for his pains; but, finally, he joined in the laughs and 'set 'em up.' [53]

The fame of Bodie's scintillating rise as the latest golden wonder of the West was generally acknowledged by mining investors in the eastern stock exchanges of New York and Boston. The latest news from the camp was eagerly sought after. When B. B. Minor, a well-known San Francisco businessman with heavy interests in Bodie mines and banks, arrived in the East, he was interviewed by a reporter of the New York American Stock Exchange. Minor was quoted in all the leading eastern financial organs of the day, with unreserved optimism. "There is no mining camp on the Pacific Coast where so many mines are in successful operation. . . . The milling capacity by January 1880, will total 115 stamps. In addition to this, The Spaulding Company has commenced grading for a 10 stamp mill. . . . With these stamps running, the monthly production of Bodie should rise to $5,000,000 a month."[54] Minor's enthusiasm and confident words of prophecy, that portended a bountiful dividend harvest, were shared by mining investors both east and west as 1879 readied its exit.

The *Daily Bodie Standard* of Monday, December 22, proudly announced that the camp had a population "of more than 7,000, and has not had a death for nearly two weeks." While this was comforting to the plague worried citizens who now counted their good fortune at surviving the grim reaper during the pneumonia-ridden days of early fall; it cast a shadow of uncertainty for A. C. Friend, who only three weeks before had confidently taken delivery of a magnificent new $2,900 hearse.

That December a well-known young man about town, who was a clerk and a sports enthusiast to the core, could hardly wait for the first good snowfall. When it arrived a few days before Christmas, his enthusiasm knew no bounds. In his subsequent adventures, by the narrowest of margins, he missed the dubious honor of having the first ride in Bodie's magnificent new Black Maria. His exploits, as recorded in the local press of the twenty-third, are as follows:

> . . . He is better known for his champion connecting snowshoes. He had learned to use them in a San Jose flower garden. So, he mounted on his new pair at the mine and started down for Main Street. Things went along smoothly for a 100 yards or so, the snow being soft and the descent gradual; but pretty soon, the hill got steeper and the snow comparatively harder. Then the snowshoes acted as if they were bewitched. Starting at breakneck speed, the rider managed to hold his balance for a couple of hundred yards, 'til the snowshoes collided with the stable. There, he made a flying leap of some 25 foot radius, alighting on the roof and crashing through to scare a pensive cow nearly to death. When the boys came to his rescue and were bearing him tenderly to his lodgings, he said, as soon as he could catch his breath, "Too smart, too cunning, and write on my tombstone, He died in a successful attempt to put a skylight in a cowshed."[55]

Christmas Eve, '79, was celebrated by the opening banquet of the new Grand Central Hotel, Bodie's finest hostelry. A sentimental free-loading member of the fourth estate reported the glamorous occasion and the superb provender: "The attendance was large, including many ladies; and a more sociable and happy assemblage has never been seen in Bodie. The tables groaned under a load of luxuries which were highly appreciated by all; and wine and wit flowed freely.

"When all were seated and the viands were being discussed, a quartet in the hallway adjoining the dining room struck up Christmas Carols which were followed from time to time during the banquet with songs filling the building with melody. After supper the party adjourned to the parlor above where songs and general merriment were indulged in for an hour or so while the dining room was being cleared for dancing which was kept up till a late hour."[56]

Christmas Day was a big occasion for the camp, and an exuberant daily, flushed with the strong wine of exaltation, rushed into print with:

THE NOONDAY MILL—30 MORE STAMPS—THUNDERING AWAY

> The splendid new 30 stamp mill of the Noonday Mining Company was started up for the first time yesterday, Christmas afternoon, in the presences of a large number of people, and amid the popping of champagne corks. A lady visitor sounded the whistle for the start; and when the ponderous machinery moved off like the works of the most delicate watch, other ladies seized the whistle cord and made the hills ring with a prolonged whistle. The visitors included members of the press, merchants, bankers, and others; and all seemed delighted with the fine success of the start, as if they had been personally interested as builders. Mrs. John Parham, wife of the Superintendent of the Noonday Mine and Mill, presided in the engine room, by personally opening several bottles of champagne. Toasts were drunk; but the noise of the heavy machinery was too great for any extended remarks and reply. The mill is situated near the mine with mine car tracks running from the hoisting works to the battery for the transportation of ore.[57]

Later in the week the camp was blanketed by one of the worst snowstorms to ever hit in the district. For several days the miners were unable to go to work at the Bodie Bluff Consolidated and several other mines on the hill. The old-timers always referred to it as the Great Storm. It heralded the start of a long, hard winter, and its coming marked the end of wheel traffic into the camp for months to come; and prudent citizens rechecked with care the stove wood in their woodpiles.

In some neighborhoods a sharp lookout was kept for the ever-present wood pirates, who if not watched could heist the contents of a woodpile in a night or two. A local sheet carried a veiled warning to these thieves: "Those citizens who have been loading wood with giant powder cartridges say they don't care a straw if they do fire the houses of wood thieves, by blowing them up."[58]

The camp sped into the new year with a nostalgic backward glance at the corridors of memory. A sentimental scribe with a fleeting sense of the sweep of Western history gravely chronicled:

> OLD AND NEW—TRANSIT OF THE ARGONAUTS. Reunion and Banquet of the Pioneers at the Grand Central Hotel, New Year's Eve.—The New Year's Eve reunion and banquet of the "Pacific Coast Pioneers Society of Bodie" at the Grand Central Hotel was one of the co-mingling of old comrades and new friends which marked an epoch in the social history. . . . The arrangements were perfect; and for this, the officers and their guests are indebted to Mr. M. H. Harrington, The Marshall. The splendid dining hall of the Grand Central was filled to its utmost capacity with Pioneers and invited guests. Some private dining rooms were brought into requisition for the accommodation of those who could not gain admission to the main dining hall. The feast was of the bountiest and of the very best. Waiters glided about noiselessly and were prompt and polite. The whole management being under the efficient personal supervision of Mr. S. N. Pritcher, manager of the hotel. By 9 p.m., the parlor of the hotel was filled with ladies and a half hour later the "old boys" filed down from Judge Peterson's office and entered the large reading room of the hotel. When the band struck up "Marching through Georgia" the dining room doors were thrown open; and the ladies from the parlor above with their escorts marched down and took seats at the tables—two tables, one on each side, extended from end to end of the hall. A table placed across the hall near the entrance was assigned to the members of the press.

After music by the band, the feast began, and wine and wit and sentiment flowed for hours. First, and greatest instrumental musical treat of the evening, was the duet from the opera, "The Barber of Seville," on the violin. A. Petroni and A. Berlinger at the piano, both being masters of their respective instruments. President Hunt and Maurice Greggory then sang "The Seven Soldiers" and "Little Boy," a touching and beautiful little ballad that elicited rounds of applause. Mr. and Mrs. Molinari rendered, in Italian, and with wonderful sweetness and power, "Ah, Si, Coll'-essere" from the opera "Il Trovatore." . . .

Vice president Folger, at the tick of twelve o'clock, arose and, with great earnestness, wished the assemblage a "Happy New Year." Mrs. Hetsel then recited Tennyson's ringing recitation to the New Year and was loudly applauded. "Yankee Doodle" by the band and "Free and Easy" followed. There were humorous speeches by Col. Jackson and Dr. Davidson. The latter said that he presumed everybody like himself was prepared to turn over a new leaf—he had been thinking the matter over for four or five days, but couldn't make up his mind which leaf to turn over. . . . At this stage of the proceedings, several men walked in with their arms full of champagne bottles with the announcement that Jessie Summers, the cattleman, wished the entire assemblage "A Happy New Year," and desired them to take a glass of champagne with him. When the champagne corks ceased their rattle of musketry, a sweet little nine year old girl, with a wreath of golden hair, flowing down like a mantle below her waist, appeared upon one of the tables and recited and acted to perfection, "A Snack in School." The self-possession and dramatic power displayed by this little fairy, Miss Florence Molinari, took the audience by storm, and the recitation was frequently interrupted by rapturous applause. "John Brown's Body" then sprang spontaneously from the grave and went marching on. One after another followed into the chorus, until the whole audience and band joined in; and with every foot on the floor beating time to the sweet swinging air. . . .

Vice president Folger [*Chronicle*] proposed a toast to the Press of Bodie and called upon the band to respond with the "Rogues' March." The band failing to respond, Mr. H. Z. Osborne [*Free Press*] was called upon. He responded briefly that the press—especially that of Bodie—was made up of that class like Mr. Folger whom he wouldn't object to seeing marching to the tune of the "Rogues' March." After this there was much applause. . . .

Alexander Hunt, an accomplished elocutionist, favored the

audience with a recitation of "The Fellows Apology to the Judge." He received rounds of applause. . . .

One of the gems of the evening was an original poem recited by the author, Maurice Greggory, entitled

"THE OLD SLUICE BOX"

"Where the rocks are gray and the mountains steep,
And the gulch below looks dark and deep,
Where the gnarled pines in their rugged pride,
Loomed gloomily up on either side,
Where the manzanita is crooked and thick,
Where once was heard the shovel and pick,
Where the shadows lie heavily upon the rocks,
There lies, half buried, The Old Sluice Box.

. . . .

From the moss-grown rock on which I lean,
I gaze down into the sluggish stream.
The face that I see has graver grown,
And my voice has a somber tone,
And the wanton wind, with my hair at play,
Shows that my locks have all turned gray.
So, I love to think of the days long gone by
When spirits were light, and my hopes were high,
And I could welcome again, the rough hard knocks,
To be mining once more with The Old Sluice Box."

Judge Hetsel, in a very appropriate and eloquent speech, returned the thanks of the guests for the hospitality extended to them by the Pacific Coast Pioneer Society of Bodie. "But a few minutes ago," said the speaker, "We passed a milestone, an epoch, broadly and strongly marked; and we thank these old veterans, not for their hospitality extended us; but that we are here. Thirty-one years ago, this place was a howling wilderness, inhabited only by the coyote and Piute."[59]

And so, echoing these and other remarks made by various speakers, the first two hours of the new year were passed in Bodie. The finale came when the band discovered "Home Sweet Home" and the happy audience marched out of the dining room and into 1880.

CHAPTER VI

The Camp in Its Magic Hour - 1880

The year was but a few hours old when Thomas Travis lay sprawling and choking in his own blood on the snow-covered board sidewalk in front of the Concert Hall dance house. Officers Markey and Black arrived on the double and collared the knife-wielding antagonist, Tom Dillon, whom they forced away from the fallen man. Travis was pulled to a sitting position. With blood pulsing from severed arteries in his side and back, he raised his pistol and with the last remnant of his ebbing strength fired one shot, which ripped into Dillon, felling him like a poled ox into the already crimson-spattered snow.

An eyewitness, James Mulligan, recounted that "Travis then sang out to me to 'run down and tell Dolly to come and see me.' As he fell back he remarked that he was dying. . . . He was then taken into the dance house, and did not live over four or five minutes."[1]

Dillon, though critically wounded, managed to pull through and a few months later, in March, was tried for killing Travis; but lack of evidence and his strong plea of self-defense brought his release.

Not all was blood and violence in Bodie on that first day of 1880. The merry sound of sleigh bells carried the intoxicating joy of the holidays and the bright new year in chiming harmony back and forth across town, as friends and neighbors kept the old tradition of open house and the happy exchange of New Year's greetings. The local press with sly artfulness noted, "As 1880 is a Leap Year, young ladies will have the privilege of making New Year calls."[2]

The first week in January the following news items were served up in a "Brief Mention" column:

"A Mexican woodpacker on the Bridgeport-Bodie road had nine mules frozen to death during the late storm.

"The cable at the Bodie Mine broke yesterday morning, precipitating a water tank to the bottom of the shaft and smashing it to atoms.

"The Bodie Social Minstrels will perform in Aurora on Friday and Saturday evening."[3]

The merchants and citizens of the camp were bending every effort, in spite of adverse weather conditions, to perfect a high-pressure water system for fire protection for their bustling new city of 7,000. The *Daily Standard* of January 7 called attention to

> . . . the progress of the work of pipe laying made by Gilson-Barber and Company, the contractors who are furnishing and laying the pipe for the new water works. They, and the ditch contractors as well, deserve the greatest credit for the energy expended in preparing the town for defense against fire. The ditch being contemplated will run the whole 1800 feet along Main Street. As the pipe is all ready, the laying will be completed within a week should the threatening storm blow over. Yesterday 500 feet of pipe properly secured were placed in position from the Standard Mill crossing to Main Street. The latter street was closed, but during the night the crossing was restored for teams.
>
> There are to be eight large hydrants, or fire plugs, placed along the line; one at the Standard Mill crossing; one at the northeast corner of Mill and Main Streets; and one every 300 feet along the 1800-foot line of pipe on the west side of Main Street. This will embrace the whole populous portion of the main thoroughfare. The two hose carts, manufactured in San Francisco to the order of Gilson-Barber & Co., have arrived, together with 1,000 feet of hose. The hose will be kept on the reels and can be dispatched to any threatened point at a moment's notice. Gates are to be put in near Mill Street so that the water may be cut off from either end of the town, and then let run to the other end.[4]

The dubious distinction of being the most litigated mining company in the district was held by the Rustler. The *San Francisco Stock Report* of the sixth commented: "The Rustler Gold Mining Company of Bodie is the champion mine for law suits. No less than eleven different suits have been commenced over

Mrs. Patrick Reddy, an early "arbiter elegantiae" of Bodie society. *(Grace P. Crocker Collection)*

William H. "Billy" Metson, as he appeared in one of his ast courtroom battles, nearing eighty and full of fight. *(San Francisco Examiner)*

H. Z. Osborne (right), editor and publisher of the Bodie Free Press in the "Heyday." Photographed with Major M. Stedman, N.C. (C.S.A.) when they were the only surviving members of the "Blue and Gray" in the House of Representatives. *(Raymond G. Osborne Collection)*

The Standard's five-pounder. This is the one that survived the Glorious Fourth, '81.

A buggyload of Bodie belles. Fourth of July at the race track.

Sixteen-mule team, straining at a heavy load of mining machinery, arrives at Camp. *(Los Angeles County Museum of Natural History, by permission of J. McLaren Forbes)*

Freighting over the Sonora-Mona Trail. *(Tuolumne County Museum)*

A Bodie-bound wood train pauses for a brief stop at Warm Springs on the eastern shore of Mono Lake before starting the long uphill trip to Bodie. An "old-timer" pointed out that this ancient wood-burning locomotive should be the Tybo. *(Ella Farrington Mattly Collection)*

"The Bodie," the most powerful locomotive put in service by the Bodie & Benton Railroad. (Sadie

Main Street. Bodie in the winter, lighter than usual snow pack. *(Sadie Moyle Palany Collection)*

William H. "Billy" Metson visits the Lent Hoisting Works. Its shaft, over 1,200 feet, was Bodie's deepest. *(Francis H. Frederick Collection)*

Early Bodie fire companies' captains. *(Francis H. Frederick Collection)*

Nine-passenger open Henderson coach on the Independence-Bodie run. *(Los Angeles County Museum of Natural History, by permission of J. McLaren Forbes)*

"Spanish Joe's" jackass wood train arrives on the double from Rough Creek with bulging packs of pinon to fire the boilers of Bodie's first stamp mill. *(Los Angeles County Museum of Natural History, by permission of J. McLaren Forbes)*

A trail-weary, charcoal-laden pack train makes for the Standard's blacksmith shop. The superintendent's house is on the right. After the turn of the century it was called the Hoover House for Theodore Hoover, brother of the thirty-first U.S. President, who lived there when he was superintendent. *(Los Angeles County Museum of Natural History, by permission of J. McLaren Forbes)*

The Leavitt House. Ninety years ago, its hospitality was sought eagerly by stage-weary Bodie-bound travelers. Now it is known as the Bridgeport Hotel-Motel. The authentic historical quaintness of its parlor and the comforts of its rooms still refresh the hurried traveler. *(Grace P. Crocker Collection)*

Lundy—Fourth of July, 1900. Mrs. W. O. Lundy and W. O. Lundy, seventh and eighth from left. (Grace P. Crocker Collection)

The Tioga Pass Road. Long before the advent of the automobile, it was a two-day trip by pack outfit from Mono Lake to Yosemite Valley. *(Los Angeles County Museum of Natural History, by permission of J. McLaren Forbes)*

ground held by the Rustler by eleven different companies. . . . The Rustler ground promises to be a bonanza for the lawyers." Meanwhile, the mine itself was in borrasca and paid only "Irish dividends [assessments]."[5]

As the freezing days of January sped by, a multitude of rumors rode the shifting winds of speculation concerning the status of the Bodie Consolidated. The mine workings had been closed to any and all visitors for months. On January 20 a Bodie daily in a probing article attempted to draw aside the veil of secrecy and silence with the following article:

> There is something so mysterious about this mine and its management that it is attracting general attention and, to some extent, distracting all other attempts to fathom the mystery. Private letters are pouring into Bodie from New York asking for information concerning the present condition and the prospects of the mine. . . . All kinds of stories are floating about, "The dividends are played out, and, many people here think the mine has come to a standstill." The dividend last declared was 25¢. It is said that the company shipped $109,000 in bullion yesterday, and certain it is that within the past 48 hours a new find was made in the mine deemed of sufficient importance by the superintendent to have it recorded as the Fortuna. This new vein was discovered in the east crosscut on the 433 foot level. Altogether it would seem that the outlook for the Bodie Consolidated was more encouraging than at any other period in the history of the Mine.[6]

By mid-January the town was upset by the utter disregard for law and order shown by the riffraff element of the camp. A local sheet cried out that "a Mexican was knocked down and robbed inside of The Old Tuolumne Stables about one o'clock this morning. And footpads and garroters ply their trade in the streets of Bodie, and, perhaps, this is why the officers keep off the streets late at night."[7]

The growing disenchantment of the solid citizens of the town with certain members of the constabulary was further fanned into action when

> . . . a troop of hoodlum boys, ranging in age from 8 to 20,

> crashed the theater last night. A number of them climbed in a high window, and in doing so broke several panes of glass. Once inside, their noise was deafening, and their language disgusting. One officer, we presume he was an officer, climbed up among them at one time and quieted them for a few minutes; but as soon as he left their presence, the acts of hooliganism broke out with renewed vigor. One boy, 12 or 14 years of age, was passed over the heads of the hoodlum men and boys from the rear and elevated over chairs occupied by ladies on the floor. In making the attempt to pass another boy over, the intended victim braced himself against the wall, and down came the whole tier of seats, men, boys, lumber falling down with a crash. Several persons were severely bruised and skinned about the feet and legs, and it seemed simply miraculous that no limbs were broken. While all this was going on, an officer stood in the aisle quietly smoking a cigar.[8]

The *Daily Bodie Standard,* applying the well-known power of the press, helped to crystallize public opinion and bring things to a head when they publicly offered a fine Chromo as a prize for the first garroter or footpad who could catch an officer out in the street at night. This stung the night patrol into publishing a card of denial and denunciation against the editor of the *Standard.* He immediately squared off with the four irate officers in a cleverly prepared blast in the edition of January 28:

> That Chromo wakes up the night watchman. . . . It is now on display in Ike Philip's Saloon under the Standard office, and it will be given to the first garroter or footpad who complies under the conditions imposed and no questions will be asked. The offer was not only made in good faith; but for a good purpose in order to bring the officers and the garroters in close contact with each other, as there appears no other way of getting them together. We have never heard of them coming together, though it is darkly whispered that they do possibly meet in back rooms and dark alleys after a successful garrotering operation has been performed. . . . If we are rightly informed, Mr. Markey's beat extends along Main Street, southward from Mill Street on which two recent cases of garrotering have occurred. One of them was within 40 feet of Mr. Markey. The beat patrol led by Messrs. Black and Farnsworth extends along the Main Street from Mill Street northward to the Hurdy Houses on which garroting and similar pursuits are actively carried on. Mr. Hitch-

ell guards Chinatown where assaults are far more numerous than arrests, and opium smoking is carried on, on a large scale; the dens appear to be especially guarded against disturbances from others than their patrons.[9]

An aroused citizenry took action, and by mid-February most of the above-mentioned deputy constables had been replaced, and within a few weeks Bodieites walked their streets without fear of molestation from the rough elements who were curbed for a time.

Also in February the preliminary organization of Bodie's unit of state militia "was completed, 75 members being sworn in by F. P. Willard, A. A. G. The following commissioned officers were then elected: Captain William A. Irwin, Jr., First Lt. M. B. Kelly, Second Lt. T. H. Smith. Non-commissioned officers will be appointed. It is presumed that the Adjutant General of the state will immediately forward arms to the company. And then, let the Piutes attempt a raid on Bodie, if they dare."[10]

As February came to a close a simmering newspaper war broke out into the open. Bodie with its bustling population of 7,000 had four daily papers fighting for a toehold and a piece of the advertisers' dollar and the readers' interest. By March first choosy readers could take their pick of one evening and three morning news sheets. Hostilities between the inkpots started out in a mild manner as earlier in the year the *Daily Standard* casually referred to the *Chronicle* as its "gulch" contemporary, or to the new and vigorous *Free Press* as the "little press in the alley." The *Standard,* on January 29, stung by many barbs and the loss of more than a few subscribers to the *Free Press* and the *Chronicle,* took dirty aim at the latter morning rag's affinity for coining jingling verse with: "The Warbler of the Waste Dump turned the crank of his rhythm mill today and, as usual, round smooth chunks of poetry rolled out like sausages from a sausage stuffer. It trickles in rhythm rills over the sensibilities of the tenderly susceptible, with a sort of splash—

'Mary we shall always miss you
Gone will be your pleasant smile.'

Had the oilcan been much larger you would have gone about a mile. 'Whom the Gods love, die young,' is an old and truthful saying, and we shudder when we think of the early and untimely fate of the sweet singer of the Waste Dump. Gone will be his feet-like hams, misty will be his watery rime, he will twang his harp in canta; but nobody cares a dime." It was a nasty little vendetta, a feud with no holds barred; and the lusty rough-and-tumble Bodieites loved it.

The *Chronicle* struck out with: "The Chronicle has stuck to its old-fashioned hand press, paid its debts according to the contract, and can see its ways clear, although its contemporaries with steam engines and big presses and debt cannot see beyond a day. So say the people of Bodie."[11]

A few days later the *Chronicle* reloaded and let fly at its contemporaries with:

> There is the Free Press. On its Websterian brow there is emblazoned, Official Press of Mono County. For sometime it floated at its masthead that it had paid its telegraph bill. Certificate of honesty? It is a bigger man than Grant even if it is "puss and boots."
>
> That fellow in the gulch is the News whose mission is to expose fraud and corruption, and meddle with other people's business. They claim the largest circulation of any paper in Mono County. Advertisers, please take note that this circulation is larger than that of the combined papers (and that's not saying much) and is steadily increasing; 200 copies were sent to the schoolhouse with an admonition for the school marm—"Rawhide for the children." It reminds us of a town in China where there is no water for 13 miles, and the dogs are all day going after it and all night coming back. It is all night blundering and all day correcting it, and a lively fight is going on in the back alley.
>
> There—is the Standard, the staid and solemn grandmother around the corner. . . . It is waiting for the great Hugh McCohn, the young Irish orator whose masterful effusions in its columns, and its immense circulation and influence carried Bodie, San Francisco, and the State for the republicans, to say who will become President.[12]

In mid-March, in a heated ink-slinging duel with the *Chronicle* over who paid its compositors the accepted union rate, the *Standard* referred to its contemporary as "The Rat Sheet."[13]

The *Standard* of March 25 in its "Brief Mention" column noted that "there were eight men in the Bodie branch jail yesterday, Wednesday, including the City Editor of one of our contemporaries." (No names mentioned.)

And so it went on for several months. The first to retire from the lists was the *Chronicle,* whose editor had boasted that "the *Chronicle* intends to continue in Bodie as long as the town and Folger Brothers last."[14] By January, 1881, the *Chronicle* had fled from the Bodie press war and set up shop in safety at the county seat. And with the Folger brothers turning the crank, Bridgeport had itself a newspaper now called the *Bridgeport Chronicle Union.*

Colonel Dunn, president of the Maryland Consolidated Mining Company, at the extreme south end of the lode, was justly proud of the speed and precision with which his veteran crew of miners were sinking the company's main shaft. His timbermen on the day shift were experienced miners, the best in the business, and they prided themselves on the number of shaft sets they could place per shift. These shaft timbers were cumbersome and heavy, and man-killing to cut and fit into place. The safest way to do this operation was to timber from the bottom up to join with the completed sets above; but Fitzpatrick, Brennan, and Fitzsimmons were speed burners, and they always managed to place more sets than any other timber crew. Unfortunately for them, this trio of hard-pressing "Micks," in their "zeal to put in as many sets of timbers as possible before the three o'clock shift went on, were careless in wedging up,"[15] with the sad results that the timbers and scaffolding on which they were working carried away and crashed eighty feet to the bottom of the shaft, crushing and killing Fitzpatrick and Brennan, and badly injuring Fitzsimmons.

This horrible accident didn't seem to tighten up safety procedures in the least. In every mine in the camp it was the order of the day to push things to the limit. Every outfit was pressing on with everything they had, to try and find and garner their share of the treasure horde. So, in the following three weeks of February, Martin King was killed in the McClinton Mine. A. C. Robertson, foreman at the Spaulding, lost his life trying to thaw out a batch of giant powder in his oven. The last victim of these slapdash days was a hardy but inattentive native of Ireland, named Peter Burke, who walked into the Standard shaft at the 500-foot station and fell three hundred feet to his death. The stunned and appalled reporter who viewed his broken body commented: "This is another of those fearful and fatal accidents which have marked the mining history of Bodie with bloody details and dotted its hillsides with new-made graves, adding to its annals."[16]

Most of the unfortunate victims were members of the Miners' Union, under whose auspices their funerals were conducted. In the sad case of foreman Robertson (whose cookstove and cabin went skyward with him) the generous heart of Bodie's citizens was manifested once again. A big benefit, at the Miners' Union Hall, raised $405 for his bereaved family in Oakland.

A few days after the flying exit of their foreman, the Spaulding Mining Company proclaimed to their stockholders that their new mill, with its ten 800-pound stamps powered by the latest thing in a 60-horsepower Corless steam engine, was beginning operations. The Etna Iron Works of San Francisco, its builders, pronounced it the last word in stamp-mill construction. By the end of February, 1880, the shrill tones of its throaty whistle were added to the growing chorus of smoking mills and hoisting works that each day partitioned starting and quitting time in the camp.

The lure of outside mining excitement in the late fall of '79 siphoned off a score or two of Bodie's hardiest prospectors. Jim Slack was one of the rough-and-ready crowd who went over to scenic Mill Creek and with Jim Monahan, J. M. Jones, and Lawrence Homer took part in the formation of the Homer Mining District. This new district was located about twenty-one miles southwest of Bodie in a picturesque, rugged U-shaped valley, the mighty handiwork of a gouging, grinding Pleistocene glacier long since gone. There was plenty of enthusiasm among the Mill Creekers, as they were then called, about the glowing future of their district. Some very rich quartz veins had been found; however, many of the newly located claims were high up on steep granite ridges 10,000 to 11,000 feet above the sea. The prospecting and opening up this Alpine District took a special breed of tough, hardship-immune rock hound. This was Jim Slack to a T—he was tough enough for anything. In his description to the *Bodie Press* of how it was that first winter at Lundy in Mill Creek amid the gold and snow and how rugged were the trials of his winter's jaunt on horseback to and from that embryo camp, are experiences that should certainly heighten the respect of a present-day button-pushing, throttle-mashing, convenience-ridden reader for the tough, resolute old pioneers who took everyday hardships in their stride and bulled their way through.

A Bodie daily in February carried the wintry tale:

> Jim Slack, a well known miner and prospector with large mining interests in the Homer Mining District at Mill Creek . . . left here to look after his property in that region. . . . Slack journeyed on horseback, and, after several hours of hard riding in the face of a furious snowstorm, he reached Lundy's ranch, and he found in its neighborhood between 50 and 60 men and two women, outside of Lundy's family and miners, engaged in the Homer and May Lundy Mines. . . . At Lundy's, Slack found a number of men camped under the trees and in tents, and also W. E. Stevens and Billy Rabajon, who went out last Monday to start a lodging house, chop stand and saloon. They had improvised a cabin by placing a scantlon from the gable end of a log cabin to the fork of an adjacent tree and had leaned slabs against it. About nine o'clock yesterday morning when Slack was ready to start back, he called to Stevens and Rabajon to say goodbye. The two men were engaged at that time in sinking through the snow for foundations for the purpose of a new building and had gotten down about eight feet. Billy Rabajon placed his shovel across the trench and climbed up on it, so that he could get his head above the surface of the snow, and sang out to Slack in cheery tones, "Jim, tell the boys in Bodie this is a 'bully' country." . . . Riding 23 miles on his horse through a blinding snowstorm, Slack had to walk nearly half the way in order to keep on the trail, for every time he

would get off from it, both he and his horse would go down. Two sleighs that came in contact with Slack reached Bodie about dark last night. One of the sleighs brought in four and the other two men. The coyotes along the route have become so hungry and ferocious that yesterday several of them made demonstrations as if they would attack one of the sleigh teams. They trotted along side the horses for 150 yards, barking and snarling, and paying little attention to the shouts of the men in the sleighs. The hands of the men were so nearly frozen that they could not draw their six-shooters to kill the animals.[17]

It was in just such a storming and wintry scene twenty-one years before, that the blizzard-fagged old Argonaut, whose cognomen the camp now carries, yielded up his high hopes and exhausted spirit to numbing cold and exhaustion.

The ardent enthusiasm for the new Homer Mining District by mining adventurers from Bodie mushroomed a lively little camp almost overnight. A Brodieite who moved to Lundy less than a month after Jim Slack's snowstorm visit reported:

> There are 12 log cabins, one frame house, eight canvas houses, and any amount of brush and stone houses occupied by prospectors who are there to protect their claims from the crowd of jumpers and "bee hunters" flocking in. . . . There is one chop and oyster stand, The Gem–one hotel, Lundy's–one saloon, Rabajon and Stevens–a general merchandise establishment–a lodging house, beds $1.00 per night–one livery stable, Scott's–whiskey, one and two bits per drink–and everything else in proportion . . . Hill and Hill Saw Mill will soon have lumber for all. . . . The Homer Mill and Mining Company have completed the survey for their millsite and started grading today. . . . A Justice of the Peace and a Constable will probably be the next addition to our camp. As a petition, looking for such an end, went to the board of supervisors last week. There are two candidates for Justice of the Peace, Rabajon and Homer. Mastretti came here last week with a petition for Constable, and got only a few names; as the camp was unanimous in favor of Jim Slack, who is a lion with the boys here.[18]

Old John Striker was one of the Bodie crowd who caught Mill Creek fever that snowy spring, and like a soaring eagle, he zestfully swept into the Alpine District, yearning to better his fortunes and get in on the ground floor. He made a hasty survey of Lundy and found that the boys had grabbed off all the best sites. So John struck out on his own, "ascending to Mill Creek Canyon, and some distance above Lundy Lake came upon a level field of deep snow. There he concluded to locate a townsite, or a place for a desirable ranch. After weeks of hard labor and considerable expenditure he succeeded in getting his ranch fenced in; but, a week or two ago, the snow disappeared, and with it, the ice that supported it. Striker's ranch vanished like a dream. The level field of snow, upon which he had located, turned out to be the covering of a lake. He consoled himself with the reflection that he has a good trout ranch at least."[19]

This new district generated plenty of excitement and had its ups and downs. In June a letter from Lundy was received in Bodie which in part read: "The boys are havin' a war dance tonight, with powder salutes, bonfires, and a grand Jubilee all over town. They have struck it 'richer 'en hell' all over the district. Yesterday they struck it richer than the Boston Consolidated opposite the Homer Mine. . . . The boys are too much excited and too busy to attend the Fourth Celebration in Bodie this year."[20]

There was one dark cloud on the horizon for the exuberant citizens of Lundy. In their zeal to found their town they brushed aside the protest of Jonathan Boomershine and his neighboring rancher, Lundy, who owned the land under an agricultural patent. The old bean-eaters and prospectors from Bodie and elsewhere, with their natural disdain for sod-busters and ranchers, told Boomershine and Lundy to go to hell. They then hired the spellbinding lawyer General Kittrell as legal adviser. The case, a famous one in its day, wound its rocky path through numerous hearings before Federal Land Commissioners. It was finally settled in January, 1881, by a decision in Washington, D.C., by the Registrar and Receiver of the General Land Office, in favor of Boomershine and Lundy. This decision left many a Mill Creeker red-faced and disgruntled.

Bodie's fame as the new pacesetter of the mining West was

publicly acknowledged by eastern capital in mid-March, when Mr. B. B. Minor was invited to speak before the famous Bullion Club of New York. The *Daily American Exchange* carried his rosy remarks:

> A year ago the reputation of the Bodie District of Mono County was confined and local; but it is now world wide, and the developments made from day to day promise to give it as great a prominence as is enjoyed by the well known Comstock Lode of Nevada. . . . About one year ago, Bodie had a population of about 2,000; but it has increased since to 7,000 or 8,000. There are 31 steam hoisting works, four newspapers, many banks and stores, etc. The places of business at the present time number 450. There are now seven quartz mills and 125 stamps with a crushing capacity of 250 tons per diem. The estimated output of the ore is about $250,000 per month or $3,000,000 per annum, and is steadily increasing. A railroad, branching from The Virginia & Truckee Road, is projected to Bodie; and the managers of it state that the construction will begin at an early date. . . . The geologists who have examined the Bodie District all concur as to the permanency of the deposits. The gold found here carries a percentage of silver. Though differing in the various mines, the silver ore averages about $5.00 per ton in silver and $55.00 per ton in gold, and it is thought that in time large silver deposits will be reached.[21]

While Minor from his pink cloud ballyhooed the camp's investment virtues before the attentive eastern capitalists, the hardy citizens who blasted, dug, milled and hauled Bodie's commerce met the hurly-burly zestful life of the place head on; and the results of the daily scuffle ran the gamut of the human comedy. One of the red-necked characters was McCarthy, a Don Juan of sorts and a man of action. In fact, it was because of an overabundant supply of the latter that he stood before Justice Peterson, who arbitrarily outlined his immediate future as twenty-nine days in the pokey. The unabridged tale as it unfolded in the evening paper of April 5 was eagerly read:

> James McCarthy was arrested Saturday after beating a frail, fat French damsel, not overly fair, probably forty years, named

Louise Du Barr, who resides on Bonanza Street. McCarthy and Madame Du Barr rejoiced in a mutual love in the wicked city of the Comstock; but in time, the fair Louise felt the fires of love cooling in her avoirdupois tissue and endeavored to give her James, in the classic phrase of the hoodlum, "the shake." The lineal descendants of the McCarthys of Loc Vallashaney could ill brook with such treatment. He felt the blood of his noble ancestors, who had helped St. Patrick club the toads out of Ireland, surged with wrath at being cast off, and banged the object of his affections in a forceful and affectionate style peculiar to his line. The stony-hearted Louise did not appreciate the high spirited McCarthy methods of rekindling the flames of love, and had him arrested for assault and battery; and an unfeeling Virginia magistrate sentenced the fiery James to 29 days in the Comstock dungeon. While he was languishing in it, his lady love cut stick for Bodie.

As soon as McCarthy was released from duress vile, he followed Louise to this place. Seeking out her abode, he demanded her to take him back into her bed and affections or soothe his lacerated feelings with the healing salve of a golden poultice. The recreant Louise refused to do either, whereupon the irate McCarthy whammed her most beautifully. Officer Farnsworth, being in the neighborhood with an eye to preventing anybody from giving the peace and dignity of the people of the State of California a black eye, so to speak, scooped the belligerent James into his official net and flung him into the dark somber recesses of Kirgan's bastille.[22]

The severe winter of '79–'80 and its continual succession of raging snowstorms that had persisted past mid-April had closed the roads to most wheel traffic for months. So, by the third week in April, a serious wood famine developed in Bodie. The concerned local press worried into print with: "Several mines have been compelled to shut down for lack of wood with which to run their hoisting works. . . . It is now proposed to call a meeting of the citizens at Johnson's Bodie House, corner of Main and Green Streets at 7:30 this evening for the purpose of discussing the subject, and devising ways and means of opening the roads to the nearest principal source of supply. . . . Wood thieves broke into the Gold Hill restaurant and stole $10.00 worth of wood, that's about one fourth of a cord."[23]

The "Brief Mention" column of the same sheet related: "A bookkeeper in one of the leading grocery houses in Bodie rejoices in the wood famine because he can now get a drink for a barrel stave."[24]

In April the generous citizens of the camp turned out in large numbers in the face of miserable weather and fuel shortage to attend benefits given by the Ladies' Aid Society and the Bodie Social Minstrels for the aid of Honorable R. D. Ferguson, the ailing attorney who had so ably delivered the graveside address when the town paid its last respects to W. S. Bodey, that past fall. Ferguson had been stricken by pneumonia which left him so broken physically that he had been confined to his hotel room for twenty weeks. His health and money gone, his doctor warned that he must leave "these Snowy Peaks" and changeable climate and go into the valley sunshine below before it was too late. The kindly effort of the Bodie ladies netted $122 and the Social Minstrels turned over $113 to his cause. With the good wishes of the camp ringing in his ears, Ferguson was able to leave Bodie and journey to Siegler's Springs in Lake County, where he partly regained his old vigor.

The *Daily Bodie Standard* of May 14, 1880, carried a story of more than passing interest: "The steam-propeller for Mono Lake will arrive from Carson tomorrow, Friday, and will be immediately dispatched to the lake and put together. The vessel is to be called the Rocket and is 36 feet in length by 10 feet of beam. It will be of great convenience, not only to excursion parties who desire to visit the island in the lake, but to others desiring to cross and reach distant points on the shore. The little steamer will, also, be of incalculable benefit to lumber dealers in towing barges from the vicinity of the saw mills to the shore near Bodie."

A conquering hero was given a rousing welcome in the first week of June, when his stage rolled up Main Street. He was Bodie's greatest athlete. Hundreds of men eagerly awaited their chance to shake his hand. Duncan A. McMillan had worked as a miner in the Standard Mine for the past three years. Lithe and quick as a panther, with tremendous strength and timing, he was a natural athlete. He was a member of the Bodie Caledonian Club. Having won the local contests—putting the heavy and light stones, as well as the hammer throw—the club chose him to represent Bodie at the annual California Scottish Games in Oakland that May. He distinguished himself and his town by making a clean sweep of four first places in winning both the heavy and light hammer throws and putting the heavy stone and putting the light stone. The jubilant *Bodie Press* applauded: "This gives Bodie the championship of the Coast."[25]

The greater part of the adult citizens of the camp were the pure distilled product of the rough-and-tumble West. Ex-ranchers, border ruffians, Indian fighters, soldiers of the Blue and Gray who had worked their shifts and drawn their pay on the C.P., U.P., mines and mills, and businesses of every camp from Aurora to the fabled Comstock. All were familiar with the ebb and flow and combustible situations of mining-camp existence. Claim-jumping, lot-jumping, and similar shenanigans had been witnessed as common occurrences. They were men who could be surprised without being dismayed.

The surprise arrived about 11 o'clock on June 4 with the persistent clanging of the fire-alarm bell that alerted the town. When it became apparent that there was no fire, hundreds massed at the engine house, where they quickly learned that someone had jumped Standard Avenue during the night. It had been fenced off at Main Street, and as far back as the fire house, and a small building erected in the center of the appropriated thoroughfare.

The story of the quick disposal of a knotty civic problem by the action-ready Bodieites in the heyday was reported in the *Chronicle* the following day:

> Our citizens were highly excited and indignant yesterday morning when it was discovered that Standard Avenue had been jumped . . . and fenced in, and a small building erected in the center. It was soon ascertained that Dr. Blackwood and some others had committed this outrage on the public. . . . Harvey Boone, of Boone and Wright, stated that the object of the meeting was to act on the matter of the street obstruction and nominated

> T. A. Stevens chairman. Mr. Stevens was elected and J. W. Wright, of Boone and Wright, was appointed secretary. The Chairman stated political steps could be taken to remove the obstruction, but the meeting was not disposed to wait for the law to remove it, and a motion was made to find the parties who erected the obstruction, and give them ten minutes to remove it. Mr. McVarish was appointed as a committee of one to notify them of the sense of the people. Mr. McVarish waited on Dr. Blackwood and notified him, but that gentleman gave him no answer whether he would remove it or not, and he so reported to the meeting. A motion was then made, that the building in question be removed instantly. The motion was adopted with enthusiasm, and a rush was made for the enclosure which was soon thrown open again to public travel, amidst the cheering of the hundreds assembled. The hooks of the Hook and Ladder Company were put upon the building which was quickly torn down, and the lumber thrown into a cart and hauled off. Three cheers were then given and the crowd then started for the office of Dr. Blackwood in the Mono House where he was greeted with B-o-o-s! And thus ended an outrage on the rights of the people of Bodie. . . . Standard Avenue has been a county road and a public thoroughfare for the past fifteen years, and no one up to Thursday night has had the cheek to think of locating it as a town lot. And we think that the public feeling shown yesterday morning will effectively deter any others attempting a like outrage.[26]

The building boom in the camp was well into its third year by mid-June, 1880. There were several new downtown buildings scheduled for early erection.

The new Odd Fellows Hall was completed that month, and an observing reporter noted: "It is 25 feet by 60 feet, including airy rooms, and will have a seating capacity for 200 persons. The seats are upholstered, and comfortable as well as attractive. The interior is ornamented in the Corinthian style of decoration, with columns and statuary. On the right as you enter, is observed statuary representing Europe, Asia, Africa, and Australia. On the left, Faith, Hope, and Charity. The Hall occupies one of the most eligible sites, being next door to the Miners' Union Hall."[27] With the completion of this hall and several other buildings, Main Street took on an imposing city atmosphere. There were signs, however, that the construction peak had been reached; in fact, it was beginning to taper off as most of the eligible sites of the downtown area were being rapidly filled.

A new stirring of civic pride was noted when, with the completion of Leo Scowden's townsite survey, Alexander Hunter, a local painter, began scurrying about soliciting orders for house numbering.

Bodie's boardinghouses down through the years have been the butt of some pretty rancid stories. By her own admission Mrs. Chestnut kept the finest lodging house in the camp during the heyday. Her rates were a dollar a week higher than at any other table in town. Catering to the taste of the more sophisticated boarders, she advertised in April that "her elegant boarding house on the east side of Main Street is prepared to furnish the very best board by day or week, also lodging. Her table will be supplied with the choicest dishes on the market, and the prices will be in keeping with the times. $9.00 per week or 75¢ per meal; no Chinese cooks employed."[28]

At the other end of the gastronomical ladder was the calculating provender provider whose modus operandi appeared in the local press with no names mentioned: "A washed out looking woman stopped before a butcher stall and began eyeing some poultry with pensive interest. 'Are these chickens tender?' she inquired. 'Oh, yes, Madam,' said the butcher, alert for a sale, 'as tender as young quail, I assure you.' 'Then I don't want them,' she said languidly. 'Why, Madam, don't you want tender chickens?' asked the astonished dealer. 'Well, you see I keep boarders,' answered the lady. The butcher soon convinced her that he was fibbing before, and consummated a sale. Tomorrow some unfortunate boarder will be picking his teeth with a scratched awl, and swearing that Bodie chickens are fed on steel wire."[29]

The *Nevada Press,* somewhat envious of Bodie's glamorous rise to the heights in the mining firmament, was always ready to take a dirty dig at the exciting new camp. In keeping with this left-handed policy, the *Carson Appeal* in June let fly with a derisive barb: "In Bodie the burial ground is so wet, they have to bail out the freshly dug graves to get the coffin in, and then pile rocks on to keep it from floating until the funeral services are over. . . . At some of these funerals, a preacher is frequently at a loss to know whether to read a baptismal or a burial service." A Bodie sheet sadly quipped a brief retort: "Only too true."[30]

The evening of June 29 was one of spectacular enchantment for the citizens of the camp, both young and old. As a curtain raiser for the coming excitement of the Fourth of July celebration, the town turned out to witness its first balloon ascension. After about an hour of preparation, the big hot-air balloon was released, and to the Oh's and Ah's of the populace, it shot up to about 1,000 feet above the town "when it suddenly took fire and came down in sparks."[31] This thrilling event coupled with almost perfect weather kindled a glow of enthusiasm for the preparations of the coming patriotic holiday.

The Fourth of July celebration of 1880 (held on Monday the 5th) was by far the largest event of its kind ever held in the history of Bodie. The camp was at the peak of its fame. The last three years of its history had been a scintillating series of excitements. The hamlet of thirty-six months ago was now a roaring camp of over 8,000 people whose name was a household word across the land. Its flushed and success-ridden citizens looked on the world as their golden oyster. And just about the hardest thing to find in the camp in its magic hour was a pessimist.

At the stroke of midnight, thirty steam whistles shrilled their welcome to the 104th Independence Day. At 4:30 that morning, Hoskins Brass Band "took position in the observatory of the Belvedere Iron Works and played 'Hail Columbia,' 'The Star Spangled Banner,' 'Red, White and Blue,' and 'America.' At sunrise the Standard cannon was brought out and belched forth a welcome to the day of days. Flags were flung to the breeze, and our city put on its best 'bib and tucker.' And then, the rest of Sunday was allowed to pass quietly,"[32] except for the spectacular but fatal efforts of Paddy Carrol, a liquored-up Irish gunslinger who succeeded in terminating his worldly sojourn of forty years.

Paddy was a member of the Miners' Union and attended the special meeting Sunday evening on the Fourth called for the purpose of "rescinding a resolution adopted at a previous meeting which opposed a parade of the members of the Union in the coming Independence Day Celebration." (This action had been taken because a segment of the union was hostile to an officer of the day.) Paddy had his own definite ideas on quashing this legislation. He kept the floor with loud and abusive name-calling oratory and refused to take his seat. This was too great a cross for President Shaughnessy to bear, so he ordered five miners to throw him out of the hall. Paddy's unceremonious exit didn't dent his determination in the least. A few minutes later, after securing ample reinforcements from Demon Rum and a wicked-looking dragoon pistol, Paddy attempted to forcibly run the blockade of six well-heeled guards at the door of the Miners' Union Hall, who promptly returned his broadside with a well-aimed volley that ventilated the charging "Mick" and freed his turbulent soul to warmer regions. The *Chronicle* of the tenth laconically commented, "Carrol was said to have been a 'bad-man' and his sudden taking off is not regretted by those best acquainted with him."[33]

Monday the fifth dawned a perfect day. At an early hour "the thunder of the Standard M. & M. Company's artillery banished sleep, and our streets were soon filled with those anxious to take part in all the glorious celebration. Main Street presented a gala and patriotic appearance with its innumerable decorations of evergreens, flags, and festoons of bunting."[34]

The big features of the day were impressive.

Two brass bands with stirring martial music stimulated the holiday throngs.

They thrilled to the advent of the Standard's cannon, a snooty five-pounder, drawn by four snow-white horses under the command of Captain Jules Renault (a grizzled old artilleryman, ex-officer of the deposed Emperor Louis Philippe of France). Captain Renault, who worked as a trusted guard of the Standard's bullion room, had personally supervised the construction of this showy piece of ordnance (the gun barrel having been turned from a spare piece of 6-inch shafting) and had also made certain that the gun carriage and accouterments were perfect in every detail. So, with proud military bearing and an inbred esprit de corps, he wheeled Bodie's homemade gun past the dazzled sidewalk-packed crowds that lined the parade route.

Bodie's four fire companies—Babcock Engine I, Pioneer Hook & Ladder I, Champion Hose I, and Neptune Hose II—with their engines brightly burnished and all the firemen in spanking new uniforms, were reviewed with pride by the assembled citizens.

Probably the cleverest feature of the parade and the one best remembered by the old-timers was the miniature brass-mounted cannon contributed by the Booker Mine. Colonel Ellingsworth, the mine's superintendent, had it made in their shop. "It was drawn by ten boys in uniform under the command of Master Charlie Irwin, who was mounted on a fine pony, richly caparisoned."[35]

"Thousands of people lined the streets, and greater enthusiasm had never before prevailed, singing and cheering from the balconies and re-echoing from the column being continuous from the commencement to the ending of the march."[36] Countermarching was necessary to bring the long procession before the grandstand which had been erected in front of the Gold Brick Saloon. Captain Messick, the grand marshal, and his richly mounted aides and the 214 members of the Miners' Union who marched as an honor guard to the car of state were all given a thunderous ovation.

In the afternoon the program of events included a track meet. It drew a huge crowd that admiringly followed the movements of Bodie's great athlete, Duncan A. McMillan, who won the 15-pound hammer throw with a toss of 92 feet 9 inches. He was closely pressed by H. Bell with a heave of 92 feet 2 inches. The great Duncan that afternoon took three other first places and tied Lee De Camp in the standing high jump at 4 feet 5½ inches. Dennis Keefe took the hop, step, and jump with 40 feet 8 inches, and Rod McGinnis picked off a first place in the hitch and kick at 9 feet 2 inches high. Some of these events may not be hot stuff to the modern sports fan, who very probably never saw a hitch and kick contest, but to the track fan of a century ago this was a track and field contest worthy of his closest attention.

Back in the "good old days" no Fourth of July celebration in any American city was complete without a funnybone-tickling and rib-cracking parade and oration served up by a collection of local clowns, known as the Horribles. Wearing grotesque masks and outrageously dressed, they lampooned anything and everything in town. Teachers, lawyers, editors, saloonkeepers—all were in for it when their speaker staggered to the rostrum.

C. Staley, the Horribles' orator of the day, drew roaring rounds of guffaws from the crowd as he larruped the atmosphere with:

> Fellow rounders, cheek gorillas, amateur actors, hoodlums, knights of the poppy, and superintendent of the finest and best free lunch routes in Bodie.
>
> We, today, represent the highest phase of triple X and double distilled cussedness to be found on the coast. When I see your opium-bleached, boozy-inflamed mugs gathered around this rostrum, I feel that I was perfectly right in demanding in advance the $500.00 Mr. Pope [chairman of the program committee] offered me to deliver this oration. . . . In this camp our mines are the most ably managed on the coast. Our superintendents know more today about sour mash, Santo Pedro, poker, back streets, and scrub horse racing than any other class of men in the country. They are broad in their views, painstakingly conservative, and hold on to a four bit piece like a burdock burr in a bull's tail. They are men of great understanding, wearing number 5 hats, and number 10 boots. . . .
>
> Think, four daily papers in a town of 7,000 inhabitants. Pause for a moment and regard the mental caliber of their editors and compositors. . . . Turn your attention, I pray you, to our saloonkeepers, all men of means . . . self supporting, making all their own liquors, except gin. It takes too long to make—fifteen minutes. . . . The various ranch men who come here have been known to take four straight drinks, and then go out and steal their own horses, saddles, and blankets and hide them in the sagebrush.

> One poor creature accompanied by two riding and pack animals in passing through Bodie on his way to Mexico unfortunately stopped at the Senate Saloon. He hoisted in half a dozen drinks, filled a gallon jug and continued his journey. He said to the Bishop Creek Vigilance Committee, who were anxious to know how he came into possession of 300 head of horses between this place and Independence, that it was Bodie whiskey, and he was afraid it would choke him. He didn't lie about it either. . . .
>
> When I look around on your rum-sodden countenances, soulless opium eyes, like two gobs of putty in a pan of starch, I solemnly promise and speak it with tears in my eyes, that I will never do it again. Oh! my beloved, continue in the paths you have marked out, don't miss a trick. See if you can't ruin some other saloon and drive the proprietor into bankruptcy. Be as tricky as you can; remember, the world owes you a living.[37]

Another feature of the celebration was an elimination tournament featuring "Cornish style wrestling which commenced at the Bodie Hay Yard on the Fourth, lasting three days. James Snell won the first prize of $100. Jake Palkingham second prize $30. Con Driscol third prize of $25."[38] Hoskin's Brass Band was in attendance and rendered three days of thumping music.

The grand flop of the celebration was the scheduled display of fireworks in the evening. A sarcastic reporter suggested "it must have been made of sawdust or badly damaged powder. . . . There was scarcely enough force in the powder to carry the Roman Cannonballs above a man's hat."[39]

Of the many extracurricular events that were not in the official program but by virtue of their interest secured a headline in the news stories of the day, none produced more chuckles or lasting comment than the plight of a well-known, personable young Bodieite, elegantly arrayed in the latest creation from his favorite tailor and sporting a "two-story Plug Hat," who proudly took his seat of honor in an open carriage alongside gorgeously dressed ladies and their handsome escorts. He was totally unaware that a thin slice of limburger cheese nestled under the sweatband of his magnificent new chapeau.

A practical joker, "a brother of his profession, with malice aforethought, had inserted the limburger on the sly."

In the glowing warmth of the Fourth the carriage and its gaily dressed occupants took its place in the procession which slowly wound its way toward the grandstand:

> . . . The day was hot and whenever our hero raised his Plug to wipe the heat below, a murmur of disgust passed along the line. The little wind that was blowing carried the effusion of the cheese. "What in the thunder have you been doing with yourself?" inquired his companions in the Carriage. "That scent you gave us is death." "I believe it's me," said the good man, "or else it's the breeze coming down that Gieger Canyon [location of the slaughterhouse]." He sat and groaned, and whatever way he turned, he saw men and women holding their noses. He knew all his toggery was fresh from the tailor's hands and the store. . . . "How he could smell so outrageously," he could not conceive, "unless he had taken suddenly some fearful disease."
>
> The procession over, he rushed to his room and flung himself upon the bed in deep despair. His landlady, hearing his groans, rushed to the room and inhaled the smell and started for the door in dismay. "Where did you get into it?" said she. "Get into it," said the man, "I have not got into anything, but some deadly disease has got hold of me, and I shall not live!" She told him that any disease that smelled like that was going to be chronic. . . . She got his clothes off and soaked his feet in mustard water, and he slept.
>
> The landlady sent for a doctor and told him all the particulars, and that the man was used to handling cattle and meat, etc. The doctor picked up the patient's new Plug Hat, tried it on, and got a sniff. He said that the hat was picked before it was ripe. The doctor and the landlady held a post mortem examination of the hat and found the slice of limburger. Few and short were the prayers they said. They awoke the patient to prepare his mind for the revelation that was about to be made. The doctor asked him if his worldly affairs were in satisfactory condition. He gasped and said they were. The doctor asked him if he had made his will, and he said he had not and he wanted a lawyer and sent for one. The doctor asked him if he felt as though he was prepared to shove off. The man said he had always tried to lead a decent life; but he wanted a minister to come anyway to help him take account of his stock.
>
> The doctor then brought to the bedside the sweat band and showed the dying man what it was that smelled so. The patient

pinched himself to see if he was alive, jumped out of bed, called for his revolver; and the doctor couldn't keep up with him on his way downtown.[40]

A story of a crowd-gathering event on the Fourth, handled with great delicacy by the local press with no names mentioned, was reported about "a lady who owns a Brownstone Front uptown and one who is the chief engineer of a double bay window mansion downtown were impregnated with too much Fourth of July patriotism and bad whiskey. The consequence? An overturned buggy, a few bruises, and lots of words that Deacon Parkinson says 'Are not in the Bible.' "[41]

Just twenty-four hours after Paddy Carrol's bad judgment had brought him a place of quiet repose on the mortician's slab, another liquor-laden character, by the name of James Kennedy, spied his current enemy, Bill Baker, on the sidewalk in front of the Comstock Saloon, where his fumbling draw and bad aim promptly landed him a spot on the same slab. There have been many versions of this killing, but in the August trial of Baker at Bridgeport, where he was ably defended by Pat Reddy, a defense witness, S. F. Hoole, testified that Kennedy drew on Baker first and that Baker fired in self-defense. Reddy's adroit tactics and the pleas of self-defense brought Baker's acquittal.

It must be remembered that not all life in Bodie was killing and violence. There were thousands of hard-working, peaceable, law-abiding citizens in the town who daily engaged in a fruitful and rewarding life and took great pleasure in attending the various social functions. The *Daily News* of the ninth glowingly reported the Strawberry Festival:

> The benefit given by the ladies to the Reverend Father Cassin last evening at the Miners' Union Hall was a complete financial and social success. It is estimated that the net proceeds will amount to about $1,000. That is something like a benefit. A pleasing feature of this benefit to Father Cassin was the presence of a large number of Methodists, Episcopals, Congregationalists, Baptists, and other denominations, being a tribute to the Reverend Father's merit seldom paid by the opposing denominations.
>
> The arrangements were of the most perfect character to

insure satisfaction to the visitors and a good financial success to the enterprise. The tables were spread in the most artistic manner and were loaded with the choicest dishes, viands, and condiments. The supper table at the head of the hall was a model of artistic beauty. The coffee and chocolate and rich cream was the subject of praise from all. The music added additional pleasure to the enterprise. Several ladies and gentlemen favored the audience with singing, etc. . . .

During the second week of July a Chinese businessman in a moment of blind rage fired both barrels of a double-barreled shotgun at "Chatto" Encinos, a Mexican herder employed by "Spanish Joe" Alcraz, the wood packer. The murderous attack occurred at Chung's Rough Creek hangout (about six miles northwest of town) where he had an unfenced garden back of his cabin. The succulent rows of vegetables attracted the pack mules being herded by Chatto. The mortally wounded man was brought into Bodie for medical aid. He died within a few hours.

Sam Chung was arrested and tossed into Kirgan's bastille. Later in the day the sheriff, sensing an impromptu necktie party, shackled Sam to a deputy and sent him under cover of darkness to Bridgeport. This maneuver on the part of the law was made just in time to prevent a lynching. The reporter who interviewed the deputy sheriff and jailer recounted:

. . . between one and two o'clock this morning, Jailer Kirgan heard a rap at the prison door. Supposing the visitor to be an officer with a prisoner, he opened the door. Instead, four masked men rushed into the jail room. Kirgan inquired, "What do you want?" One of the men replied, "We want Sam Chung." "He's not here," replied Kirgan. "Where is he?" inquired the masked spokesman. "I sent him out into the mountains with good guards," replied Kirgan. "Open that door!" said the spokesman of the party pointing to the door of the cell from which Sam Chung had been removed. The door was opened, the man entered, scrutinized the two or three other prisoners in the cell. Coming back into the room, he demanded that the door of the other cell be opened. This was done. The man checked the cell, stepped back into the front room, motioned his companions to the outside, and then politely bowed himself out. Jailer Kirgan says the men were heavily armed with pistols. . . . Outside the Jailer saw eight other men similarly masked. He is of the opinion that the men were Mexicans although the spokesman used the plainest English.[42]

The riled-up editor of the *Daily News*, who had formerly been a member of a 601 committee in Virginia City, splashed into print with:

> It is our opinion that a little "hemp practice" would be beneficial in this town. Although the majesty of the law should in all cases be sustained, there are circumstances which occur that compel the law-abiding citizens to band together for protection and wrest from the official clutches, cowardly assassins and set a signal example of them and so strike terror into the hearts of cowardly murderers, highwaymen, and robbers. Vigilance committees are sometimes an absolute necessity, and it is the general opinion of the tax paying citizens of Bodie that the sooner a 601 organization is instituted the better for this section of the country. During the past few weeks several dastardly murders have been perpetrated.
>
> Businessmen have invested their all in this and adjoining mining camps, but have they any protector against the incinerary torch? None! A man whose life is worth much to himself and to his family and associates is apt to be shot down while passing a lawless mob on the Bodie sidewalks. . . . It is high time that the people assert their rights and determine on self protection.[43]

During the days of her glory Bodie could exult over the presence of almost all the fraternal orders, each with a large and dedicated membership. In addition there were several active patriotic societies—the Irish-American Land League, the Junta Patriotica Mexica de Bodie, and the Scottish Caledonians, and not to be outdone, the proud issue of *la belle France,* of whom there were a great number in the camp, always managed to let off plenty of steam on Bastille Day.

On July 14 an observer chronicled: "Our French residents made Rome howl with the Standard's five-pounder at sunrise this morning and will partake of a banquet at the Grand Central Hotel this evening . . . 21 guns were fired at sunrise—21 guns at noon—and the same will be fired at sunset. . . . The French tricolor is seen waving from the staff of Bodie Peak and the French citizens are jubilant."[44]

In mid-July the operations of a high-grading gang was broken up with the arrest of an assayer. He had been cornered on one of the levels of the Bodie Mine where some very rich quartz had been taken out. Some of this ore, in certain spots, was so rich that more than half of it was gold. After trapping this thief, he was trussed up and confined in one of the drifts for over twenty-four hours, while a surveillance was clamped on some of his contacts both inside and outside of the mine. Several miners were arrested as accomplices.

Incidentally, thousands of dollars' worth of rich specimens was probably stolen from both the Bodie Mine and the treasure-house section of the Standard Mine. All kinds of ruses were used to pack it past the watchful scrutiny of the shift bosses and guards. Double-bottom lunch pails, carefully concealed "foxy pockets," and many a miner's big pipe were stuffed full of rich little chunks of gold hacked out of specimen rock that he had mined for the company during his long twelve-hour shift. Just how much was stolen will never be known. An old-timer who had lived in those affluent times informed me that "in certain miners' cabins you could hear the one stamp mills running all night" as the daily haul of pilfered high-grade was milled out in big hand mortars. However, this type of larceny-oriented miner was not representative of the vast majority of the workingmen of Bodie, who as a whole were as honest and hard-working as any collection of miners who ever swung a "single-jack."

On July 21 the readers of the *Daily Bodie Standard* were informed that the *Pioneer Press* of the camp and Mono County had been acquired by M. F. Hoole and the *Bodie Daily News.* Thereafter the paper would be known as the *Bodie Standard News.*

In its first edition it ran a macabre story on a weird exhibit on display in the lobby of the Grand Central Hotel, placed there by Louis Salmmons, a pioneer resident of Mono Lake. He had been impressed with the vast unknown potential of the dead sea of the West which touched his doorstep. Inquisitive Louis began conducting quasi-scientific experiments on his own by collecting several dead Piutes and pickling their bodies for two years in the strong solution of the carbonate and sulphate of soda, chloride of sodium, etc., with which the waters of Mono Lake are charged. Researcher Salmmons confidently predicted that this powerful brine would petrify his Indians. In support of his experiments, he had sawed off a portion of a scalp and lugged it to Bodie for public inspection, where he informed an astonished reporter that later on he intended to ship to the Medical Museum in San Francisco a fully petrified redman. The squeamish scribe commented, "A queer fellow is Louis, worthy of commendation for his experiments."[45]

As the wondrous days of a fleeting high-Sierra summer sped on its way, all the circus of Western politics descended on the teeming camp. 1880 was a presidential election year. Congressional, state, and local campaigns were also unfolding.

Bodie Democrats, directed by Colonel B. B. Jackson, had constructed a speaker's platform in front of the Bodie Bank on Main Street. On many evenings, while crowd-gathering bonfires blazed nearby, big-gun Democrats like General John R. Kittrell and Judge Selden Hetsel ascended to this prominent perch and lambasted the Republicans with blistering attacks. Kittrell, in particular, fired broadsides at Garfield's hinted connection with the Credit Mobilier,[46] with verbal swings for good measure at Republican corruption and the alleged whiskey rings of the Grant administration. For the edification of the Mono County voters, they paid glowing tribute to their standard bearer, General Hancock.

An amusing side effect of this high-blown eloquence was a nightly rash of soapbox orators. Being denied the privilege of venting their for-and-against gabble from the speaker's platform, they climbed on any handy box and flung their bellyaches to the evening breeze while the sidewalk crowd enjoyed the show. Occasionally a practical joker enlivened the performance by breaking out "Snorky's" fish horn. One evening "after Mr. McTrenahan had finished his address on the projected railroad between here and Reno, the stand was replaced by a slightly tight individual who attempted to refute all the previous speaker had said, but before he could state his views on the monopolies, railroads especially, somebody kicked the box from under him. Then, both orators crossed the street and, procuring another box, started to again address a large and attentive audience in front of the Standard Lodging House. By this time both speakers had indulged in too much booze, and the results were highly appreciated by the delighted crowd, but just in the middle of the fun, some congenital fool managed to gain a position on the stoop above the speakers and quietly emptied the fluid contents of a receptacle upon the latter. The crowd instantly dispersed, declaring them the strongest speakers of the season, some going so far as to assert that they could smell them for two blocks."[47]

In the first week of August, however, mining excitement outpaced politics and everything else in the town as a jubilant local press glowingly reported: "OH JUPITER—WHAT NEWS—$4,000 TO THE TON—BY JUPITER.—This morning the Standard News reporter visited the Jupiter Mine in company with several gentlemen and examined the recent strike at the 600-foot level. . . . The vein in the south drift at this level . . . carried ore of good quality, and at the face, the last shot uncovered some of the richest ore ever found in Bodie. . . . The past two days has created a stir among mining men. . . . Developments of the Jupiter character show solid merit that goes far forward, driving the chronic croakers to the wall."[48]

The same edition announced, ". . . the old Sonora Dance Hall on King Street has been converted to a Chinese Joss Temple,"[49] thus giving the "almond-eyed heathen" the jump on their Caucasian brothers in providing a house of worship for their believers. The Catholics and Protestants were still in the fund-raising stage for their church buildings.

For weeks the sporting populace of the camp had enthusiastically debated the pros and cons of the coming collar-and-elbow Cornish style wrestling match between the Bodie champion, Rod McGinnis, and ex-deputy constable Gene Markey. The agile, catlike 180-pound McGinnis had run up an impressive record of victories. His opponent, Markey, a veteran peace officer and a wrestler, was a rough customer in any kind of bout. In training for this match, he had trimmed down from 240 pounds to a mere 185 pounds. His known aggressiveness and experience brought him the backing of the sporting crowd, and with them he was the favorite.

The *Standard News* reporter, at the ringside on Sunday evening, August 8, chronicled the action:

> The Miners' Union Hall was jammed with strong hardy men to witness the wrestling match. . . . At half past seven P.M. pool selling commenced, Markey being evidently the favorite, but previous to the close, however, pools sold about even.
>
> At twenty minutes to nine o'clock, McGinnis, accompanied by S. V. Sabin his keeper and second in the contest, appeared. McGinnis wore red stockings and oxford shoes with white tights, striped trunks, and a knit shirt. He presented a fine appearance and was loudly cheered, and was introduced by the Master of Ceremonies Mr. Green. Eugene Markey, accompanied by Joe Farnsworth, entered immediately and was introduced, and the house fairly resounded with cheers. A referee was now to be chosen. [The parties selected a dozen different men each of whom declined to act; after consuming over two hours in vain attempts, they finally agreed on John Riordan to act as referee.]
>
> The ring was soon cleared and the time called. . . . For fifteen minutes, they struggled and wrestled, the active pass work being done entirely by McGinnis who made many attempts to bring his opponent to the floor, and who, at every pass, with the agility of a cat, landed on his feet. After a desperate struggle, McGinnis fairly pulled the jacket of Markey over his head and the contestants were led to their seats. Markey's jacket again replaced, the contestants took their positions. Another 15 minute's struggle resulting precisely as the previous bout, a rest of 15 minutes followed.
>
> When again the men were placed in position and after a few passes were made by each, Markey was gently laid upon his back. The referee gave the first fall to McGinnis. It was now 11 o'clock.
>
> After another rest period, wrestling was resumed. McGinnis made a terrific pass and failed, but followed it up by forcing Markey over the seats of the spectators at the stage. After a moment's rest, they again took their holds. Markey was brought

> to his knees twice, but his hold could not be broken. The last time, McGinnis, with a strength of an enraged tiger, brought him to his feet and, with a terrific rush, forced Markey to the floor. As this was not considered wrestling, it was neither allowed or claimed as a fall.
>
> The men returned to their rooms for grooming, at which time, a slight disagreement occurred between Bannon, a special officer, and deputy-constable Whiteacre. This threatened to result in a general melee. Pistols were drawn and knockdowns were prevalent. The referee, in trying to quiet the disturbance, was gently laid on his back, and being a small man and with no artillery support, he was forced to leave. For a time, this row threatened to be one of a very serious nature, many of the parties thinking there was no danger in swinging cocked pistols, but it was a noticeable fact that the house was cleared in short order of about three fourths of the audience. The trouble ended, however, and nobody was seriously hurt. The hall was again filled. And again, McGinnis and Markey were on their seats waiting for the referee to call them. The referee was called by the Master of Ceremonies, but he could not be found. The crowd gradually dispersed.

And so ended the most ballyhooed wrestling match of the year.

Interest in sports and athletics held a dominant place among the eager young men of Bodie, and many of them participated in baseball, wrestling, track, and gymnastics, which last was especially popular. Ed Wilson and his partner, Hamilton, had leased McAlpine's Hall and fitted it up as a first-class gymnasium. They installed the latest weight-lifting and exercising apparatus, and parallel bars, and erected a ring for boxing and wrestling. There were over 125 regular paying monthly subscribers, and many more who used the gym and its facilities for occasional workouts. In the evenings it was a popular hangout for the young muscle-building set. The members always worked out properly attired (custom of the time) in tights and long-sleeved gym shirts; so it was considered quite proper for young ladies, when in company with their sisters or boy friends' older sisters, to visit the spectators' box, if invited by their swains, to enjoy the workouts. Because Manager Ed Wilson saw to it that proper decorum was maintained at all times in the gym, parents generally did not object when their courting-age daughters were invited to visit.

In August a snoopy reporter came up with a lively little comedy that originated from a harmless visit to the gymnasium, which he entitled "Muscular Culture Runs Wild":

> A young man of Bodie, possessed of a magnificent physique and so modest and unassuming that he was hardly aware of it, visited the gymnasium a few nights ago in company with his truly-truly sweetheart and his sister and several of their female friends. He was surprised and astonished at the evinced admiration and delight expressed by the ladies at the feats of agility and strength and the splendid forms of the members. Oh! At last he had discovered the true secret. Her decelerating coquettish propensities had of late caused him many a heart pang. An idea took possession of him. After returning home that night and lying awake until daylight, he evolved an idea from his inner consciousness.
>
> He managed after a day or two to get his sister to invite his girl over to spend a quiet afternoon and bring her sewing. She accepted the invitation and came over. Soon the two ladies became deeply involved in discussing the comparative merits of the different fashions and other subjects dear to the feminine heart. While thus engaged, they heard a peculiar noise in the backyard and on going to the rear window discovered the cause. They saw the young man at the buck, and a stack of wood, sawing away at the rate of 40 cuts per minute clad in an extremely décolleté gymnasium shirt without sleeves, and knee britches and slippers. While his extensors, flexors, and biceps and muscles on his legs stood out like whipcords, he was perspiring profusely and out of breath, nearly played out, and wondering "why the devil he hadn't attracted the girls' attention and heard some pretty remarks on his appearance." As soon as his darling saw him, she went over backwards in a dead faint with shame and indignation—just then her paternal derivative entered the room. As soon as he learned the cause of her swoon, he made a break for the amateur wood-sawer. When the young man saw him coming, six shooter in hand, he started over the fence. Just as the old man turned loose, the fugitive fell into the arms of an officer who immediately took him before the justice where he was fined $50 for indecent exposure.[50]

The solid citizens of the camp were gratified with the news that the Hotel de Kirgan, the town's famous lockup, would have its accommodations increased to "16 prisoners without crowding." The new cells were equipped with the latest patented ventilators. In addition, a twelve-foot fence was being constructed around the prison "lot, thus enabling the prisoners to take exercise without danger of escape."[51]. The imperfection of the latter observation was blushingly acknowledged by the local press a short time later, with the sad admission that "Alexander Jones, the notorious blanket thief, and Dan Horne, who had been committed to await the action of the Grand Jury, on a charge of Grand Larceny, slipped out into the yard, placed a plank against the high wood fence at the rear of the jail, scaled the fence, and made their escape."[52]

The prisoners were boarded by Jailer Kirgan, who "exercises a personal supervision over the kitchen and, it is safe to say, not a better quality of food is found on any table in the county. The prisoners are boarded at a cost to the county of $1.00 per day, and Mr. Kirgan is paid out of the general fund with script worth the sum of 65¢ on the dollar."[53]

In late August the *Bodie Standard News,* in reviewing the mining progress of the camp, announced that the Syndicate Mining Company's new underground steam hoisting works, located some 2,200 feet from the portal of the Syndicate tunnel, had solved its draft problem in linking up with the Tioga shaft. Now, "Bodie can not only boast of the greatest gold mine, but the highest smoke stack in the world. The smoke stack of the Syndicate Hoisting Works is 1,040 feet in length, extending from the station on the tunnel level to the Tioga shaft and then up 700 feet to the surface to a point some 20 feet above the highest point of Bodie Bluff."[54]

As the month came to a close an observer noted an absence of the colorful daily spectacle of the Indians on Main Street. Their favorite corners of Main and Mill streets were left unattended where almost any day in the summer and fall from fifty to a hundred Piutes of all sizes could be seen squatting on the ground and lolling at the edge of the sidewalks. The bucks, in the cast-off hats and glad rags of Bodie dandies, and the smiling, gaily blanketed squaws with their little brown papooses in wicker cradles slung on their backs, all had departed for the Piute Fandango, as the local press narrated: "About 1,500 Piutes are gathered at the north east corner of Mono Lake holding their annual festival. This consists of feasting, drinking, horse racing, and going through the war dance. It is a sort of love feast where the dusky sons of the forest meet to select their mates. The Grand War Dance of the season comes off this evening, after which it will taper off by degrees, as each of the tribe lays in his stock of 'grub' from the lake, until the camp is deserted."[55]

This annual food harvesting event on the shore of Mono Lake by the Piutes had been a big event for hundreds of years in the life cycle of countless generations of these Indians. The grub, unpalatable to the finicky white man, was the "larvae of a small fly in the form of a 'white worm' which is thrown, in immense quantities, upon the shores of the lake. These larvae, when dried, were used by the Indians . . . as an important article of food."[56] This grub, the Piutes dubbed "Koo-chah-bee."

In 1880, Bodie was the financial, commercial, mining and social arbitrator of Mono County. It was the largest and best market in that region east of the Sierra for everything—hardware, soft goods, groceries, and whiskey; but if a citizen had legal business to transact, Bridgeport would be his destination. For a while there was considerable agitation to move the county seat to Bodie, but the movement was opposed by the rest of the county.

By the end of August, 1880, the new county courthouse at Bridgeport was going up rapidly. A scribe from Bodie who had been subpoenaed for an appearance in the Superior Court dropped by to inspect the new building, and he noted that "the roof is nearly on and ready for the shingles." However, he reserved his greatest enthusiasm for the description of his trip from Bodie to the county seat: "Taking the Nevada Stage Company's coach at 3 o'clock in the morning on a seat by that 'Prince of Whips' Joe Tobey, and with the moon shining in all its splendor, we started from the Grand Central, the stage loaded to the guards. Away we sped through the cool bracing air of the early morning which appeared to give vim to the six spirited animals who dashed onward with astonishing speed, running to the 16 mile house in short time. As we arrived there, shortly after daylight, we exchanged horses and again were off like the winds, striking into the valley as the sun with its warm refreshing rays began to peep over the mountain tops. The prancing horses rushed on and soon had the Nevada Company's Stage at the post office at Bridgeport where breakfast was had at Allen's, making all feel good-natured."[57]

Contrast this with a recent complaint of a Bodie visitor who tooled her push-button, climate-controlled, everything-automatic Detroit dream boat from Bridgeport to Bodie, and after spending all of forty minutes on the road, arrived in the old ghost town, and on alighting from her purring chrome buggy wailed, "What a horrible road."

The economy of the camp had enjoyed almost three years of continuous growth and expansion which saw the construction of over 1,800 houses, several large mills, and 31 steam hoisting works along with their numerous blacksmith shops, tool shops, etc. With the arrival of late summer, 1880, there was a rather rapid decline in all construction. As the saturation point was reached, hundreds of carpenters and building artisans were laid off. One of the first major establishments to feel the slowdown was that of Captain Porter. He was a pioneer businessman of Bodie and had done more than his share to bring the camp out of its swaddling clothes to the grand eminence it now enjoyed. The firm of G. L. Porter and Company operated the largest lumber yard and a sawmill and two shingle mills in the lumber forest south of Mono Lake. To move the finished lumber from the mills, Captain Porter had acquired the small steamer *Rocket* in San Francisco and had hauled her from the railhead at Carson by freight teams to Mono Lake, where he constructed a fleet of big lumber barges whose heavily laden hulls the hard-working *Rocket* towed to the north shore, where the lumber was loaded on big high-wheeled freighters piloted by "bullpunchers" and their oxen for the short but tortuous haul up Cottonwood Canyon to the company's Bodie yard.

The energetic and optimistic Porter, who had in the past successfully gauged the business barometer, was caught unprepared for the slowdown, and had a disproportionate amount of his business on the cuff. Many of the non-productive smaller mines were having trouble. In order to do their mining, they declared Irish dividends which their weary and hard-pressed stockholders could not pay. Consequently these mines were months in arrears on their lumber bills with the good Captain, which made it impossible for him to meet his obligations.

In late August the nervous creditors of the G. L. Porter Company, after consultation, decided to give the hard-pressed firm a chance to work out of its difficulties. The hopeful creditors designated Mr. Abner and a prominent merchant, A. F. Bryant, as well as an employee of the company, J. S. Cain, to act as signees in conducting the business.

It was the second night in September and special officer Bob Whiteacre stood with easy alertness two or three feet from the end of the mahogany bar of the Comstock Saloon. He had been hired by Mr. Williams, the owner, to keep out the "opium fiends." This undesirable element had "infested the saloons and became a powerful nuisance."[58] Whiteacre had nerves of steel and a Bodie-earned reputation of knowing no fear. Earlier in the year he and Jack Roberts had been engaged as deputy constables when the criminal elements made the streets unsafe, and between them they practically eliminated strong armed robbery and garroting in Bodie. After quitting the constable duties, Whiteacre worked for the stage companies, Wells Fargo, and others who required special security from time to time.

"Winnemucca Jack," a Bonanza Street character, had informed the Comstock management and Whiteacre earlier in the evening that George Watkins, one of the opium fiends, had been elected to ambush the officer. And when Watkins entered the saloon a short time later, Whiteacre promptly busted him over the head and chucked him into the street.

Standing at the end of the bar and sideways to the street entrance, the officer dismissed Watkins as a problem. In his business, handling this type of bum was a pretty routine affair. Shortly after midnight a thirsty group of miners shouldered their way through the swinging doors, closely followed by John Sloan, a confederate of Watkins. He stepped to the side, holding the door, and in rushed Watkins with a double-barreled shotgun, firing as he entered. The roaring blast blew out the lights as the murderous charge ripped into the officer's abdomen. Whiteacre went down in a bloody heap. This produced a monumental stampede from the saloon, and in the darkness and confusion, Watkins and Sloan escaped, but the next day they were caught and put in jail.

The incensed editor of the *Standard News* charged into print with: "It was a cold blooded assassination. . . . The town is overrun by these 'Opium Fiends' who have no visible means of support, dress fine, and have some money. Men robbed nightly, murders committed without hindrance, an officer shot down in the discharge of his duty brings matters to such a crisis that a 601 will be compelled to clean out the mess of crime."[59]

The following day Watkins, who had fired the fatal shot into officer Whiteacre, having been denied his pipe of opium, cried out in great agony for relief. His friend Sloan, in the next cell, gave him a bottle of chloral hydrate and told him to take two teaspoons to relieve his spasms. Instead, Watkins committed suicide by downing the whole bottle of poison.

It was the first Saturday night in September and John Hackwell and his friends headed for the hurdy houses and fleshpots on Bonanza Street. Payday had been a recent event. So, after belting a round of Shannon's Bourbon that braced the boys, they swung down lower Main Street for a roaring night on the town. Arriving in front of Ward's Undertaking Parlor, some of the crowd wanted to go in and take a look at Watkins, the opium fiend, but Hackwell and one Ed Worley said, "They'd seen enough of Watkins and his kind when he was alive." Anyway, Hackwell wanted to see Dora Burnell at the Lower Dance House, with whom he had threaded the Mazy earlier in the week and scuffled with when he found his poke and pistol missing. He'd been in liquor—couldn't exactly remember anything except that he landed sprawling in the dust of lower Main Street. As he and Worley arrived at the corner near the dance house, Hackwell announced that he intended to get his pistol. He got it all right! Two assailants rushed them in the darkness and blasted him with his own British Bulldog. Marino Castro, the assassin, had fired from such close range that Hackwell's friends who rushed up found him stone dead and his clothing on fire from the powder flash.

"Officer 'Tex,' arriving on the scene, had the body taken to Ward's Undertaking Parlor where this reporter went on hearing of the affray. A dense and excited crowd in regular post office style, two deep, pressed in to view the body and out again. After joining the line, the body was soon in sight. The unfortunate man was found weltering in his own gore—dead. . . . Inquiries revealed the facts that Hackwell was a miner and that a woman was at the bottom of the trouble. Her name was Dora Burnell. She was arrested and lodged in jail."[60]

She was a native Californian, and she admitted that Marino Castro was her cousin. The same scribe chronicled: "The woman is rather good-looking with beautiful large black eyes and if the tigress within her were aroused, this scribbler would not like to be the object of her devotion. The supposition is that she gave Castro Hackwell's pistol for the purpose of killing him in cold blooded murder. . . . The woman had said on Saturday in the presence of two men that she would have Hackwell killed by Marino Castro, her cousin, at eight o'clock on Saturday night." And that was the hour of his demise.

It was after midnight and a weary undertaker was vainly trying to close the doors on the dwindling remnants of the curious crowd. Out on the sidewalk a friend of Hackwell's by the name of John Rann was set upon and surrounded by Manual Costello, Dave Bannion, Flannery, and another "bad man" known as Old Red. Rann, a hard-working woodchopper, had ruffled these gorillas when he vented his opinion on the cowardly killing of Hackwell a few hours before. As they threatened him he backed into John

Wagner's Saloon, and in the wild struggle that followed, in self-defense he shot and killed Costello.

As the sun rose Sunday, September 5, the well-worn slang expression "A man for breakfast" was hardly in keeping with the booted tally laid out on the cold mortician's slab.

At the very hour that the bloody, brangling turbulence erupted in Bodie that Saturday night, forty-odd miles to the north road agents collected their toll in the classic manner of "Stand and deliver." The Carson to Bodie stagecoach lurched and jolted swiftly ahead of its rolling cloud of dust. As it neared Sulphur Springs, it was brought to a sudden stop by the strident cry, "Halt!" "The driver stopped and two masked outlaws . . . came up, one on each side of the coach, and ordered the passengers riding outside to 'stick 'em up and come down.' . . . They were disarmed and ordered to stand with their hands up. The door of the coach was opened and the passengers ordered out. . . . One of the robbers guarded the passengers with a Henry Rifle while the other took the Wells Fargo box from the boot, dragged it about 20 feet and broke it open. Then, taking the contents, he ordered the passengers into the coach."[61]

As the highwaymen faded into the night the driver cracked his whip, and the packed and jiggery coach jounced on its way. Near the Elbow Ranch, the northbound Bodie to Carson stage pulled over to let the heavier-loaded Bodie-bound coach pass. During the moments of this brief stop driver Billy Hodge and express messengers Mike Tobey and Woodruff, on the northbound coach, learned the nerve-tightening story of what had happened and were alerted for trouble ahead. A few hours later as they approached Dalzells Station, the rifled Wells Fargo and Company box was spotted. The stage stopped and Billings, the agent of the stage company, got down to retrieve it. . . . Mike Tobey jumped off and was looking for tracks on a side road that forked behind the stage. One of the robbers, concealed in the brush, sang out, "You S.O.B., you're sneaking up on us."[62] He fired, missing Tobey and killing the near lead horse. Tobey ran around the side of the coach, and Billings tossed him his gun. Tobey told the other messenger Tom Woodruff, who was inside, to come out and they went to the back end of the coach. One of the robbers came up to the head of the horses where the coach light flashed full upon him. Tobey fired, killing him instantly. As the other robber came up on the other side of the coach, Tom Woodruff took a shot at him, but failed to bring him down. This outlaw then fired and wounded Tobey in the left arm. At this juncture, Billings and Woodruff left the coach with the wounded Tobey to seek aid at nearby Simpsons; however, after proceeding a short distance, they discovered that Mike's wound was not as dangerous as it first appeared. So, after administering first aid, they started back in the darkness to the stage. In the meantime the remaining robber came out of the night, and getting the drop on driver Hodge, forced him to hand over a Wells Fargo box, which he broke open and plundered before fleeing into the darkness. This section of the Bodie-Carson road near the old Dalzells Station, about eighteen miles this side of Wellington, Nevada, was a favorite "toll station" of the road agents of 1880.

The following day a fighting Bodie editor with strong vigilante overtones lashed out with: "Four men killed in two days is rather too much even for Bodie, and it is high time our people should awake to their responsibilities that must come of cleansing our town of men who are a terror to the community. . . . It is but a short time since the rough elements of Bodie threatened to burn the town. This everybody knows, and in our judgment an ounce of prevention is worth a pound of cure and the quicker it is applied, the better it will be for every decent man and woman in Bodie."[63]

Another observer caustically remarked that "the reputation of Bodie will soon equal that of the bloody ground of Kentucky unless the quietus is placed upon the disturbing elements."[64]

In mid-September the famous Wells Fargo special agent Sam Hume, working on a hot clue, arrested the surviving highwayman of the Sulphur Springs stage robbery in San Francisco. Fifteen days later Lincoln Anthony Sharp, a shackled prisoner of Wells Fargo's ace sleuth, Hume, and messenger H. C. Ward, was brought to Aurora for trial and deposited in the Esmeralda

County jail for safekeeping.[65] To make doubly sure of getting brigand Sharp out of circulation the practical folks of Wells Fargo retained Bodie's famous trial lawyer Pat Reddy to handle the prosecution. But the wily, Houdini-like Sharp, "part Cherokee and part French, possessing all the cunning of the former and all the intelligence of the latter race,"[66] crossed up these well-laid plans by skillfully unchinking a few bricks from the wall of his cell in the Aurora pokey and evaporating without a trace, except for the deft false trail clue of his shackles that were found on the Benton road.

Life was cheap among the reckless ruffians of the time. They fought over the slightest provocation at a word, almost at a look. Early that fall two of these short-fuse characters, both in liquor and complete strangers to each other, were having a big night of it whirling the Mazy Waltz with a couple of Bonanza Street virgins, when one of them, accidentally or on purpose, jolted the other. Page, the man who was bumped, ripped out a volley of insults and threatened to stomp his adversary Keough down. He drew his Colt, but he was a wee bit slow. Keough's lightning draw cut him down with a ball through the right temple. "Page fell to the floor—dead, and Keough made his escape."[67]

The searing impact of the bloody September doings of the camp's bad men and the eagerness with which the country's paper-selling editors depicted the rampant violence helped to install the Bad Man From Bodie to his pre-eminent place as a genuine imperishable legend in the sanctified gallery of Western bad men, where, with his boastful, vaunting, trigger-happy cussedness, he would have his niche forever.

The connotation of being a Bad Man From Bodie was a frequent boast of the toughs and highwaymen of the day. When one such character, Joe Fisher, alias Foster, who had shot Harry Diamond in San Francisco, was arrested in San Jose in the fall of 1880, he, with swaggering, publicity-seeking bravado, claimed to be the Bad Man From Bodie. The judge was unimpressed and set him up with a permanent residence in San Quentin.

Journalists, alert to sell copy, were quick to capitalize on the fame of the latest Western bad man, which news items they spread before the big-city subscribers. E. H. Clough (a well-known Sacramento Valley journalist whose effusions into certain pistol-totin', hell-for-leather aspects of Western life had gained for him a modest distinction) published his version of the Bad Man From Bodie in an October issue of the *Sacramento Bee*:

> One of the peculiarities of the "Bad Man From Bodie" is his profanity. A "Bad Man From Bodie" who never uses an oath, is as impossible as perpetual motion or an honest election in Nevada. This trait is especially noticeable whenever he kills a man or endeavors to kill one. Whenever you hear of a man from Bodie who did not swear when he pulled his gun, you may depend on it that he is base metal, tenderfoot, a man from Pioche, or Cheyenne, or Leadville. The oath of the "Bad Man From Bodie" is like the cheerful warning of the rattlesnake and, like that warning, the blow follows close upon its heels. Whenever a "Bad Man From Bodie" dons his war paint and strikes the bloody trail of carnage, he is prepared for every contingency. His little gun nestles cozily in his right hand coat pocket, the latter being lined with velvety buckskin to prevent the hammer from catching and frustrating his purpose of converting his enemies into full fledged angels. . . . His language reaches out and grasps the irresistible and terrible in nature, lifting it, as the Titans lifted the mountains, and flinging it with awful force against those who listened to him. I have seen him leap upon a billiard table and shout his defiance in the following stirring manner, "Here I am again, a mile wide and all wool. I weigh a ton, and when I walk, the earth shakes. Give me room and I'll whip an army. I'm a blizzard from Bitter Creek. I was born in a powder house, and raised in a gun factory. I'm bad from the bottom up, and grit plumb through. . . . I'm dry! Whose treat is it? Don't all speak at once for I'll turn loose and scatter death and destruction. . . . Your treat, is it? Well, stand in, boys. The Red Headed Woodpecker from Cow Creek is going to liquidate." . . . "The Bad Man From Bodie" is drifting down into the valley. He is located in the metropolitan centers where he may enjoy life without the inconvenience of always dreading a vigilante committee, that mushrooming tribunal of justice from which there is no appeal. . . . Besides, the winters in Bodie are very severe. . . . "The Bad Man From Bodie" . . . occasionally dies with his boots on, but never within the memory of man has

> one been hung by a civilized hangingman. He may accidentally drop down to oblivion through the instrumentality of an 18-inch Bowie. . . . When the warm weather beguiles the flitting swallow back to his last year's nest, "The Bad Man From Bodie" will return to his stamping ground up in the high Sierra or again to the wilds of southwestern Nevada. His lungs will once more expand with oath burdening winds, his cheery voice will ring out defiance to the trembling auditors. The short sharp yelp of his Derringer or Whistler will send the echoes flying, and the people of the camp where he takes up his abode will smile grimly and rub their palms as they remark in sotto voce tones, "Wreckoes gonna live it up this spring. I see the bone breakers got in." The undertaker dusts out his gorgeous death wagon. . . . The coroner gets ready his jury lists and makes a bargain with a particular physician in regards to holding of the autopsies. The grave digger buys a new spade, and the man whose job is epitaphs for dead men on imperishable marble lays in a stock of new chisels.[68]

The month of September witnessed the start of the big three-compartment Lent shaft, a joint venture of the Bodie and Mono Mining companies. Its purpose was to enable these companies to undertake the development of deep mining in both their properties. This shaft ultimately became the deepest working in the Bodie lode, attaining a vertical depth of more than 1,200 feet.

The month of September also saw the opening of Pat Reddy's elegant new law office that occupied the entire top floor of the new Molinari Building on the triangle block at Main and Mill streets. It consisted of five large rooms. And an observer noted that they are fitted up in magnificent style "and it is the most imposing law office outside of San Francisco."[69] Reddy's able and efficient new law clerk was young W. H. "Billy" Metson, who had arrived in Bodie shortly after the Fourth of July, fresh out of high school. Under Pat Reddy's masterful guiding hand he would become a giant in the annals of Western mining law. In Nome, Alaska, years later, at the turn of the century, the lessons in courage and careful preparation of his cases that he learned from the brilliant, redheaded, one-armed Reddy would enable him to win an almost hopeless case for his placer mining clients—a case so spectacular and famous that it was the basis of a great novel, *The Spoilers,* by Rex Beach (later made into a motion picture of the same name). The hero of the story was a young attorney, Bill Wheaton, none other in real life than Pat Reddy's junior partner, Bodie-trained Billy Metson. He had received his early legal training in the rough-and-tumble two-gun years of the camp's heyday.

And the last of September saw the hullabaloo of the fierce final rounds of politicking in the presidential campaign of 1880 descend on the camp. The Republicans, in their campaign to corral the Bodie voters for Garfield, held a torchlight procession up Main Street on the evening of the seventeenth which the *Standard News* (local clarion of the Democratic party) described as being "composed of 84 men supposed to belong to the Republican Club of Bodie, 60 'Boys in Blue,' 14 of 'em were in the last war, but 44 little boys ranging in age from 15 to 5 years. There were four bonfires on the street. The procession was strung out in the street and extended 376 feet at the Grandstand. These 188 men and boys were joined by about 2,400 Democrats who were attracted to the spot by the bonfires. . . . The band played, and Colonel D. M. Riordan, commander of the 'Boys in Blue' called the meeting to order. . . . The speaker of the evening was visiting Congressman, Renaldo Pacheco. He addressed the audience and at the conclusion of his speech spoke in Spanish, urging Mexicans and Spanish-speaking Americans to be loyal and true to the Republican principles and to vote the straight Republican ticket."

Nine days later the same sheet extolled:

> GRAND RALLY. The Largest Assembly Ever Seen in Bodie. Democrats Jubilant, and the Republicans Correspondingly Democrats Jubilant, and the Republicans Correspondingly Despondent. Reception of Honorable Wallace Leach, an Imposing Democratic Demonstration.—Bodie put on all its holiday attire yesterday afternoon. Large flags floated from the top of High Peak, and from the Standard Mill and Hoisting Works. . . . When darkness fell, seven large bonfires were lit on Main Street, and a huge one was kept up on High Peak, illuminating "Old Glory" as it floated from the staff above. . . . The streets were filled with thousands of people desirous of participating in the recep-

tion of Wallace Leach, the Democratic nominee for Congress. . . . A large body of mounted horsemen led by Grand Marshall Ned Reddy were followed by marchers with flags and torches, and the Bodie City Band. This was followed by a wagon from which a stream of lighted Roman candles ascended. . . . As Mr. Leach's carriage made its way up Main Street to the Grandstand, the earth fairly trembled with deafening cheers from the multitudes, and whistles shrieked from the Mills and Hoisting Works of the Mines, for two miles along the lead, and the cannon boomed. There were a number of transparencies [signs on glass] in the procession, each bearing a motto, such as first side—"Succession perish by the sword"—Hancock, second side—"The Union is saved"—Hancock, another read—"Our candidate needs no white-washing," second side—"Credit Mobilier"—James A. Garfield, ten shares, another read—"Chinese must go," second side—"American Soil for American Working Men."[70]

From the eminence of the bunting-draped grandstand conspicuously lighted by hundreds of torch bearers and the vaulting glare of the crowd-beckoning bonfires, Wallace Leach harangued the assembled throngs. It was a great show. The moment of truth came thirty-five days later when the votes were counted and the nation elected the twentieth President, James A. Garfield. Bodie's two precincts rolled up a total of 640 votes for Garfield and 553 for Hancock. The camp also stood for Renaldo Pacheco, 612 to 422 for Wallace Leach for congressman.

Of interest is the ratio of voters to the population. W. A. Mather, the careful Federal census enumerator for Bodie, in the nose count of 1880 came up with a tally of 5,375 for the entire population of Bodie township during the heyday. This is rather severe on writers who have rushed into print flatly handing out a figure of 10,000. They have obviously assembled many of their yarns from the elastic statistics of the hot-stove and spittoon legends of the following decades. How amusingly inaccurate this hearsay can be is shown when a quick check of the census of 1880 reveals that the entire population of Mono County was 7,499 and the combined totals of Inyo and Mono counties' inhabitants were 10,427.

Admittedly, census taker Mather, in spite of his known diligence, would have found it impossible to count all the inhabitants of Bodie, numbered among whom were many scores of outlaws and picturesque ruffians who in the booming camp found a temporary base for fruitful operations after having successfully eluded the swift retribution of Judge Lynch's court elsewhere. And there were many who never gave their right names. They were known only as "Big Red," "Wild Bill," "U. P. Jack," "Naughty Nellie," etc., or any other cognomens they fancied, but this element by the wildest stretch of the imagination never exceeded 20 percent of the camp's population.

The enthusiasm and civic pride over its exciting new position as the fastest-growing and most-talked-about mining town in the American West was further enhanced in San Francisco that fall when the proud Knights Templar of the Bodie Commandery received a magnificent banner for having the largest representation, according to membership; because of this they were chosen to carry it at the triennial conclave at Chicago, and a big delegation of this fraternal order made the trip. The wholehearted civic pride that all Bodie took in this junket was manifested on September 26 when the news came by telegraph from Aurora that the three Knights Templar who were delegated to return the banner to Bodie had arrived in Aurora. The *Bodie Standard News* chronicled the story: "Yesterday afternoon, the famous 'Whip,' Jim Mooney, was dispatched to Aurora with a six-in-hand to bring back the distinguished gentlemen in style. And at nine o'clock this morning flags were flying from every flagstaff in town and along the ridge. While the Bodie Commandery was assembling to receive their brother representatives in a becoming manner. At 10:20 A.M., the whistles of the Bodie and Syndicate Mills, two miles below town, announced the approach of the party, and their music was echoed by the whistles of the other mills and hoisting works for a distance of two miles along the ridge. The Standard cannon occasionally drowning the sounds of the whistles with its booming. This was the signal for Burlinger and Frank's Brass Band to strike up a stirring air at the corner of Main and King Street,"[71] where the Knights Templar of the Bodie Commandery were marshaled, in full regalia, ready to escort the carriage bearing the banner and the three Sir

Knights, William Irwin, J. H. Caldwell, George Warren. When the carriage arrived, their ranks wheeled into line, and with the band playing, proudly marched down Main Street to the Masonic Hall.

One day in early October an earth-shaking explosion rocked the camp. Many who felt the shock thought that another powder magazine had gone skyward, but as the fire company rushed south on Main Street with dogs and kids in hot pursuit, the wrecked and burning Bodie Foundry was seen to be the cause. At the five-o'clock pour the two Potter brothers and Norton Pine had tapped the cupola, drawing off some of the molten metal. "The latter threw a bucket of water upon the red hot mass, suddenly chilling the surface and generating heat in the interior. . . . An explosion occurred hurling the men for fully 30 feet and scattering the molten iron in all directions. . . . The men escaped with a few slight burns and bruises, but one side of the building was blown out and the foundry set on fire."[72] However, the prompt arrival and diligence of the fire department in extinguishing the flames saved the other buildings and the pattern shop.

A prominent Bodieite who paid a visit that month to Mill Creek and Lundy reported: "There is now one five-stamp mill and three arastras running in the district, and Jim Townsend's big arastra will be started up tomorrow. Rosets' arastra is crushing from two to three tons per day. The California Company's arastra at Wasson crushes about the same quantity. The Halloran brothers' arastra crushes about three tons. . . . The new May Lundy Mill is also running but will have to be shut down for alterations. . . . The sawmill at Lundy is running full handed, and the scream of steam whistles up and down the canyon and the general air of activity that pervades the district has infused new life and hope into the inhabitants."[73]

Not long after the reassuring echoes of the regular midnight whistles had faded on a bitter-cold Monday, November 8, a ghastly red glare lit the sky a quarter of a mile to the south of the Mono shaft and high on the ridge east of the town. The frantic clanging of the fire bells and shrill blasts from the Mono, Bodie, and Lent whistles quickly aroused most of the camp's inhabitants, who watched in horror as the vaulting flames devoured the Goodshaw Hoisting Works. It made an eerie and terrifying silhouette against the eastern sky. In this holocaust four miners perished. They were working in the east crosscut on the 600-foot level. Captain Buckley, the superintendent, and Mr. Hood, his foreman, after several hours of frantic labor were able to rig a temporary hoist frame, and with a donkey engine for power they succeeded by 9 A.M. the following morning in "lowering the bucket with a light in it to the 600-foot level and raising it again to the surface with light still burning, and a rock in the bucket. About 300 men were gathered about the shaft anxiously awaiting the return of the bucket. Upon receiving the cheering news that a rock was in the bucket, probably placed there by the miners, a sigh of relief escaped the crowd and hearty cheers were given. Mr. Oliver, superintendent of the Champion, and Mr. Steel, one of the Goodshaw men, immediately got on the bucket and descended the shaft; arriving at the 600-foot level, they entered the east crosscut . . . and found the bodies of Duncan McRay, Arthur Jackson, Hugh Smith, and John Blake lying upon their faces. . . . Writing a dispatch to the effect that the men were dead, they placed it in the bucket and signaled to hoist. On arrival of the bucket, the dispatch was read, and the bright hopes of a few minutes before were dashed to the ground."[74] This sad tragedy left three fatherless families to face the world without breadwinners.

The exact cause of the fire was never fully determined, but on November 14 a letter was received by Ross Culcord, superintendent of the Syndicate Mine. It had been penned by the hoist engineer who was on duty that fatal night at the Goodshaw Mine and had been missing since the tragedy. This engineer was well known and highly respected by Mr. Culcord and had worked for him both in Bodie and previously on the Comstock.

Mr. R. Culcord:

On a bed of sickness I write these lines, praying that you and the public may not judge me too harshly. On Monday evening after everyone had left, I made the usual rounds. . . . About 10 o'clock, Captain Buckley and Mr. Hood came in and went down into the mine. After they came up, Captain Buckley went into the change room and as soon as they left, I again turned down the light next to the shaft; but did not look in the change room. . . . If the candle had been left burning in the change room, I think it would have been seen, unless some clothes were hung over the window, it being a small one. Clothes containing matches may have fallen down on the steam pipes used for heating the room and smoldered away for a long time. . . . I was reading when the midnight whistle blew. About half an hour later, I went out of the fireroom to the privy. How long I was there I cannot say. The mental strain in close attention on the sick for the previous three days was too much.[75] Abused nature could not stand it any longer. I was startled by a cry. Rushing out I saw the building on fire. As I went through the fireroom door, I heard Mr. Hood cry out, 'Send that tub to the bottom.' Reaching the engine I started the tub down and the top of the change room and the beams and rafters over my head became one sheet of flames. . . . When I realized that no human being could stand by that engine, nearly crazed with the thought of those below, I left the building, just as Captain Buckley rushed in. Of 22 years' experience in the shop and engine room, this is my first accident. With conscience free from any criminal intent and strickened with pain and remorse, I remain

Yours truly,
L. PARKER.[76]

The frozen breath of King Winter iced the camp, sending the mercury skidding to 18 below on November 13, an event that sent many an old-timer out to carefully compute the size of his woodpile. Needless to say, the price of stove wood nosed up to two dollars per cord. The following week the local press carried a brief notice that "from and after this date, the price of baths in Bodie will be 75¢ each."[77]

On Thursday, November 25 a Grand Thanksgiving Ball was held at the Music Hall on the second floor of Silas B. Smith's store. And Berlinger and Frank's Quadrille Band furnished music for a packed floor of happy celebrating merrymakers until morning.

The local press carried a unique card the day after Thanksgiving which read: "We, the boarders of the 'Hotel de Kirgan' express our heartfelt and sincere thanks and gratitude to the proprietor of said institution for the courteous manner and bountiful feast of which we partook for Thanksgiving Dinner. The table was complete in every particular, and with the proprietor's supervision and the ability of our excellent cook, assisted by that war-stained veteran, the hero of 40 battles, General John Flynn, O'Commander of the First Negro Brigade of Virginia—they got up the most sumptuous meal that was heartily enjoyed by all.

"Hoping that Mr. Kirgan may live to enjoy the good of this world and Thanksgiving dinners for many years, we remain, Respectfully, 'The Boarders' [prisoners in the Bodie jail]."[78]

As those wondrous rip-roaring final days of 1880 turned the corner of Western history, another boom year went into the record. Bullion production topped that of '79 with every indication of bigger things to come.

The gun-slinging blood-letting violence of which there was more than enough to go round had been played up by the outside press as they pounded out paper-selling stories of doings of the Bad Man From Bodie.

In the camp itself the economy held a prosperous course. True, some two thousand fewer citizens thronged the streets than at midsummer, but many of these had been carpenters and construction workers who had left when the building boom subsided.

In the bitter printing machine war that had erupted back in March when the *Bodie Chronicle* came out as a daily, the new and skillfully edited *Free Press* of Osborne and Cleveland emerged as the top dog of Bodie's newspaperdom. The *Daily News,* which had so confidently assimilated the *Daily Bodie Standard* in midsummer, now found itself hors de combat as its subscribers swarmed to the *Free Press* fold, forcing on it a change of management and a six-month suspension of operation. The other losers in this Armageddon of the inkpots were Uncle "Bob" Folger and his brother, who fled the field and the wicked city of Bodie. Stopping to catch their breath in Bridgeport, they decided to begin all over again with the *Bridgeport Chronicle Union.*

CHAPTER VII

The Heyday Rolls On - 1881

The new year was just fifteen days old when the hard-working Folger brothers grabbed the handle of their little press and ground out their first big story:

> Again Bodie comes to the front with another murder, the foulest of many that have disgraced that town. Yesterday morning at half past one o'clock, Joseph De Roche, a French Canadian, shot to death Thomas Treloar, a Cornish miner. It appeared to have been a cold-blooded murder of a peaceful and harmless citizen. . . . The custody of the prisoner had been intrusted to a drunken constable from whom he escaped. . . . De Roche had attended a ball at the Miners' Union Hall and danced with Mrs. Treloar against the request of her husband. About the close of the ball, De Roche left the Hall and laid in wait for his victim at the corner of Main and Lowe Streets where Treloar was shot through the head. Intense excitement prevails in Bodie against the murderer and the constable from whom he escaped.[1]

Seven days later the same mountain oracle carried the sequel:

> De Roche, the murderer of Treloar, was captured on Saturday night, eight miles from Bodie on the Goat Ranch Road and hanged by the 601 on Monday morning. We clipped the following account of the lynching from the "Free Press"—Judge Lynch held his first court session in Bodie early on Monday morning and passed judgment on a criminal whose crime was already recorded and impressed upon every mind in this community. . . . Between 1:30 and 2 o'clock A.M. Monday morning, a long line of masked and unmasked men were seen to file out of side street into Bonanza. There must have been 200 of them. As the march progressed to the jail, the column increased. In front were the shotguns carried by determined men. . . . When the jail was reached, it was surrounded and the leader made a loud knock at the door. All was quiet and dark within. The call had the effect of producing a dim light in the office, and amid loud

cries of "De Roche, bring him out! Open the door," etc. Jailer Kirgan appeared and responded by saying, "All right, boys. Wait a minute, give me a little time." In a moment the outside door was opened slowly and four or five of the men entered. Here, under instructions, the door of the cell in which the condemned lay was swung open. The poor wretch knew what this untimely visit meant and prepared for the trying ordeal and humiliating death. It was some moments before he was brought out, and the crowd began to grow impatient. Some imagined that the prisoner had been taken away by the officer. If this had been the case, what would have followed can only be imagined. All these doubts were put at rest by the presence of the man. He wore light-colored pants, a colored calico shirt, and over his shoulders hung a canvas coat, buttoned around the neck. His head was bare, and as the bright rays of the moon glanced upon his face, there was a picture of horror visible. It was the look of dogged defiance and submission. With a firm step, he descended the stairs and came out on the street in a hurried manner, closely guarded by the shotguns and revolvers. The orders, "to fall in," were given and all persons not members of the mysterious committee to "fall back." The march up Bonanza Street was rapid, but not a word was said by the condemned man, and his gaze was fixed upon the ground. He was hurried up the back street to Fuller, the corner of Green was turned and when Weber's Blacksmith Shop was reached, a halt was made. In front of this place was a huge gallows frame used for raising up wagons, etc. . . . Now it was to be used for quite a different purpose. "Move it up to the spot where the murder was committed," was the order. And immediately it was picked up by a dozen men and carried to the corner of Main and Lowe Streets. The condemned man glanced at it for a moment, and an apparent shudder came over him, but he uttered not a word. From an eye witness we learn that the scene which followed was awful in its impressiveness. Snow had just begun to fall, and the moon which had shone so brightly during the early part of the night shed but a pale light on the assembled company. When the corner was reached, the heavy gallows was placed on the ground and the prisoner led up to it. The prisoner's demeanor still remained passive, his hands incased in irons were clasped, his eyes occasionally were turned upward, and his lips were seen to move once or twice. On each end of the frame was a windlass with large ropes attached. The rope placed around the prisoner's neck was a small one. When the knot was made it rested against the left ear. This did not suit De Roche particularly and he changed it, so that it would be more to the rear. Some suggested that his hands and limbs be tied. This was immediately done. The large iron hooks of the frame dangled near the prisoner, and the grating sound produced a peculiar and eerie feeling. It was at least three minutes before everything was all ready. De Roche was asked by the leader if he had anything to say. He replied, "No, nothing." In a moment he was asked the same question, and a French-speaking bystander was requested to receive his answer. The reply this time was, "I have nothing to say only, oh God!" "Pull him" was the order. And in a twinkling, the body rose three feet from the ground. Previous to putting the rope on, the overcoat was removed. The second after the body was elevated, a sudden twitch of the legs was observed; but with that exception, not a muscle moved. While the body hung to the crossbeam . . . it swung to and fro like the pendulum of a clock. The crowd remained perfectly quiet. After a lapse of two or three minutes, a voice sharp and clear was heard in the background. "I'll give $100 if twenty men connected with this affair will publish their names in the paper tomorrow morning." The voice was immediately recognized as that of a leading attorney. And a yell went up from the crowd, "Give him the rope, put him out," and similar sentences that drowned out his voice. His retreat was as dignified as the extenuancies of the case would permit. While the body was still hanging, a paper was pinned on to his breast bearing the following inscription—"All others take warning, let no one cut him down—Bodie 601."

At the expiration of thirty minutes, Dr. Deal was summoned and he pronounced life extinct. The body was then cut down and placed in a plain box and taken to Ward's undertaking rooms. The mysterious committee had completed its work and the Captain gave out the order, "All members of the Bodie 601 will meet at their rendezvous." In a moment the scene of death was deserted. To use a familiar expression, "De Roche died game." He was firm as a rock to the last. He passed out into the unknown without a shudder.[2]

That same week another Bodie Bad Man had his earthly stay abruptly terminated. Dave Bannion, a beetle-browed bully with a long record as a troublemaker, swilled on his nightly round, and in this rum-soaked condition he hiccuped his way to the bar in the Divide Saloon, where he chanced to run afoul of a pleasantly "swacked" but durable Irishman, in the person of Ed Ryan. In the quarrel that erupted Bannion drew his six-gun and tried to pistol-whip his man, but before he could wallop his antagonist, Ryan polished him off with a quick shot as he fired from the hip, killing the bad man almost instantly. Bannion had managed to get off a tardy but wobbly shot which winged Ryan in the right side. A medical man's probing verified that Ryan had a fifty-fifty chance of survival.

A few days later, as if to relieve the bloody grimness of the times, the *Free Press* published a little poem by General Kittrell.

TO MARY

Mary had some little skates.
    She, with them, went out to slide.
She slipped, and therefore had a fall
    As also did her pride.
Her heels flew up—her head went down
    And struck upon the ice
Displaying both her striped hose
    Which surely was not nice
She jumped up quickly on her feet
    And said she did not care.
But on those hose, a card was seen
    Marked fifteen cents a pair.[3]

By early March the camp was full of rumor over which route the projected Bodie Railroad and Lumber Company's narrow gauge would take. The *Free Press* of March 9, 1881, speculated that the "proposed route along the west shore of Mono Lake would develop considerable freight business from the Jordon, Homer, and Tioga Mining Districts," and pointed out that Yerington and Bliss (directors of the railroad) had ordered 200 tons of hay from the King Ranch to be delivered to a point south "of Mono Lake where they will have a new sawmill running in four weeks."

On the first Sunday in March, Major John Kirgan, the tough and courageous old Texan who had been the camp's greatest peace officer through the wild and turbulent years of '78, '79, and '80 harnessed up his powerful and spirited gray horse and sprang into his sulky to enjoy a brief afternoon's ride.

As he swung down Main Street the high-stepping gray suddenly became frightened by a bounding football which had eluded some youthful player, and bolted. Kirgan, clutching the reins and fighting for control, swept southward on Main Street. At a ditch crossing opposite the Mono County Bank the pitching sulky crashed into an open trench, throwing the old deputy sheriff with terrific force upon the frozen street, where he sustained "some fearful injuries to his head, and he was picked up unconscious." A reporter who visited him on March 13 sadly chronicled, ". . . his condition has now grown worse, and he is unconscious much of the time, and the doctors are not extending much hope for him."[4] A short time after this visit the gallant spirit of this grizzled old pioneer took leave of his beloved Western landscape forever.

On the second Saturday in March the clattering telegraph key carried, in a private dispatch from San Francisco, the news that in the case of the Jupiter against the Bodie Mine, the jury in the U.S. Circuit Court had ruled in favor of the defendants. This was another victory for Pat Reddy, Bodie's great lawyer, who convinced the jury that the Apex rights to the rich Fortuna vein were in the Bodie ground, thereby knocking down the Jupiter Company's claim to the rich ore being mined from this vein.

Wednesday, March 23, 1881, was an important day for Mono County. The first trial in the new courthouse at Bridgeport was held, with Honorable R. M. Briggs, judge of the Superior Court, Department I, presiding. It was the trial of George Morton, and began and ended on the same day. He was accused of stealing bullion from the Standard Consolidated Mine in Bodie. The case unexpectedly blew up in the face of the imposing legal array assembled by the prosecution, W. O. Parker, district attorney, and Pat Reddy, retained by the Standard Company. When their key prosecution witness, a miner named Height, was placed on the stand, he promptly "denied the truth of what he had told before the Grand Jury"—a yarn which had implicated Morton. At this abrupt turn of events "the prosecution had to throw up the case and consent to Morton's discharge. Mr.

Reddy favored Height with a good tongue-lashing for his perfidy. Upon his acquittal, Morton remarked to the court that he had been eight months in jail and was destitute. Whereupon the Honorable Pat Reddy, a prosecuting attorney, quietly handed him a $20 gold piece"[5]—a simple act that conveyed a little of the milk of human kindness which endeared this brilliant counselor of law to a legion of friends and contemporaries of his enchanting era in Western history.

Reddy's courtroom manner was superb. His astuteness, his careful preparation, and his almost total recall made him a frightening opponent in any case. A leading member of the San Francisco bar once described to me how he and other young law students during the Gay Nineties eagerly went to observe his courtroom manners. They were, along with the judge and jury, fascinated with his correct diction and faintly purring Irish brogue, which came out in picturesque sentences of winged words that plainly captured the members of the jury one by one. As an orator he had no peer. Some years ago an old-timer who attended a public function in Bridgeport shortly after the current courthouse was completed recalled a gleaming phrase of Reddy's speech as he whimsically referred to his local legal contemporaries. "Like eagles, they came over these mountains sharpening their claws on the rough edges of $20 gold pieces."[6]

As March came to a close all speculation on the exact route of the new Bodie Railroad and Lumber Company's narrow gauge was swept aside as J. T. Oliver's survey of the route had been completed and approved. It skirted the eastern shore of Mono Lake and passed Warm Springs, running in an almost straight line southerly for a little over ten miles to the company's 12,000-acre timber forests and their new sawmill. The *Free Press* of April 30 noted that the builders of the new railroad were Robert N. Graves, Seth Cook, Dan Cook of San Francisco, and H. M. Yerington of Carson City, Nevada. Graves was listed as president, and William Willis of San Francisco, secretary. "Capital stock is $1,000,000 and a term of existence of 50 years." The estimated cost of the road in running order, with equipment, was $400,000. Construction was scheduled to begin at once.

On Saturday afternoon, May 17, at Boone's corral, a capacity crowd of 1,200 witnessed the Cornish-style wrestling match between Rod McGinnis and James Pascoe. From the standpoint of attendance and interest it was the greatest sporting event in the history of the camp. The sports-minded *Free Press* of the eighteenth summarized the spectacle: "A draw battle—Pascoe and McGinnis in the ring—After five hours of hard work, neither man had given a fall. . . . Even stocks were ignored, and the small trifles of everyday life were swallowed up in the battle between McGinnis and Pascoe. . . . The stakes were $500 a side. . . . When time was called, nearly all the seats were taken. The law and the clergy were represented. Men from the mines, the shops and the stores were on hand, and the scene was invigorating to witness. A brass band played at intervals throughout the afternoon. While the wrestle was on, the Main Street and the balance of the town was extremely quiet. Scarcely anyone could be seen and the whole town appeared deserted. . . . Every man who could raise any money put it up on the results. The Fourth of July was not half so much a holiday as was Saturday."

Dave "Tex" Hitchell, a former Bodie night officer and ex-deputy constable, got himself riddled with lead in a King Street opium den. Hitchell had put the bite on quiet, easygoing James Stockdale for a buck in an uptown card room, and on being refused he went off in a huff. The *Standard News* of June 7 recounted their seamy meeting in the opium den a few hours later:

> It is not known what passed between the two men in the room. It is stated that Hitchell began abusing Stockdale, knocking him down with a six-shooter, an opium pipe, or some other equally dangerous weapon. There was a commotion of considerable magnitude. At any rate, Stockdale left the den and procured a revolver. When he returned, he found Hitchell in a bunk, considerably under the influence of the deadly narcotic. Immediately upon Stockdale spying him, he began to shoot. The first ball

> struck Hitchell in the abdomen, another ball struck him in the right groin, and the third ball also entered his body. . . . The wounded man staggered up and rolled out on the floor. The Chinese and other inmates of the house were terror strickened. Chinamen could be seen running in all directions, yelling and shouting as though the house were about to fall and crush them all. Some drew pistols, others drew knives, and within a few minutes King Street was alive with celestials, white opium fiends, and frequenters of the Chinese quarters. Hitchell was removed to the County Hospital where Doctors Van Zandt and Blackwood were sent for. The wounded man was in great pain, but did not display much concern as to his injuries. He died at one o'clock this morning.

Stockdale fled to Aurora, where he was apprehended by the sheriff of Esmeralda County, acting on a telegram from Bodie authorities requesting his detention.

That same day Norman McSwain, a highly regarded Canadian miner, worked his first and last shift on the 500-foot level of the Bechtel Mine. In loading a round of holes to blast, a premature explosion occurred, blowing the top of his head off. By some quirk of fate his shift partners working beside him escaped without a scratch.

As Bodie readied itself for the Fourth of July in '81, it was the focal point and northern terminus of a $500,000 railroad construction project. On July 2 a delving *Free Press* reporter interviewed Dan Cook, prominent San Francisco capitalist, and his brother Seth, who were major stockholders of the Standard Consolidated Mining Company, the camp's foremost bullion producer, and were also chief bankrolling directors of the new Bodie Railroad and Lumber Company's narrow gauge. When asked what his opinions were on the future of the Bodie District, financier Cook replied: "The best answer that could be made to such a query would be to call attention to the fact that we are building a railroad to supply the mines of Bodie with lumber at the expense of $600,000 to $700,000. We would not make this outlay if we did not anticipate that the district would enjoy a sufficient length of life to make the investment a profitable one. Bodie today is the best and surest Camp on the coast. Its bullion output, in my judgment, will be as large or larger ten years from now as it is at present. In the 1,000-foot level of the Standard, we are not far enough in to strike the ledge, but we expect to find it."[7]

Almost within the hour of the *Free Press's* interview with capitalist Cook, a dispatch hummed over the wires to Bodie that fell like "a pall": " 'President Garfield Shot by a Chicago Nihilist.' And immediately the news spread like wildfire. As nothing could be obtained, the wildest sort of speculation was rife. No news was received during the afternoon. At six o'clock the *Free Press* began to receive telegrams. By eight o'clock, its extra edition appeared on the streets and was bought up immediately. . . . That evening all other public topics were ignored. And while no great excitement was manifest, a feeling of deepest sorrow prevailed."[8]

Because of the President's grave condition, the Fourth of July committee of arrangements held an emergency meeting on the third, at which it was agreed to put off the parade and celebration. However, early on the morning of the Fourth several telegrams indicating an improvement in his condition were received, and after a hurried meeting it was decided to hold the parade and celebration as planned.

As the Fourth dawned "nature fairly outdid itself. . . . The sun rose in a cloudless sky, and not a breath of air stirred, and everything was enveloped in sunshine and warmth. The day was simply lovely. Such a beautiful sunrise has seldom been witnessed here. For ten minutes before the orb of the day appeared above the peaks, the eastern heavens were clothed in a garnet of the deepest red, the reflection was extremely exquisite. Presently, this red changed to a yellow hue and in time faded away as the sun moved on its course." At daybreak the Standard artillery was brought out and the salute was fired by Jules Renault, the veteran French soldier. Upon this occasion "the new cannon recently made at the Standard Mill was brought into use. Five pounds of powder were used in every charge, and the echo along the canyon was remarkably distinct. At an early hour the town was all life and activity. The small boys were out with crackers and bombs, making all the noise possible, frightening horses, timid ladies and dogs."[9] Nearly all the business houses on Main Street were gaily decorated.

Officers of the day were Thomas C. Ryan, President; Reverend F. M. Warrington, Chaplain; Judge R. M. Briggs, Orator; and William Irwin, Grand Marshal. The parade was smaller than that of 1880. There was only one brass band. A big feature was a second Standard cannon. This new piece of ordnance, as it rumbled down Main Street followed by its slightly smaller but capable-looking predecessor built in 1880, gave the Standard Mining Company unquestioned affluence in the artillery department, a position it enjoyed until the sunset salute was fired. On the thirty-eighth shot (one for each state), gunner Renault and his enthusiastic crew poured in an extra charge of powder for good measure and socked home the wet wad, good and tight. The result was the biggest bang of the evening, splitting the gun from "butt to muzzle, and blowing the carriage to kindling wood."[10] The only injury was that suffered by the pride of Standard's machine shop, which had built the piece.

After the parade and at the conclusion of the literary exercises, the rush for the race track on Brooker Flat began, as some six hundred patriotic celebrating members of the sporting fraternity pressed in to service "express wagons, handsomes, buckboards, jerkwaters, mud-wagons, two-wheel affairs, and quartz carts with every conceivable style of animal hitched to these vehicles and dashed off," at something between a trot and a gallop that sent boiling clouds of dust into the warm, still air of the Fourth. Most of this jovial dusty cavalcade swung around to the south side of the 600-yard oval track where the judges' stand was located and a commodious bar dispensed a wide variety of thirst-quenching lubricants.

This was the first meeting of the newly organized Bodie Jockey Club, and President Stevens and Secretary Rankin had done their best to line up the speeediest hay burners of Mono and Inyo counties. There was some disappointment, however, when Black Harry, the Bishop flash, failed to show up.

In the first race of the day a horse named Joe Kennedy

sponsored by J. C. McMillan won by three lengths over the favorite, Nelly O'Malley, a mare entered by T. W. Smith and J. S. Cain.

A celebrating reporter who was on hand observed that the track was "dusty and of course no speed could be made. But what was the difference, one horse stood the same chance as the other. Later in the afternoon, a heavy shower of rain dampened the ground and the clothing, but not the spirits of the crowd."

The second race was won by Buckskin, owned by Will Irwin. The other two entries jumped the track at the halfway mark, "and as a fair start was not given, and owing to the darkness, the race was declared off until Tuesday, the fifth."[11]

The same scribe who favored the ponies over the grunt and groaners of the mat observed, "So many people attended the horse races on the afternoon of the Fourth, that the wrestling matches were put over until Tuesday."

On the third Monday in July the Bechtel Mine had its second fatality of the summer. Alex Larson was a strapping Swede who had survived the powder explosion that had decapitated Norman McSwain. In the short weeks since that miracle Alex had quaffed many a glass of schnapps as he pondered the trick of fortune and the frivolous caperings of fate that had conducted him through this holocaust without a scratch. In midafternoon the liquid consolation and reveries of this hard-working Scandinavian were terminated forever as he stepped backward from a passing ore car and plunged two hundred feet in the darkness down a yawning incline to his death.

A conscientious news hound who was responsible for the local intelligence reported that the Bodie Sunday school, which had boasted 29 children in '79, now had an enrollment of 130. "The concert last Sunday evening reflected in a fair degree what the little folks had been taught by their kind and devoted teachers."[12]

He also felt constrained to call out for fair play for "the manager of a certain boarding house that had lost all her boarders the other day. She bought ranch butter and put it on the table. The roast beef demolishers noticed a change in the cow fruit, and not being used to a good article, they thought the madam was trying to ring in oleomargarine on them. So, in a secret caucus, it was resolved to seek out a new place. In offering up prayers for the President, let not the landlady be forgotten."[13]

And while on the topic of groceries he called attention to the fact that "gull eggs from Mono Lake are in the market, and those who eat them say 'They are loud.' "

In the closing days of July certain sections of the county were troubled with a worrisome phenomenon of nature. A lamenting cattleman who had just driven a supply of beef on the hoof to the Bodie market reported:

> Never since the county was settled have grasshoppers been so numerous as they are this year around Mono Lake and Adobe Meadows. The Free Press man who spoke with genial loquacious Frank Shaw of Adobe Meadows was informed, "The ground is absolutely black with them, all over the valley, in some places from two to six grasshoppers high." Mr. Shaw said, "From two to six feet in depth," but in order to put the statement on a truthful basis, the reporter prefers grasshoppers instead of feet. He says that they absolutely wipe out everything in their way, and in the valleys laying adjacent to Mono Lake not a green blade of anything will be left standing. The hoppers are now laying their eggs preparatory to a plentiful burden next spring. Frank saved over a lot of choice thoroughbreds from last year's visitation of these pests, and he thinks that by crossing the breed he will be able to produce a few swarms of these industrious little workers that will contract to clean up Inyo County with several days' labor next summer. He will guarantee to strip Bishop Creek and Owens Valley within 24 hours after starting some of his choice bands southward.[14]

Early in August, Elly Orrum—Mrs. Sandy Bowers of Washoe and Comstock fame but now widowed and playing hide and seek with poverty—operating as the "Washoe Seeress," arrived back in Bodie with her Ouija board and bunco accessories. After a few so-so weeks of prophecy-for-pay among the more gullible citizens of Mill Creek, she again set up shop in Bodie for a two- or three-week stand on upper Main Street in a building opposite the post office. The camp had been a regular port of call on her fortune telling circuit for the past few years.

The local press noted that a grand social affair was in the making for the coming Friday evening: "Mr Joseph Silva, an accomplished musician well known to the Bodie Public, will give what promises to be one of the most successful social entertainments ever given in Bodie. His selection of musicians deserve special notice, including as it does Professor E. Burlinger, piano; John King, violinist; John Prior, cornet; Charles Hayes, clarinetist; and Joseph Silva, flute. The admission price has been fixed at one dollar, and it is anticipated that a large and select assembly of ladies and gentlemen of Bodie will attend."[15] This was Silva's last musical. The popular Portuguese fell victim to typhoid fever; sixteen days later his many friends attended a large and imposing funeral and paid their last respects to him.

By mid-August, Superintendent Thomas Holt had the construction program of the Bodie Railroad and Lumber Company's narrow gauge and sawmill running just about on schedule. The labor troubles that had plagued the start of this project in late May had blown over. Disgruntled, out of work Bodie miners, accustomed to three and four dollars per day, had balked at the company's wage of $1.25 per day plus board, and at their hiring of some five dozen Chinese.

Twenty-five 14-mule teams were hauling a steady stream of rails, sawmill machinery, and railroad iron from the new terminus of the Carson and Colorado Railroad at Hawthorne, Nevada. They geed and hawed southward across Whiskey Flat and around through the low hills and west across the almost level desert plain to Warm Springs on the eastern shore of Mono Lake, which had become the hub of the construction project.

"Twenty-two miles of grading had been finished on the second of August." And the *Free Press* of Saturday, August 6, glowingly recounted a trip that their reporter had made over the grade at the invitation of Superintendent Holt. Starting at the Bodie terminus some 600 feet east of the Mono shaft, it departed "along the eastern slope of Silver Hill to a point between the Defiance and Red Cloud Shafts." Here it turned east across the flat and skirted the western slope of Nevada Hill, and then easterly to an intersection with the junction of the Syndicate and Noonday wood roads. The grading on the right of way over this four-mile stretch was completed, the grade being a gentle 70 feet to the mile.

In the next seven miles 260 white men and 68 Chinese were working with picks and shovels, drills, horses and scrapers, carving out the grade, which now increased to a precipitous 200 feet to the mile. There were "two switchbacks or Ys about a mile and a half apart, and the roadbed zigzaged and curved down the mountain sides. Over these switchbacks, the "trains will have to be backed up both going down and coming up." Driving the work on this stretch to completion were the three bull pushers (camp bosses) Hugh Drum, Thomas F. McMillen, and H. C. Technor, chief of the railroad commissary and supply department. The men were housed in four separate camps, consisting of "a boarding house and dining room and kitchen, with white walled tents scattered about."

Near the foot of the mountain and at the beginning of this steep seven-mile stretch, a 260-foot-long wooden trestle spanning a 50-foot-deep gully was in the preliminary stages of construction. The reporter found sixty-eight Chinese whose camp was located just below the trestle site, working on the foundations and abutments for which eight two-horse scrapers were bringing in fill.

In the next two miles the grade gradually tapered off, as the roadbed reached the "level of Mono Lake plain." No work had been done on the next five-mile stretch. However, in just a little over three months puffing locomotives would be hauling trainloads of lumber for the mines of Bodie over this roadbed for which the ties were still lying uncut in the forest and at the site of the rapidly rising sawmill, a tribute to sweat and toil, Yankee know-how, and the organization and driving ability of Superintendent Holt.

By '81 most of the Bodie shaft mines had encountered a perplexing and pocket-denting problem in the unbailable water table that remained all too constant at about the 450-foot level. The hopeful future of deep mining was challenged by this physical barrier. As the year wore on, many of the smaller mining companies, especially in the saddle of the lode and in the south end, were forced into an economic cul-de-sac. Having failed to find sufficient good milling ore in the upper levels, they embarked upon a program of sinking their shafts deeper, hoping to strike "it" at greater depth. But the water table whose lowering called for costly outlays for huge steam pumps could only be had by levying big assessments on their already jittery tax-ridden stockholders, who had seen nothing but promises and Irish dividends for years. So several of the weaker companies had shut down entirely, victims of the faltering faith of their backers. The big bullion producers, like the Standard and the Bodie Mine and the well-financed Red Cloud and Noonday companies in the south end, also felt the bite as they installed and put into operation the huge costly Cornish pumps with which they would attack the problem of dropping the water table ahead of their sinking operations. However, these companies were well entrenched behind the profits from the rich ore that they were extracting from their upper levels. So they accepted the challenge, installed the most powerful pumps available and drove downward. The results of the dewatering achievements in mid-August galvanized a mining expert of the *Free Press* into a glowing pronouncement that sent his pen racing:

> The fact that the water has been so far conquered in the Bodie District that levels are being run in four deep shafts, 200 to 300 feet under the old water line is a most gratifying circumstance. It would seem that very shortly we are to get a glimpse of rich ores which have hitherto been guarded by what has been an impassible barrier; but which now has given way to the indomitable pluck of the leading spirits of the district. The Lent Shaft has reached the depth of 700 feet and within a very few days a drift will be running for the famous Fortuna ledge which will thus be developed at a vertical depth of considerably more than 100 feet below the lowest point worked, and on the dip and strike of the vein perhaps 200 or 300 feet deeper. The Fortuna is a vein which the best judges of mines who have examined the district do not think will ever quit. Its discovery on the new levels in good shape will give an immense back of ore in addition to that now being found in the upper levels. It is one of the interesting points in the mining situations here just now. The

> Red Cloud is the other. There a crosscut is already in, 67 feet west from the shaft on the 600 foot level running for the Concordia ledge. This ledge is the Veta-Madre of the silver hills series. It resembles, in many respects, the remarkable Comstock Lode. In size, it is immense. Its width being from 50 to 200 feet. And this great quartz vein is the pudding in which our bonanza plums must be found. Successive rich ore chimneys have been found along its course in the Concordia, Oro, Adenda, and Dudley Mines. We believe these chimneys will make into a bonanza below, crowding the clay and filling the vein to great width with rich bodies of silver ore. The water difficulties that have hither-to-fore crowded out many of the weaker companies who, with good prospects, it may be anticipated will resume work at an early date.[16]

As August came to a close it brought news of an Apache Indian massacre in New Mexico. A controversial old Bodieite, rugged individualist George Daly, former superintendent of the Mono and Jupiter mines, fought to the last against Victorio's band when some three hundred White Mountain Apaches without warning attacked miners and settlers and attempted to ambush several small isolated detachments of U.S. cavalry in western New Mexico. The *Free Press* reprinted a glowing tribute to Daly that had appeared in the Denver *Rocky Mountain News,* lauding his coolness and courage under fire and the fine leadership that he exhibited during the thirty days' reign of terror in Leadville, Colorado, when he was superintendent of the Little Chief Mine there.

The early weeks of September moved quickly past, each with its daily current of newsy trivia:

A rock-throwing gang of small boys flushed a big rattlesnake with thirteen rattles and a button from among the sagebrush and headstones in the graveyard, and from a safe distance polished him off with several ragged but well-aimed rock showers.

At a meeting of the Bodie chapter of the Irish American Land League, President Hennessey made a stirring plea for every patriotic Bodie Irishman to put his name on the roll and accompany it with an initiation fee of one dollar, adding that it was "the duty of every Irish American and every friend of

"Cel'brat'n' " the Fourth. *(Los Angeles County Museum of Natural History, by permission of J. McLaren Forbes)*

Bodie's Fourth of July Celebration in 1903. A long, thin line. Their patriotism never faltered though their numbers dwindled. *(Sadie Moyle Palany Collection)*

An empty string of mule-drawn ore cars at the portal of the Bulwer Tunnel. *(Los Angeles County Museum of Natural History, by permission of J. McLaren Forbes)*

This surrey carried happy couples on many a Sunday drive. *(Francis H. Frederick Collection)*

Moyle & Gilkey's first pneumatic-tired stages. With flags flying and draped in bunting, the Hawthorne-Bodie run was inaugurated. *(Sadie Moyle Palany Collection)*

Motoring on the primitive, twisting Lee Vining Road (now Route 395) in the brave, dusty, gear-mixing days of "Billy the Wind." *(Los Angeles County Museum of Natural History, by permission of J. McLaren Forbes)*

Panoramic view of the town, and north along the lode from Silver Hill toward Bodie Bluff. *(Francis H. Frederick Collection)*

Bodie, 1931. The downtown area before the Big Fire of June 23, 1932 wiped out most of the buildings. *(Francis H. Frederick Collection)*

Bodie, after the Big Fire. *(Francis H. Frederick Collection)*

Aftermath. The brick vault of the Bodie Bank building sits in a smoldering ruin. *(Pomona Library, Frasher Fotos)*

J. S. "Jim" Cain's eyes purr with glinty satisfaction as he takes a quick "hot look" at the miraculously intact contents of his bank vault. *(Frasher Fotos, Grace P. Crocker Collection)*

Old "Jim" Cain assesses the "plunkin'" value of the old piano. *(Pomona Library, Frasher Fotos)*

Open-pit mining by the Treadwell Company's power shovel, 1931. *(Francis H. Frederick Collection)*

The snowy giants of the mighty Sierra. View from the Bodie shaft. Left to right: Ritter and Banner, Mt. Warren, Dana *(center pyramid)* and Conness march across the south horizon on a cold spring day. *(Francis H. Frederick Collection)*

OFFICE OF THE DEPUTY POSTMASTER GENERAL
WASHINGTON, D.C. 20260

September 14, 1966

Mr. Warren Loose
180 Camino de Herrera
San Anselmo, California 94960

Dear Mr. Loose:

The last postmaster of Bodie, Mono County, California was Mrs. Edith Van Ciel. She assumed charge on July 25, 1939 and served until the post office was discontinued November 13, 1942.

I am returning your stamped self-addressed envelope.

Sincerely yours,

Geneva C. Chancey

Geneva C. Chancey
Librarian, Post Office Department

Last post office and postmaster of Bodie, Mrs. Edith Van Ciel, and author. Circa, summer of 1942. Verifying letter below from librarian, U.S. Post Office Department, Washington, D.C.

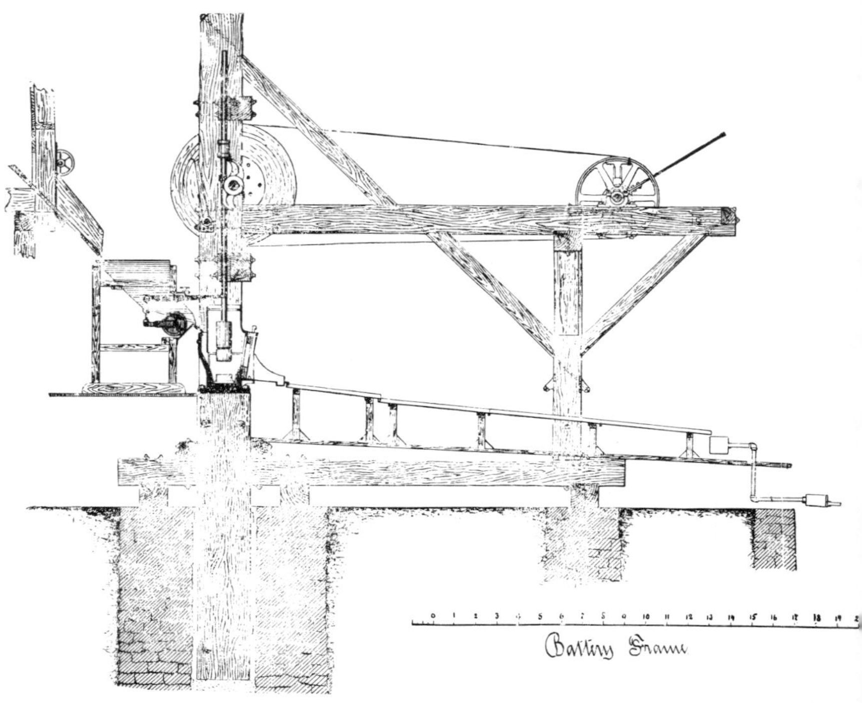

Schematic profile drawing of a stamp mill, battery and structural layout. *(California State Mining Bureau—Eighth Annual Report of the State Mineralogist for the year ending October 1, 1888)*

the oppressed to assist in the work of liberating Ireland."[17] A highlight of the evening was the recitation of a patriotic Irish poem by a smiling son of the Emerald Isle with the intriguing name of Frank Hollywood.

Professor Coutrie announced a select soirée for Bodie's best society, and "all those who love dancing will enjoy themselves." The best music in Bodie would be in attendance. "Admission, $1.00 and none but respectable people will be admitted."[18]

A Bodie editor caustically noted that "very few firemen responded to the last two alarm fires, so few in fact that it was difficult to move the hose carts along the streets. . . . Turning out for dress parades should not be the chief end of the fire companies."[19]

The parade of trivia was abruptly terminated when early in the evening of the nineteenth the clattering telegraph key brought the melancholy news of President Garfield's death. "The sad tidings gradually spread through the town. As soon as the news was confirmed, businessmen along Main Street began to drape their buildings in mourning, and by eleven o'clock the entire street gave evidence of the sorrow that filled every heart."[20] On the twenty-first a public meeting was held at the Miners' Union Hall to work out a suitable memorial program and funeral service to be held on Monday, September 26.

On that day "the sun rose in a cloudless sky," and as it attained its zenith it looked down upon the most imposing spectacle of pomp and circumstance ever witnessed in Bodie. "Not a breath of air stirred the flags that hung from the numerous staffs." The day was soft and balmy and an Indian-summer glow drenched the camp with golden radiance. It was almost high noon when 34 Knights Templar in full uniform marched out of the Miners' Union Hall and mounted their horses closely followed by 73 Master Masons. They formed the head of a long procession that included 39 Knights of Pythias, 40 members of the Odd Fellows, 107 stalwarts of the Miners' Union, and the Champion, Neptune, Hooks, and Babcock fire companies all in uniform, followed by 28 veterans of the Blue and Gray.[21] And then came the hearse drawn by six coal-black horses, alongside of which marched 12 distinguished pallbearers. This solemn and imposing cortege, followed by many citizens in carriages and on horseback, moved east on Green Street to Wood, and then turned north to Standard Avenue. Swinging west to Main, they turned and marched south on that thoroughfare along which several thousand sad and reverent citizens stood in silent ranks on the sidewalks and along the street in front of the black-and-white-draped buildings. The slowly moving column turned west on Green Street to Broadway and swung south to the cemetery, where Dr. J. W. Van Zandt delivered the funeral oration at the graveside ceremony honoring James A. Garfield, the twentieth President of the United States, who on that very day was being buried in far-off Cleveland, the lingering victim of an assassin's bullet.

On the day following the obsequies an Indian rode in from Mono Lake astride his pinto pony and noticing that the front of every building was draped in mourning inquired of a bystander, "What for hang 'em up black and white stuff?" He was then told that the Great White Father was dead. "How he die?" Upon being informed that a white man had shot him, the Piute was silent for a moment, then, with an expression of apparent sadness on his face, observed, "He all a' same Apache. You catch 'em new father pretty soon?"[22] Upon being assured that the President was to be succeeded, he rode off relieved.

The Bodie fire bell clanged furiously and the boys of the Babcock Company rushed their little hand-pumper cart down West Green Street to the burning residence of Mrs. Reed. They were followed by the Neptune Company, who quickly attached their hose to the plug at the corner of Main and Green streets, but their hose was not long enough to reach the fire. So they were forced to helplessly await the arrival of the Champions, who had charged off to Chinatown by mistake. By the time this red-faced and winded outfit had loped back from Chinatown and hooked up to the hose of the frantically waiting Neptunes, the "residence was almost in ashes. The Babcock was out on time and had a stream of water on the fire in good session, but nothing substantial was accomplished."[23] The building, which was owned by A. F. Bryant, was a total loss, and the Reed family lost everything they owned. Here again Bodie showed its big heart. Within one hour Dan Wagner, a prominent businessman, raised $300 to help the burned-out family, and a benefit ball given later in the month raised the total contributed by the generous citizens of the camp to $719.00.

With October came a change of weather and a change of pace with the pronouncement in the press that "a thoughtful family man is now laying in his wood supply."[24]

One of the raciest shows of the season, with standing room only, was in progress in Justice Phlagar's court. A well-known "keeper of a gilded palace of sin on Bonanza Street" battled with one of her "soiled doves" over the ownership of a much traveled trunk and its assortment of lingerie and glad rags. The jury and the audience loved the spicy and entertaining revelations that were made as the case unfolded. And the ever-present reporter observed: "Upon exhibiting the wearing apparel which embraced a number of undergarments, the audience was very much excited as many of them never saw such curious articles. Several of the jury men blushed and one or two wanted to be excused, but they were forced to see the thing through. Several witnesses were examined and the prices of drygoods were carefully discussed as were all the points in the case. For fear they would be called as witnesses, several of our best young men kept out of reach of the constable."[25]

The foregoing may sound a bit odd to the reader in the second half of the twentieth century accustomed to Hollywood nudies and topless waitresses, but in the Victorian age the mere accidental sighting of a prettily turned ankle was enough to cause the hardiest miner to forget his lunch bucket.

During the second week in October the sporting element of the camp discussed nothing but the coming Go-As-You-Please foot race to Hawthorne, Nevada and back for a purse of $300. The Cousin Jacks backed their wonderful little athlete, James Pascoe, to the hilt, while many a discerning Bodie sport laid his dollar on the long-striding George Wilson. At six o'clock A.M. on Monday, October 10, with a sizable crowd of their respective backers on hand, they answered the starter's gun in front of the U.S. Stage Company's office and reeled off with an amazingly fast pace for Hawthorne, some thirty-seven tortuous mountain miles away. They were followed by four referees in a buggy, Harry Bell and Duncan McMillan representing Wilson, and John Rundell and Joseph Tonken acting for Pascoe. Wilson made the first ten miles in an hour and five minutes. And at one o'clock a telegram from Hawthorne flashed the news to Bodie, "Wilson just arrived, feeling rather shaky." At this point in the race Wilson was several miles ahead of Pascoe. After a brief pause Wilson picked up his second wind and legged it back up the dusty road for Bodie. He met the weary Pascoe as the little Cornishman wobbled into the three-mile house, still trying to make Hawthorne. Pascoe tossed in the sponge and gave up the race, and signed a statement which read, "I hereby acknowledge myself beaten and renounce my claim to the stakes."[26] It was witnessed by Henry Seabeck. Wilson climbed on a Bodie bound stage and arrived back in town at 10:30 that evening to claim the purse. So ended this mountain marathon.

In mid-month Deputy Sheriff Showers, acting under a new California law, closed all the opium dens on King and Bonanza streets and notified the dealers in this traffic that they would be subject to a $1,000 fine for selling the dope, and anyone found "hitting the pipe"[27] would face a $500 penalty. With this traffic curbed, the death knell was sounded for Bodie's Chinatown. Its few remaining inhabitants, consisting of good Chinamen, engaged in laundry, wood, and restaurant business.

A celebrated temperance lecturer arrived in the camp that month, and opened a bare-knuckle attack on John Barleycorn. That, acording to one observer, did much to relieve the temporary "monotony and dullness of the times." On Tuesday night Colonel C. M. Golding went after the saloonkeepers, many of whom were present in the overflowing house at the Miners' Union Hall. The editor of the *Free Press,* whose roving reporter covered the lecture, carefully noted that "the Free Press is not strictly a temperance paper. Its mission being the advancement of our mining interest and a careful compilation of the news of the day. . . . Bodieites are willing to listen to a dissertation on any given subject. . . . They will listen to a sermon, visit a wrestling match, attend a horse race, enjoy a boxing bout, listen to the ear piercing shrieks of the political speakers, and even an ordinary dog fight will not fail to draw an appreciative audience. There is nothing mean about Bodie. Bodie has a large heart and is liberal in her views, and liberal when the hat is passed around. . . . The Colonel hit the liquor dealers very hard, but they stood their punishment manfully." A reporter sounded out "Master Mixiologist" Joe McDermot, who acknowledged "the lecture is good, possessed of argument and no man in Bodie could pass a more pleasant and edifying hour than by listening to it, but if they think they can deliver more temperance lectures than I can sell whiskey, why just let them keep it up." Another well-known saloon man acknowledged: "So far as his shooting it up to us fellows so hard for being in the business, that was all right. It was true, we deserve it. If I don't sell liquor, someone else will, but I felt grieved, sir, when the speaker exposed the mode of manufacturing the whiskey. The stuff that's put into it. How simple and how cheap the cost. I really thought it was unfair in the Colonel to give that away."[28]

As the month came to a close the *Free Press* eagerly reprinted a statement that appeared in the *San Francisco Post* by Messrs. Boyd and Lent on their return to the Bay area after a critical examination of the Bodie Consolidated Mine in which they emphatically stated that "it is looking better and showing more ore than at any time since the last Bonanza gave out."[29]

The same Bodie news sheet sputtered at the snide utterances and insinuations of the *Daily Report,* which had printed the following: "A second-hand monument has been knocking around in Bodie for some time without finding a purchaser. The times are rather dull up there and as no prominent, popular and gentlemanly ruffian has been shot lately, so there has been no need for imposing monuments. The enterprising owner of the marble has, therefore, started a subscription to buy it and erect it somewhere in the cemetery to the memory of Garfield."[30]

In November, 1881, two railroad companies dreamed of

getting to Bodie. On the first the Modesto and Tuolumne and Mono Railroad Company was incorporated with a capital stock of $5,000,000—50,000 shares of $100 each, of which 1,500 had been subscribed. Charles Crocker, A. M. Town, and W. B. Huntington were among the directors. The road was to be 150 miles in length, running from the San Joaquin branch of the Central Pacific Railroad, thence through Stanislaus County, Tuolumne County, and Mono County to Bodie.

On Monday, November 14, at about 3 P.M. the rail-laying crews of the Bodie Railroad and Lumber Company drove the last spike at the Bodie terminus, and two puffing little wood-burning Mogul locomotives shrilled their whistles as they inaugurated the iron horse's entrance into the economy of the camp with the two carloads of lumber for the mines. To celebrate the completion of the road, Superintendent Holt that afternoon gave a turkey dinner to all hands and local dignitaries. The latter railroad is an accomplishment in the history of Bodie; the former is still a dream.

The weather that night, as if in a fit of jealous rage at being shunted to a minor consideration as the camp celebrated its new status, erupted into a raging Sierra windstorm that tore over the ridges and swept sand and dust "in all directions and Main Street looked as though it was in the midst of a gritty fog. The street lamps shed but a poor light upon the passing humanity. Those who were out hurried along and those indoors remained there as long as possible."[31]

In the last week in November the *Free Press* boasted that "Engine No. 3 for the Bodie Railroad & Lumber Company made a trial trip from the Mound House to Dayton, hauling two new cars #5 and #6 for the Carson & Colorado Railroad. The engine is a powerful six-wheel connected. It is not so fast as the four-wheelers used on the C. & C., but it is more powerful—as it has to be—to do the work on the extraordinary grade and curves of the Mono Lake Road."[32]

The same issue noted that Bullfinch and Clasby have opened the "Music Hall Roller Skating Rink, and propose to keep it in such style that ladies and gentlemen and misses and boys in Bodie can attend it at proper hours and enjoy the exhilerating practice of genuine roller skating. The best of order and decorum will be maintained."[33] Their ad stated: "Admission to Gentlemen—25¢, Admission to Ladies—Free. For the use of the skates —25¢. Skating hours—from 2 P.M. to 4 P.M. and 7 P.M. to 9 P.M. No questionable characters will be admitted."

In the first week of December the new and unpopular state Sunday law had its first local test. Most of Bodie's saloons had bowed to the blue law and closed for the Sabbath, but A. I. Weiler kept his cigar store in front of the Molinari House open. He was promptly hauled up before Justice Newman. He asked "for a jury trial, but after exhausting two venues, only six men could be found competent to try the case."[34] The public wrangle that would ensue in the months to come over Bodie's resistance to this unpalatable statute would cost a popular district attorney his job.

As the chilly days of early December arrived, seats that had for years gone begging on the fast outbound freight wagons were at a premium. With the big layoffs at the conclusion of the railroad construction and suspension of operations in many of the smaller mining companies and the quick demise of Chinatown with its unwanted characters, the daily exodus that began in mid-November continued. Out-of-work men, discouraged miners and prospectors, and others who preferred a less rigorous winter climbed aboard the jolting springless high-wheelers with their baggage.

A big surprise in early December was the 50 cents per share assessment levied by the Bodie Consolidated. The editor of the *Free Press* rationalized: "Life is made up of unexpected events, and the true philosopher bears up under each one, and draws a lesson therefrom. The Bodie Consolidated Mining Company has of late been forced to expend a great deal of money for new and powerful machinery, and this assessment will assist in keeping the mine in good running order. The company is doing some good prospecting proving the way for deep mining in the district."[35]

A hard-working local theatrical group announced that they

were rehearsing the "truly remarkable drama, 'Ten Nights in a Bar Room.' W. C. Lawrence will sustain the leading part and Florence Molinari will also appear. The production will be presented for the first time to a Bodie audience on New Year's Eve." A reporter dryly quipped, "Most of our people have seen this play produced on the stage . . . and many have put in ten or more nights at such popular resorts. However, this old play will, no doubt, be received with applause."[36]

On December 9 the Bodie Tunnel Mill went into operation. It featured a revolutionary new crushing principle that its inventor, W. F. Howland, claimed would do the work of twenty stamps; however, after a breakdown-plagued run of nine days, Howland's Pacific Pulverizer was declared a failure. The management announced that the ore was too hard for this high-speed roller mill which turned at 175 rpm and that it "would be replaced with a reliable battery of stamps."[37]

The *San Francisco Bulletin* of the twelfth carried the news that the matchless Standard Mine had just dispensed its fifty-third consecutive dividend in 51 consecutive months. This time it "paid the regular $75,000 with an extra dividend of the same amount."[38]

Intense excitement had prevailed for some weeks among the local sporting fraternity over the Greco-Roman style wrestling match between Joe Farnsworth and H. C. Bell. Farnsworth was a rough-and-tumble character. He had been a Bodie peace officer and by virtue of an earlier victory over Ed Wilson was considered the favorite. The sports reporter of the *Free Press* observed: "He is as fine as they 'put 'em up.' Joe's weight is 170 pounds. In activity, he is quick as a cat and a perfect master of the Greco-Roman style of wrestling. His opponent, H. C. Bell, weighs 205 pounds, and is one of the finest built men that has ever graced the streets of Bodie. He works in one of our leading mines every day. He has never before entered the ring. . . ." On Sunday, December 11, McAlpin's Old Opera House was jammed to the rafters. Ed Loose was selected as the referee. It was a terrific contest, Farnsworth's skill and agility against Bell's strength. After an hour of struggle "Bell threw his opponent in a very neat manner. An effort was made after the first fall to have the match a draw, but the referee refused to entertain the proposition. The second fall was given to Farnsworth after a short and active struggle. The third and last fall was taken by Bell who was declared the winner, and the verdict was received with deafening applause."[39]

In mid-December the California and Nevada Railroad Company, the brainchild of an enthusiastic but rather modestly endowed group of railroad dreamers began making noises in the direction of Mono County. Their scheme was direct and simple—a railroad from Oakland via Stockton and across the Sierra to Bodie. The high-water mark of their efforts was an 1881 eyeball survey of a route running east from Sonora in Tuolumne County, in a probing effort to stake out a right-of-way across the Sierra. They located five gaps or passes that would enable them to push a line easterly in search of what lay beyond the mountains. On November 24, 1881, their survey party located the easternmost pass attained that fall and dubbed it New Strawberry Pass at an elevation of 5,775 feet. They placed it about "1½ miles more or less southwest from what is known as Patterson's Pass on the Mono Wagon Road."[40] This, however, was the grand termination of this railroad to Bodie.

A day or so after Christmas a strolling Bodie news hawk on his rounds, led undoubtedly by his trencherman instincts, gazed at the bountiful ingredients for gastronomic splendor placed on mouth-watering display by the Bodie meat markets and came up with:

> As has been the custom in the holidays, the meat markets of Bodie are handsomely decorated, and the display of meats will compare favorably with any other town in California. . . . The City Market had a display of carefully dressed beef on the east side while the mutton and pork occupied prominent places. In front of the market was also displayed a large deer. A great many people admired the tastefulness of the collection, and in the evening an illumination was in order. . . . At the Central Market just how the collection of meats could have been improved upon, it is difficult to conceive. . . . The dressing of the carcasses was carefully performed by a master hand, and a motto

wishing all "A Merry Christmas" hung in the center of the room. . . . The Union Market, Killgore's Place, as upon all similar occasions, was so attractive that hundreds of people stopped to admire the immense stock of beef, mutton, pork, and sausage. The interior of the room resembled a New York market. The quality of the meat was A1. Fat, well dressed and hung in such a way as to bring out the pleasing effects in the best possible manner. At the present time, the markets are still attired in their holiday costumes and have lost none of their attractiveness. It is a treat to just gaze on the display.[41]

The camp's homemakers could provide their hard-working spouses with porterhouse steaks at 37½ cents a pound or round steak at 16 cents a pound. And just before payday when the exchequer was a bit low, she might serve up a bountiful repast of corned beef for 12 cents a pound. And if things were extra tough, she could ladle up plenty of mutton stew for a mere 8 cents a pound or maybe a tasty pan of pork chops at 25 cents a pound.

The twelfth month of 1881 came to a close and Bodie recorded its biggest year in the production of gold and silver bullion with a whopping $3,160,067. The Standard Consolidated disgorged the lion's share of the riches with a dividend-fattening $2,168,575, followed by the Bodie Consolidated, which dropped to a mere $372,800, a far cry from the state-leading production this mine had attained in 1878. The other Bodie mines that contributed to the record year of '81 were the Noonday and North Noonday with $244,000, Syndicate $134,706, Bechtel Consolidated $123,751, Oro $14,155, Bodie Tunnel $10,626, and Concordia $5,670, with $85,780 in scattered production and shipments from banks, including gold dust from Bodie placers worked by the Indians.[42]

But even as this production record was chalked up a weakness in the district was apparent. Ten other well-known mines failed to record any production, and kept going only by levying heavy assessments on their hopeful stockholders. Among those properties relying on Irish dividends were the Summit, Black Hawk, New Standard, Bulwer, Consolidated-Pacific, Belvedere,

Mono, Dudley, Red Cloud, Boston-Consolidated, and three or four smaller mines.

In the last week of the year, one of the most costly and destructive single fires in Bodie's history lit the December sky:

> At 10:20 o'clock Thursday evening, fire broke out in the Bodie Foundry, and in a very short time the entire building and its valuable contents were in ashes. The alarm was sounded, and the fire companies responded promptly to the call. The foundry being outside of the fire limits, the hose of both companies was of no service so the water was not turned on. The Hook & Ladder men labored hard, but yet they were unable to save but little from the flames. The Babcock engine was on hand, but it proved to be almost useless. So rapidly did the fire consume everything in its way that in half an hour from the time the fire bell first rang, the building was in ashes. The loss will not be less than $25,000. Over $10,000 worth of patterns were destroyed with the castings and machinery. The patterns were the accumulations of four years and many of them cannot be replaced without great labor.[43]

As the last days of that year peeled off the scroll of history, plenty of enthusiasm over the camp's future was apparent, but it lacked the "Where will lightning strike next?" magic headlong flight of reason that infected the stockholders and inhabitants throughout '78, '79, and '80.

The costly dewatering problem, generally encountered below the 450-foot level, and the frustrating geology, with its complex faulting that dislocated whole sections of rich quartz veins in the south end mines, caused many doubts among the backers and stockholders of these properties. However, a new bright hope was the completion of the narrow-gauge railroad. It was a great boon to the camp's economy in its assurance of plenty of timber for the mines, and wood for the smoking steam engines of the mills and hoisting works. And so with a new production record and mixed emotions, Bodie awaited 1882.

CHAPTER VIII

The Cruel Year

There was an anger in the wind when that fateful year began. As January wore on, everything east of the Sierra felt its bitterness. Bodie on its high plateau was swept by its phantom forces that swirled through the camp's frozen thoroughfares piling snow against yard-fences and buildings.

The rails of the camp's new showpiece and economic prop carried no burden heavier than ridges of frozen whiteness. To the east of Nevada Mountain where deep side-hill cuts and switchbacks carried the narrow-gauge rails down the steep grades, drifts of fifteen feet were common, a condition that in the absence of snow-removal equipment strangled for months Bodie's rail link to its lumber and wood supply.

Howling like a restless nomad, the wind swept the rooftops, slamming and buffeting whatever lay in its anguished path. From the doors and windows of the town's growing inventory of vacant buildings, it dislodged a melancholy listless banging, a sound the inhabitants vainly turned from their ear; but this dismal residue of uncertainty persisted in the growing numbers of empty houses that forlornly expressed a tattered testimony to the crumpled hopes of their departed builders.

The rawness of weather, as the winter progressed, irritated everybody and everything in town. Early snowfalls were not too heavy, but the incessant and pitiless icy wind that scythed across from the crest of the Sierra kept the mercury in the minus scale. The editor of the *Free Press* shiveringly observed: "It's cold! Damn cold! And disagreeable. This is the kind of weather a coyote gets up and runs down a rabbit before breakfast. A late spring is predicted, and stage travel is a freezing experience again. 'Road Agents' are scarce these days, and stocks are at the bottom of the ladder."[1]

Another abomination that winter was the Sunday closing law. The majority of Bodie's hardy miners, after putting in six 12-hour shifts in the week swinging single jacks as they drilled in solid rock by the flickering light of a tallow candle, mucking, timbering, tramming, eagerly looked forward with famished hankerings to the seventh day and its promise of diversion and conviviality. They prized the chance this day afforded them to down lip-smacking rounds of "Tom and Jerries" and unwind with the rest of the hard rock fraternity, as they plunked pocket-burning gold pieces on the polished bars and called for another round of mighty hookers of their favorite whiskey. The miners looked with a jaundiced eye on this new law. They regarded it as a legislative ambush to their personal rights when on their day off they found their favorite saloons, cigar stands, and watering holes closed.

The general feeling in the camp was that "it was a 'Hell-of-a-law.' " The well-liked district attorney of Mono County more or less agreed with this summation. And he stood his ground manfully, even when his former deputy in Bodie signed a complaint against him for his failure to prosecute violators of this law. In mid-January he testified that the reason he "discontinued the prosecutions for the violations of the Sunday Law was that he considered it a fruitless and useless expense to the county."[2] However, Judge Briggs, who presided at the D.A.'s ouster trial, was unimpressed and ruled that he be removed from office.

On the second Sunday in February, 150 members of the sporting crowd attended a dog fight staged in the gymnasium between James Summer's dog, Nig, and Ed Green's Butch for a purse of $100 aside. The battle lasted for fifteen snarling minutes, with 46-pound Nig whipping his older and heavier canine opponent.

Early that month the editor of the *Free Press* sounded a warning to the citizens over a growing matter of local concern (which was in a way prophetic):

> At present, there are a number of vacant houses in Bodie, some of which have no one to look after them. As a result, petty

> larceny thieves find a field for their labors, in stripping these uncared for places of anything and everything of value. Not even overlooking the joint of stove pipe nailed to the roof. Locks are being taken from the doors and doors from their hinges. And small youths, poker players, Indians, and zephyrs are at liberty to roam through the deserted and doorless halls wrecking and bringing to ruin everything on the premises. . . . The use of these dry frame houses for gambling and lodging places by the Indians and youthful portions of our population could be the means to touching them off sometime and probably bringing upon the town such a catastrophe as a wholesale conflagration.[3]

A recalling Bodieite, now departed, who was a very young lad that year, had childish fun sneaking out to play in nearby vacant houses. Once he and his playmates were trapped by the quickly falling darkness. The night and the strange noises that arose in the empty building as it was buffeted by the wind's anguished refrain that howled past the eaves, and shrieked through the broken windowpanes, filled the romping band of urchins with fear. The darkness outside seemed crowded with mountain lions, coyotes, and things. When all seemed lost, they were rescued by their mothers, who hustled them home to supper. Their alibi-hardened parents paid but scant attention to their sobbing stories that the shrieking wind had sounded like a band of hungry coyotes and they had been afraid. From their unfeeling parental rulers they received the dubious comfort that what they heard was neither the howling wind nor ferocious coyotes, but "Bill Bodey's Ghost," and they had better not stay out after dark again.

It was well into February when the *Free Press* sprang a bizarre and gruesome whodunit on its readers. It immediately created a furor and was the main topic of speculation in the winter-ridden camp for days. On Monday, February 20, J. J. Currey, a compositor on the *Free Press*, learned from the night watchman of the Champion Mine that a gunny sack soaked with blood had been found laying on the center piece across the mouth of the Ajax shaft, which was located about a hundred feet east of the Champion Hoisting Works. Currey informed a reporter who was a good detective. This ferreting scribe by checking around learned from Robert Watts, a miner at the Bodie Mine, that a few nights before as he went on shift, he saw two men unloading a box from a sled and toss it into the Ajax shaft.

> Returning to the town the reporter and his companion sought Mr. Whalen [night watchman at the Champion] and proposed he produce a windlass and rope, and all three men explore the shaft. This proposition was readily accepted. The shaft is well timbered nearly to the bottom. Repairing to the Champion Works, lumber, nails, a reel and rope were obtained. And in ten minutes a respectable windlass was constructed over the deep and now interesting hole. When everything was in readiness, the reporter put his foot into the loop of the rope and was gradually lowered 120 feet to the bottom. . . . which was covered with snow and ice. Wedged in between the cakes and a big box, a portion of a human arm and elbow was discovered. The flesh was white and firm but could not be moved. . . . The box had no lid on it and one end was securely frozen in the ice. Here and there were several pieces of bed sheet and a large piece was found in the opposite compartment of the shaft. In this cloth was a large quantity of flesh. One piece weighed nearly two pounds. as everything was frozen, a pick and axe were ordered. When these implements arrived, active exploration commenced. . . . Near the box, deeply buried in ice and water, a tobacco pail was dug out. It was considerably broken and in it was found a human hand, small, without doubt that of a woman. . . . After a little more picking, the upper portion of the leg was found. It was taken out of the water and was in a good state of preservation. . . . Still further research revealed a human trunk from the neck to the hips. The internal organs were all missing. There was no flesh on the bones, and it had evidently been removed either with a knife or by the use of fire. . . . All of the body uncovered was placed in the box and the order was given to hoist. The surprise of those on top, when the box reached daylight, can be imagined. The reporter was next raised to the surface, and in the light of the sun the spectacle was even more sickening and horrible than at the bottom of the shaft. The news that portions of a body of a woman had been found in the bottom of the shaft, created quite a sensation in town and on the hill. In a short time, dozens of people could be observed walking to the scene of the horror. . . . Coroner Deal was notified and the box and its contents were removed to Brown's Undertaking Rooms. Hundreds of people looked at the remains, and some of them returned a second time, and seemed unable to

leave. . . . It may be a foul murder, and it may be nothing more than a case of body snatching. The box bears the label of Reddington and Company, wholesale druggist of San Francisco.[4]

On February 24 the *Free Press* chronicled:

Who did the dirty work? How matters stand at present. After a lapse of three days, the mystery regarding the human remains found in an abandoned shaft by the Free Press reporter is partially explained, thanks to the work of an intelligent coroner's jury. A great mass of testimony has been given and the outcome, so far, is satisfactory in a measure. On December 8, 1881, Mary E. Turner, a married woman, age 19 years, died and was buried in the Bodie cemetery on the 9th. The finding of a human remains and a general description of the same, led Mr. Turner to the suspicion that they might be those of his wife. Wednesday morning he and a few friends went to the cemetery and opened his wife's grave. Before reaching the proper depth, things did not look right. When the coffin was reached, it was found to be empty. The husband's feelings can be better imagined than described. The coroner's jury after prolonged and tedious examination of obstinate and unwilling witnesses traced the remains found to Dr. Blackwood, who it appeared dug them himself or hired the disagreeable work done. He rented a vacant house on Fuller Street for the purpose it is believed of dissecting the body of the late Mrs. Turner whose skull found its way to Dr. Jones' office. A competent lady witness testified that she recognized the same, as the skull of Mrs. Turner by the teeth which were remarkably even and handsome. One witness testified that he frequently accompanied Dr. Blackwood to the dissecting room and saw him use a knife on the remains, cutting away flesh and performing other work in that direction. The man who so testified was one of the unwilling witnesses, but the circumstances were such that he was forced to disgorge a portion of his knowledge regarding the affair. Dr. Blackwood testified that he knew nothing about the remains, and jumped the town and has not been overtaken.

By early March, Joseph Wells and Alexander Kirkpatrick were proudly putting the finishing touches to the machine shop of their new Bodie Foundry, which had risen Phoenix-like from the ashes of its total destruction in the year-end fire. A keen-eyed observer noted: ". . . the new establishment is being refitted with everything new and of the most approved kind. With their increased facilities, the proprietors will be enabled to furnish Cams, Tappets, Shoes, Dies, Pans, Settlers, and everything pertaining to milling and mining machinery, cheaper than it can possibly be laid down from any other point."[5] While business in Bodie was showing definite hesitancy and retrenchment, these two optimistic foundrymen with indomitable energy and faith in the camp's future laid their hard-earned savings on the line for a new plant which they chestily announced would "employ almost a dozen men."

One midday during the first week of March, the squealing of fifes and the roll of drums heralded the assembling of a big public mass meeting in front of Boone and Wright's Store at the corner of Main and Green streets. Anti-Chinese feeling was running high throughout the West that year. Times were hard, and there were hundreds of men out of work in Bodie and on the Comstock. This same condition prevailed in almost every mining district in California and Nevada. Colonel B. B. Jackson climbed onto a box and announced to the assembled sea of faces that the purpose of the meeting was to draft a resolution setting forth Bodie's feelings on the Chinese question. Judge C. A. Richardson was elected chairman by a unanimous vote and H. Z. Osborne was designated as secretary, and a committee was chosen, consisting of Paul Bennett, Hugh Gorom, William Irwin, A. McMillan, and Andy Hunnewill; and they drew up a resolution which was enthusiastically endorsed and sent on to Washington, D.C. It read: 'Resolved, by the citizens of Mono County in a mass meeting assembled, that further importation of Chinese into this country should be prohibited and that our Senators and Representative in Congress are hereby requested to use their best efforts to have such a law enacted by the Congress as will insure the practical prohibition of Chinese immigration."[6]

At twelve o'clock noon on March 8, the stygian darkness of midnight fell on the camp. It had been preceded by twenty-four hours of violent wind and snow squalls. An observer dramatically recounted:

The storm which had sent out its sentinels burst upon us with

> great severity and on Tuesday night and all day Wednesday it raged with the greatest fury. Nothing like it has ever been experienced in these parts for years. The fall of snow was tremendous and a terrific gale from the south added to the discomfiture. The town on Wednesday resembled a Siberian Stage Station. Not two men could be seen on the streets at any one time. Those who had cabins or houses did not put in an appearance all day, and business was nearly at a stand-still. The banks could neither buy nor sell stock on account of the wires being disabled. Several times during the day it was reported that miners had lost their way and sank down exhausted in trying to climb the hill through three feet of snow on the level, and innumerable drifts from all directions in the face of a raging blizzard. . . . A great deal of the snow that fell on Bodie came from the high peaks of the main range. Down at Mono Lake a little snow fell, and those who were in that vicinity stated that immense clouds of snow could be seen hovering high in the air, drifting Bodiewards. . . . The mail coach due here Tuesday night did not put in an appearance, and the outgoing mail sled did not leave until six o'clock Wednesday morning.[7]

This Hawthorne-bound mail made it only two and a half miles down the canyon, to a point below the Bodie Mill, where the exhausted team gave out. Here the driver, to save himself and the horses, unhitched and managed it back as far as the Syndicate Mill, where he holed up.

On Friday after the storm had subsided, every man in Bodie who owned a horse was out breaking trails. Mike Tobey and Tom DeNise drove one of Earl's large mule teams down the canyon to locate the abandoned mail rig. They found it buried under three feet of snow, and after freeing it, hauled it to Bodie.

The effect of this blockbuster snowstorm on travel to Bodie is graphically given in the *Free Press* of Friday the seventeenth, which related the trials and struggles of a Bodie-bound freighter and his outfit: "James Dodson, a driver with a fast freight team arrived from Hawthorne in the afternoon. He left the railroad at 7 o'clock Thursday morning and coming as far as the Del Monte Station with a wagon. Then a sleigh was taken. When two miles this side of Sunshine (at the state line) the sleigh and its load had to be abandoned, and the team was driven through.

He reported about one foot of snow at Hawthorne, 15 inches in the vicinity of Town's place, while from Bodie to Sunshine, the canyon is nearly blockaded. In some places the snow is drifted to the height of 15 feet."

This was a killer storm, and in the weeks ahead mining camps and towns nestled close along the eastern escarpment of the white-blanketed Sierra would feel its terrible aftereffects as a series of devastating avalanches left death and ruin that crushed parts of Genoa, Nevada, Mill Creek, Lundy, and many isolated mining installations in the steep canyons of the Sierra.

The big mining excitement that spring was in the south end of the camp. Some very rich ore had been struck in a joint winze of the Noonday and North Noonday mines. And the stock of these companies and the adjoining Red Cloud enjoyed a quick spurt for a time. To satisfy the clamor for more concrete information, and probably with a weather eye to strengthening the positions of these companies on the exchange and with certain helpful financial interests in San Francisco, B. R. Taylor, superintendent of their Bodie mining operations, conducted a Cook's tour of the Young Bonanza, as it was called. On March 24 "a number of gentlemen were admitted to the mine, among them William Irwin, Superintendent of the Standard Consolidated; William A. Irwin, Assistant Superintendent of the same mine; Martin Jones, Superintendent of the Con. Pacific and Boston Con.; R. K. Culcord, Superintendent of the Syndicate; Thomas Buckley, Superintendent of the Mono and Goodshaw Mine; and H. F. Hastings, Cashier of the Mono County Bank; T. M. Luther, well known assayer; E. B. Pixley, local Secretary of the Bodie and Benton R.R. and Commercial Company; and a representative of the Free Press and others." They were shown the new

> developments in a winze between the Noonday and North Noonday mines which attained a depth of 200 feet on the vein below the 512 foot level. Some very rich ore was uncovered in sinking this winze . . . 14 feet from the bottom a drift was run north 40 feet, and south 15 feet on the foot wall of the ledge . . . where there is about 4 feet of rich ore. The balance of the vein so far opened being about

> the same quality as in the levels above. . . . The ore is of different character in many respects from any which has been found in the district, which is not surprising, considering it is found at a greater depth below the water-line than at any other point in the Camp. The metal is principally in the shape of gold and silver sulphides. . . . The rock is said to be, by those who are familiar with them, to resemble in appearance the ore from the old Consolidated Virginia and California Bonanzas. Assays made from the samples of one gentleman went as follows: average of 4 feet in drift 14 feet from bottom, gold $15.06 per ton, silver $58.13 per ton, total assay per ton $73.29. Average of 6 feet in bottom of winze, gold $20.09 and silver $72.27 per ton, total per ton $92.36. Select samples from the bottom, $816.43 per ton in gold and $1,048.05 per ton in silver, total of $1,864.48 per ton. . . . The rich ore is not stringy and confined to seams as has been so often the case, but is massive, blocky, and crumbles very soon.[8]

In the latter part of April, largely through the efforts of the warm spring sunshine, the puffing little wood burners of the new narrow gauge were snorting cockily into the Bodie terminus, where their shrill whistles daily announced their lumber- and wood-hauling activities. With the arrival of the first month of summer, the motive power of the railroad, which had been supplied by the engines Mono, Inyo, and Tybo, received a big boost with the arrival of the larger and more powerful locomotive, christened the Bodie. Their efforts soon laid thousands of feet of lumber almost at the mouth of many of the prominent mines and brought wood to the Bodie market at $12 per cord.

As this solid achievement was taking place, many economic changes were blowing on the winds of uncertainty. The much heralded west crosscut from the 707-foot level of the Lent shaft had finally picked up the Fortuna ledge, and much to the consternation of the management of the Bodie and Mono Mining companies, it was in the cold-as-marble language of the geologist, "almost completely impoverished"[9] at this horizon. This disheartening discovery was kept under wraps as much as possible, but like the news of any black eye, it seeped out. Several of the smaller mines had suspended operations and hundreds of people had left the camp. The Bodie Bank had discontinued its operation, leaving the financial field to the Mono County Bank, and the lists of vacant houses were steadily increasing. Real-estate prices had tumbled to such an extent that it was next to impossible to sell any dwellings, even for a fraction of their cost.

The Fourth of July parade and celebration, while charged with patriotic enthusiasm and color, was far smaller than in previous years. In the athletic events on the program a new feature was the foot race to the flagpole on Bodie Bluff and return. "The start was made from the corner of Main Street and Standard Avenue. The race was for a purse of $30.00. The distance to the top of the Bluff is about ¾ of a mile." The runners were Archie McMillan (the pre-race favorite), D. A. Anderson, Con Pohl, and two Indians, Lightfoot and Deerfoot. The *Free Press* of July 6 chronicled this mountain lung-buster: "McMillan and Pohl took a straight cut up the hill to the left of the Standard Mill, while the other men took an easy grade to the right of the mill. McMillan was the first to reach the flagpole, but on the downgrade, the Indians outran the other competitors and won the match easily in ten minutes. Considering the route traveled and altitude, this was exceedingly good time."

In the other athletic contests of the day the eyes of the crowd eagerly followed the mighty efforts of Bodie's renowned Caledonian champion, Duncan McMillan who won the spectacular Caber Toss with a heave of 39 feet 10 inches. Tossing this unwieldy 18-foot, 120-pound pole was an ancient sport of the Caledonians. The event dated back to the sixteenth century, when it was a favorite sport of Henry VIII, who called it "Ye casting of the Bar." Duncan also copped first prize in putting the heavy stone with a mark of 44 feet 8 inches and for good measure won the running high jump, but he was bested in throwing the heavy hammer and light hammer by D. R. McMillan, another member of this athletic clan.

In the week following the Fourth of July one of the most intoxicating and pride-provoking schemes of the camp dissolved when all work on the new rail extension of the Bodie and Benton R.R. and Commercial Company's[10] narrow gauge abruptly terminated with the grading gangs only fifteen miles from Benton. Thus ended the dream of a possible linkup with the Carson and Colorado Railroad, whose line was being constructed southward through Mount Montgomery Pass to Benton and on into the Owens Valley. This projection would have given Bodie rail connections with the outside world.

In September the *Free Press,* looking for something substantial and heartening to place before its readers, turned to the mighty wheel horse of the camp's mining economy and compiled a rather impressive list of the men—their pay scale and crafts—employed by the Standard Mine: "There are 90 miners, 17 car men, 2 skip men, 3 firemen, 4 tramway men employed at $4.00 per day; 3 blacksmith helpers, 3 station tenders, and 4 laborers, 4 watchmen, one timekeeper at $4.00 per day; 3 ore sorters, 2 woodmen at $3.50 per day; 4 carpenters, 2 blacksmiths, 7 engineers, 3 brakesmen, one rope man, 2 shift bosses at $5.00 per day; one chief engineer, one blacksmith, one carpenter, one pump man at $6.00 per day; one foreman, one office man, $250.00 per month."[11]

The speed with which the sands of hope and confidence in the district drained away was sadly reported by a local scribe on November 22: "The large and handsome building known as the Molinari House corner of Main and Mill Streets was sold at a public auction at the insistence of the owner. The bidding was not active, and the property was knocked down to A. Soderling [prominent Bodie assayer] for $625.00. The building originally cost over $3,000.00. This is like throwing property away. Real Estate and improvements are being knocked down at excursion rates."[12]

Ten days later the *coup de grâce* to all deep mining in the south end of the camp struck when the big but financially sick Noonday, North Noonday, and Red Cloud mining complex, with liabilities of over $600,000 and assets of slightly over $136,000, was attached in San Francisco by the Wells Fargo and Company Bank, to which financial institution these companies were months in arrears to the tune of $460,000. The repercussions of this attachment in Bodie threw 175 men out of work and closed down all their mining operations. The most serious was the stoppage of the Red Cloud's huge Cornish pump. This allowed the water table to rapidly climb back to its original level, choking off mining operations in the south end mines. It submerged all underground workings below the 450-foot level.

It mattered not that the mining and production records of the Noonday, North Noonday, and Red Cloud companies were chronically sad. In the years of their operations from 1878 to 1882 these companies never paid a dividend. The Red Cloud's total listed production was a measly $10,927.50, while it had levied some $155,000 in assessments on its long suffering stockholders. The Noonday and North Noonday had compiled a total bullion production of $1,023,289.50 while extracting $208,000 in assessments.[13] The sudden collapse of these bloated gems of corporate red ink, coming as it did at the wavering point in the camp's economy, was a catastrophic blow to the district's already shaky mining outlook and one that almost overnight destroyed the magic of the district's name. It marked a turning point in the camp's destiny, and from that fatal December in 1882, Bodie's days of glory faded away.

CHAPTER IX

From Then to Now

The rapidity with which the disenchantment for the Bodie Mining District grew is attested by the fact that by midwinter of 1883 all but six or seven of the larger mines had closed down, and the population of the camp had shrunk to less than 2,500.

The combined bullion production of all operating mines in the district that year fell to $1,582,667. Early in the following year the Standard Consolidated stopped its dividend payments. The Bodie Consolidated resumed payments for a few months, and then abruptly discontinued all dividends as their blocked-out ore bodies were exhausted.

Of the forty to fifty properties that were in active operation in 1879 and '80, less than half a dozen of these were working in '84. And the camp's population continued to dwindle as miners, millmen, and other laboring groups drifted away in search of employment. Stores, saloons, and businesses of all kinds emptied their shelves, bolted their doors, nailed up their windows, and left the fading camp. By 1888 and '89 there were almost three times as many vacant buildings in town as there were inhabitants.

H. A. Whiting, a field assistant of William Irelan, Jr., the state mineralogist, visited Bodie in the late summer of '88 and reported that only two mines were operating, while only the "Standard Company is still extracting and milling a fair quality of ore from old workings above its 500 foot level. . . . Of the ten quartz mills in the Bodie District aggregating 162 stamps, only 15 stamps have been in operation during the past year."[1] The total production fell to an insignificant $126,294.

The confident and roaring camp that had entered this decade with a population of 8,000 now numbered barely 500 souls. A resident of the camp noted that times were exceedingly dull with an "utter stagnation of real estate."[2] This deep-seated and gloomy economic fog had brought financial distress to most of the business firms left in town.

Bodie's surviving newspaper was the *Evening Miner,* of late called the *Mono Relief,* maybe because Jones, its bourbon-loving editor, who was having problems, felt that this was what he was most in need of. He was badly in arrears on his contract to purchase the *Free Press* plant from H. Z. Osborne and E. R. Cleveland, who had moved to Los Angeles. How things then stood in Bodie in the publishing business is aptly described by "Lying Jim," J. W. E. Townsend, editor of the *Homer Mining Index.* On his return from a trip to Bodie he wrote the following inquiring letter to H. Z. Osborne:

Sunday, Jan. 6, 1889

H. Z. Osborne, Esq.–

Friend O.–What will you take for the remnants of the "Free Press" outfit? The type is *all* gone, and nothing but two or three stands and the press remain. The roof over the press leaks and the machine is badly damaged by rust. It's a d––d shame. The last time I was in Bodie I went to the office to cover it up, simply because I dislike to see good material wrecked through the carelessness of a drunken sot, but they wouldn't let me have the key. And so it remains, subject to the moisture of God and the whims of a beast, who is drunk–drunk–drunk, and has not issued a paper for a month. Frost is here with me, fat as a balloon and apparently happy, with good grub and a fair allowance of grog.

In your own good time I would like to hear from you. I am perfectly contented in Mill Creek, though we have to wear snowshoes to bed and every thermometer has a cold in the head. But things are lovely anywhere if you steer a true course. Respects to Cleveland.

Yours truly,
J. W. E. TOWNSEND

In disgust H. Z. Osborne, now editor and publisher of the up and coming *Los Angeles Evening Express,* sold the rusty and abused wreck of the *Free Press* to Townsend for $100. Shortly afterwards "Lying Jim" transferred his journalist talents to Bodie, and after "tinkering-up" the old clamshell press, he began rhyming and editorializing once again in a news sheet he christened the *Bodie Miner Index.*

In the summer of 1892 the Standard Consolidated sued the adjoining Bodie Consolidated for $283,000 in a trespass suit claiming damages for the removal of ore from the Standard ground, a situation, it was claimed, that had been going on since 1884.

That summer a disastrous fire swept the downtown area of the camp, and almost all the business houses on the west side of Main Street were burned to the ground. However, kind providence spared the residential district and the buildings on South Main Street. And as time went on and things picked up in the mid-nineties most of the downtown sections were rebuilt.

In 1895, A. J. McCone, a well-known foundryman in Virginia City, got wind of the amazing new cyanide process (developed in New Zealand and Australia) for cheaply extracting gold from discarded mill tailings. He approached J. S. "Jim" Cain of Bodie with the idea of locating or purchasing the thousands of tons of supposedly worthless tailings lying below the camp along Bodie Creek. Jim Cain, with shrewd discernment, allied himself with McCone. And while the Virginia City man imported the cyanide expert, at $1,000 per month, to construct the mysterious new plant, Cain nimbly acquired the supposedly worthless piles of tailings.

John Parr once laughingly described to me how he and other curious Bodie mining men on many occasions (during the secret construction of Bodie's first cyanide plant) slipped out at night to glue their eyes to a handy knothole or a crack in the siding, to try and see what in thunder was going on behind the locked doors. Parr said that he had the process almost figured out by the time McCone and Cain's plant began its operations. He was stumped for a time. He couldn't figure out what material they were using as a precipitant to extract the gold from the cyanide solution. However, with the aid of some clever detective work, he learned that it was charcoal.[3] In the next few months the resourceful Parr, without the benefit of an expensive expert, constructed his own cyanide plant at the Syndicate and within a short time had it leaching away in profitable style. McCone and Cain cleaned up a fortune on their mineralogical *coup d' état.*

In the '90's Bodie was the terminus of a new 13-mile electric-power transmission line. When put into operation, it was one of the longest of its kind in the world. The power was generated at Green Creek and transmitted to the Standard Mill at Bodie to operate the newfangled electric motors that soon displaced the old reliable steam-power-driven pulley.

The original Standard Mill that had been constructed by Malter Lind and Company in 1877 caught fire and burned to the ground in 1899. A corrugated iron structure housing a new 20-stamp mill (the one standing today) was soon constructed to replace the original wooden plant.

Just after the turn of the century Ed Loose, who had struck it rich in his famous Grand Central Mine at Mammoth, Utah, formed with his brother, Warren, the New Bodie Mining Company. They consolidated Warren's mining claims with the newly acquired Syndicate Mining Company and the famous Jump Up Joe Mine at Masonic. In order to develop new ore chutes, they proceeded to drive the 1,400-foot long Whitney Tunnel, which eventually opened several excellent ore bodies that enabled them to keep the 20-stamp Syndicate Mill running through several years of profitable operations.

Jim Cain acquired control of the Standard Mill and Mine in 1915, when he won a settlement of a trespass action against that company. Their underground mining operations had blundered into removing ore from his Midnight claim, a property that in former years was known as the McClinton. This was truly an amazing mine. It had been operated, off and on, through the lush years of 1877-80 and up to 1888. During these years its total listed bullion production was a stunning $1,064. It never paid any dividends and levied a grand total of $123,000.00 in assessments on its unlucky stockholders.[4] Apparently the diligent miners of the Standard Company were far more adept at finding ore in this mine than any of its earlier owners had been.

The advent of World War I interrupted all mining operations

in the camp. In the summer of 1915 the famous old 20-stamp red-brick Syndicate Mill built during the Civil War (the camp's first) made its last run. Engineer Ike McKenna closed the throttle, and the ponderous cast-iron flywheel, weighing tons, slowly turned in its final revolution that stilled forever the 1,000-pound stamps of its ancient battery through which had passed some of the richest gold ore ever milled.

In the mid-twenties San Francisco restaurateur E. J. Clinton secured a lease from Jim Cain and tried his hand at milling Bodie's dumps. In his new plant under Superintendent Billy West, they crushed over 30,000 tons of Standard dump ore in a sad red-ink operation that ended in failure.

Two great mining companies, the Alaska Treadwell Yukon and the famous Homestake Company, in 1929 were engaged jointly in combing through several has-been western mining districts in search of "big low grade" situations where power shovels could be used in open-pit mining to feed crushing plants whose daily capacity would range in the 1,000-ton to 2,000-ton class. Oscar Hershey, the Treadwell Yukon's famous geologist, after a preliminary examination, classed Bodie Bluff, with its many enriching veins, as a mountain worthy of careful consideration. Already mined and awaiting only the consuming maw of the big shovels was over 300,000 tons of low-grade ore in the Standard dump, whose average assay was $1.86 per ton (old price of gold). The balance of the camp's mine dumps offered an additional 200,000 tons that averaged out close to the same figure.

After securing leases on all the mining properties in the district, the joint venture began with four operational objectives: (1) Mill ore in Bodie dumps. (2) Develop low-grade ores of Bodie Bluff. (3) Ore at depth in Red Cloud, Noonday mines, etc. (4) Develop new ore chutes in the south-end mines. The Treadwell Yukon Company acted as the sponsor of the operations. And they put into operation a 100-ton-per-day flotation plant. But here a metallurgical problem developed for which no solution could be found at the time. The clays and slimes of the dump ores depressed the froth in the flotation cells to such an extent that no adequate recovery could be made.

In the south end of the camp powerful new pumps dewatered the Red Cloud shaft. Several thousand feet of development work in drifts and tunnels were completed. A limited amount of good ore, some of it very rich, was mined. But the complex faulting problems that had stumped the old-timers in trying to follow the ore bodies were just as baffling to the Treadwell's expert and their miners. A great deal of time and money was spent in trying to unravel the problem, but it remained unsolved.

As 1932 rolled around, the worried management of both companies, feeling the economic pressures of the depression elsewhere, resolved that a careful review of the costly and so far unsuccessful Bodie venture was in order. So both the Treadwell Yukon and the Homestake companies dispatched their top geologists to the camp for a careful reappraisal of what their real chances were of attaining their four original objectives.

Expert Hershey stuck to his initial findings and declared that he felt the metallurgical problems could be solved; he thought that the possibilities of developing new ore bodies in depth in the south end mines were still a good bet. However, his opinions were put on the defensive by the Homestake's highly regarded McLaughlin. He was not so sure of solving the recovery problem with the current plant and held out very little hope of developing any ore bodies at depth. In his report he stated that shallow mineralization was "the habit of the district" and that to pursue deep mining in the south end was at best a very "speculative venture." Thus, in the face of the overwhelming economic pressures of the depression-ridden early thirties, and harking to the formidable negative tones of the Homestake's expert, the Bodie venture was phased out. The leases were terminated, and the costly machinery was hauled away.[5]

That June, Bodie had its biggest and costliest fire. A small boy, experimenting with a handful of matches, set fire to an old frame building. The late Francis Frederick, a prominent consulting geologist, related to me that he was a member of the singed, frustrated, and weary band of volunteer firemen who did their best to save downtown Bodie that afternoon. They probably could have confined the fire to the buildings in the area where it started, just south of the bank, if their fire hoses had been reliable. When the ancient hoses were attached to the hydrants, the full force of the water pressure, which incidentally contained considerable gravel, soon collapsed their disintegrating inside sections, blocking them completely or causing them to burst. So the helpless firemen were forced to watch the frustrating sight of the flames spreading from building to building, till all was in ashes.

Three years later, in 1935, Jack Rosekrans, husband of Alma Spreckels, caught the mining bug and joined forces with Henry Klipstein, who had been associated with the Anglo-American Mining Company. Together they formed the Roseklip Mines Company and secured a lease from Jim Cain on certain of his Bodie mines. They then set out to construct a mill, largely out of secondhand machinery, to convert the low-grade dump ores to a profit. A succession of frustrated superintendents from 1935 to 1942 battled to get the projected tonnage of ore through the tired and inadequate plant. After several shutdowns it was finally enlarged. The results of the overhaul provided its backers with somewhat greater tonnage but very little profit. The year 1942 saw its last superintendent, Frank Hartenette, presiding over the closing months of the Roseklip Mines Company in Bodie.

The plant stood idle until after the war, when new management began refitting it. While their crew of workmen were at lunch, the plant caught fire and burned to the ground, joining the ashes of the many others that had vanished in smoke before it.

In 1962, Bodie became a California State Park. And since then the old ghost town is visited each year by thousands of vacationing summer tourists, who excitedly explore the faded and splintered remnants of what nine decades ago was one of the richest and wildest camps of the American West.

As they gaze at the historic ruins of the old mining town and view the scattered diggings on the hills above, there always comes the inevitable question, "Will the mines ever come back?" "Yes, sir!" In 1968 one of the world's largest, the American Smelting and Refining Company, sent their exploration mining crews prowling the old lode. Results of this preliminary survey could have been disappointing, as they have recently turned their attention to other fields. However, rumor has it that other big open-pit operators are interested. These biggies are all spurred on by the spectacular and highly successful Mountain of Gold's[6] thousands of tons per day low-grade operations at Carlin, Nevada.

Today two mills still stand in the Bodie district: the 20-stamp corrugated iron Standard, erected in 1899, and Ed Gray's doughty little 7-stamp mill, which stands on the old site of the 10-stamp Bodie Consolidated about three-quarters of a mile down Bodie Canyon below the Syndicate.

To Ed Gray, now departed, must go the honor of conducting the last bona fide mining and milling operations in Bodie. He and his associates Holmes, Gunderson, and Bloom faithfully worked Ed's Blue Point Mine, whose gold-bearing quartz they dug and hauled down the canyon to the hard-working little 7-stamp crushing plant, where it was milled to 30 mesh and the gold recovered on the mill's amalgamation plates.

All other milling operations conducted in the last three and a half decades of the camp's history were essentially salvaging operations. The ores milled were the reclaimed product of the old discarded mine dumps.

As we near the end of Bodie's saga we humbly feel that we owe a salute to the crowded gallery of other characters who had their day on the stage of Bodie's history:

Hank Monk, the famous whip of the West, who gave Horace Greeley his memorable ride across the Sierra.

And petite Eleanor Dumont, alias Madam Mustache, the famous and respected little lady gambler of many roaring camps who lost her stake one unlucky day in Bodie and committed suicide on the Bridgeport road. Respected? Yes! as noted by an editor of the day.[7]

And Michael McGowan, dubbed "Michael, the man eater,"[8] who earned his dubious reputation when, in fits of violent rage, he bit off various and sundry appendages (fingers and snoots) of his victims, which landed him in court, where he threatened to chomp off the ear of Justice Peterson, who promptly had him deported to Carson City with the admonition to exercise his talents on the members of the Nevada legislature.

And Tom Cain, Jim's older brother, who was fondly remembered by the old-timers for his volcanic outbursts of colorful profanity. It was generally acknowledged that he held the record for the distance his bellowing oaths could be heard as they fell like smoking brimstone on the stubborn ears of his mules. In fact, it was a mule that probably brought his untimely demise.

And the "Strawberry Blonde"—she was a beauty, a wicked *fille de joie*. In her regular parade to the bank and post office, no hats were doffed, but all necks were craned, and every male eye was peeled as grudging homage was paid to the undisputed beauty queen of Bonanza Street. Her end was sad. Hooked on the poppy, she put a bullet through her heart on a New Year's Eve.

And Pat Holland, the fun-loving and energetic chief of Bodie's earliest fire companies, whose prominent proboscis wore a genuine rum blossom, and who, after migrating from Bodie in the early '80's, allegedly became the coroner of Tombstone, Arizona.

And Cecil Burkham, and Moyle and Gilkey, whose apostleship of the noisy, swarming new age of the horseless freighter and motorized stage ushered in the quickening transportation pace of the twentieth century with the former's first gas-eating, solid-rubber-tired lorry. As it lumbered up the steep pitches of Bodie Canyon the bouncing staccato echoes of its exhaust swept ahead to fall on the sensitive ears of many skittish and frightened teams, whose nervous, rein-clutching drivers breathed great sighs of relief as "the thing" chugged past. Its entrance into Bodie wrote the finish of the romantic stagecoach and the high-wheeled freighters drawn by their prancing and straining teams.

And "Billy the Wind," who, with the advent of the Pope-Hartford and the Thomas Flyer, became a gasoline jehu, the record-setting Barney Oldfield of Mono County's rutted roads and Bodie's dusty thoroughfares.

To these and countless other picturesque characters who played their parts through the exciting years of the camp's history, Hail and Farewell.

Notes

CHAPTER I

1. Dan De Quille (William Wright), *The Big Bonanza* (1876), p. 25.

2. For spelling of Bodey's name see Directory, 1845, at Poughkeepsie Village, N.Y.

3. Joseph Wasson, *Bodie and Esmeralda Publication* (1879).

4. *Daily Bodie Standard,* 10-27-1879.

5. *Poughkeepsie Journal,* 2-5-1961. Article on W. S. Bodey by Helen Myers, based on research by Mrs. Von Nooy, secretary of the Dutchess County Historical Society, and local-history librarian of the Adriance Memorial Library.

6. *Daily Bodie Standard,* 11-7-1879, reprint from *New York Times,* Poughkeepsie, N.Y., 10-28-1879.

7. The Territory of Utah was organized in 1850. It included areas now making up the states of Utah and Nevada, as well as parts of Colorado and Wyoming. Nevada Territory was not defined in 1859. See Edgar Levi Young, *The Founding of Utah Territory,* chap. xx, map, p. 223.

CHAPTER II

1. Judge J. G. McClinton's letter, *Daily Bodie Standard,* 10-29-1879.

2. *Mining and Scientific Press,* 9-23-1865.

3. *Bodie Weekly Standard,* 12-26-1877.

CHAPTER III

1. *Mining and Scientific Press,* 5-30-1868.

2. *Daily Bodie Standard,* 4-9-1880.

3. *Ibid.*

4. *Ibid.*

5. *Ibid.*

6. Julian Dana, *The Man Who Built San Francisco,* p. 309.

7. *Daily Free Press,* 11-9-1881.

8. *San Francisco Bulletin,* 4-11-1878.
9. *Reno Gazette,* 2-26-1878.
10. *Bodie Tri-Weekly Standard,* 6-5-1878.
11. *Ibid.*
12. *Ibid.*
13. *Ibid.,* 6-19-1878.
14. *Ibid.,* 7-3-1878.
15. *Ibid.,* 7-10-1878.
16. *Ibid.*
17. *Ibid.*
18. *Ibid.*
19. *Ibid.*
20. *Bodie Tri-Weekly Standard,* 7-31-1878 (reprint from *Virginia Enterprise*).

CHAPTER IV

1. "Reminiscences of the Bodie Strike," *Yosemite Nature Notes,* Vol. VII (1928).
2. *Mining and Scientific Press,* 8-16-1902.
3. *Bodie Tri-Weekly Standard News,* 8-7-1878.
4. *Ibid.*
5. Robert de Luce.
6. *Bodie Tri-Weekly Standard News,* 8-14-1878 (reprint from *Virginia Enterprise*).
7. *Bodie Standard News,* 9-18-1878.
8. *Ibid.,* 10-9-1878.
9. *Alpine Chronicle,* 8-31-1878.
10. *Bodie Standard News,* 10-23-1878.
11. *Ibid.*
12. *Ibid.,* 10-16-1878.
13. *Ibid.,* 10-23-1878.
14. *Ibid.,* 11-6-1878.
15. *Ibid.,* 11-27-1878.

CHAPTER V

1. *Bodie Standard News,* 12-25-1878 (reprint from *Grass Valley Union*).
2. *Bodie Standard News,* 12-25-1878.
3. *Daily Bodie Standard,* 1-21-1879.
4. *Daily Bodie Standard,* 2-17-1879 (reprint from *Esmeralda Herald*).
5. *Daily Bodie Standard,* 2-11-1879 (reprint from *Virginia Chronicle*).

6. *Daily Bodie Standard,* 2-11-1879.
7. *Ibid.,* 12-26-1878.
8. *Ibid.,* 2-12-1879.
9. *Ibid.,* 2-13-1879.
10. *Ibid.,* 2-14-1879.
11. *Ibid.*
12. *Ibid.,* 2-15-1879.
13. *Ibid.,* 2-27-1879.
14. *Mono Alpine Chronicle,* 3-8-1879.
15. *Daily Bodie Standard,* 6-13-1879.
16. *Ibid.,* 6-30-1879.
17. *Ibid.,* 7-5-1879.
18. *Ibid.*
19. *Ibid.,* 7-8-1879.
20. *Ibid.,* 7-14-1879.
21..*Ibid.*
22. *Ibid.,* 7-18-1879.
23. *Ibid.*
24. *Ibid.,* 8-13-1879.
25. *Ibid.,* 8-12-1879.
26. *Ibid.,* 8-13-1879.
27. *Ibid.,* 10-10-1879. Testimony taken before Judge Leavitte, Mono County Superior Court, Bridgeport, Calif.
28. *Ibid.*
29. *Ibid.*
30. *Ibid.*
31. *Ibid.*
32. *Ibid.,* 9-22-1879.
33. *Ibid.*
34. *Ibid.*
35. *Ibid.*
36. *Ibid.,* 9-25-1879.
37. *Ibid.,* 10-9-1879.
38. Judge J. G. McClinton mined at Monoville before the camps of Aurora or Bodie came into being. He had been a Nevada state senator. He was elected to the Eighth District judgeship and for a time was editor of the *Aurora Daily Union.*
39. *Daily Bodie Standard,* 10-27-1879.
40. *Ibid.*
41. *Virginia Enterprise,* 11-13-1879.
42. *Daily Bodie Standard,* 11-18-1879.
43. *Ibid.*
44. *Bodie Standard News,* 11-9-1880.
45. *Daily Bodie Standard,* 11-15-1879.

46. *Ibid.*, 11-19-1879.
47. *Ibid.*, 11-28-1879.
48. *Ibid.*, 11-15-1879.
49. *Ibid.*, 11-19-1879.
50. *Bodie Chronicle*, 11-22-1879.
51. *Daily Bodie Standard*, 11-25-1879.
52. *Ibid.*, 11-26-1879.
53. *Ibid.*
54. *Ibid.*, 12-23-1879.
55. *Ibid.*, 12-26-1879.
56. *Ibid.*
57. *Ibid.*
58. *Ibid.*, 1-2-1880.
59. *Ibid.*

CHAPTER VI

1. *Daily Bodie Standard*, 1-5-1880.
2. *Ibid.*, 12-29-1879.
3. *Ibid.*, 1-6-1880.
4. *Ibid.*, 1-7-1880.
5. *Ibid.*, 1-10-1880.
6. *Ibid.*, 1-20-1880.
7. *Ibid.*
8. *Ibid.*
9. *Ibid.*, 1-28-1880.
10. *Ibid.*, 2-7-1880.
11. *Bodie Chronicle*, 2-7-1880.
12. *Ibid.*, 3-2-1880.
13. *Daily Bodie Standard*, 3-12-1880.
14. *Bodie Chronicle*, 11-29-1879.
15. *Ibid.*, 2-7-1880.
16. *Daily Bodie Standard*, 2-20-1880.
17. *Ibid.*
18. *Ibid.*, 3-8-1880.
19. *Ibid.*, 5-21-1880.
20. *Ibid.*, 6-28-1880.
21. *Ibid.*, 3-26-1880.
22. *Ibid.*, 4-5-1880.
23. *Ibid.*, 4-22-1880.
24. *Ibid.*
25. *Ibid.*, 6-1-1880.
26. *Bodie Chronicle*, 6-5-1880.
27. *Daily Bodie Standard*, 6-16-1880.

28. *Ibid.*, 4-23-1880.
29. *Ibid.*, 3-18-1880.
30. *Ibid.*, 6-8-1880 (reprint from *Carson Appeal*).
31. *Ibid.*, 6-30-1880.
32. *Bodie Chronicle*, 7-10-1880.
33. *Ibid.*
34. *Ibid.*
35. *Ibid.*
36. *Daily Bodie Standard*, 7-6-1880.
37. *Ibid.*, 7-9-1880.
38. *Ibid.*, 7-7-1880.
39. *Bodie Chronicle*, 7-10-1880.
40. *Bodie Daily News*, 7-17-1880.
41. *Daily Bodie Standard*, 7-6-1880.
42. *Ibid.*, 7-10-1880.
43. *Bodie Daily News*, 7-9-1880.
44. *Ibid.*, 7-14-1880.
45. *Bodie Standard News*, 7-21-1880.
46. Stock scheme devised to finance construction of the Union Pacific Railroad.
47. *Bodie Standard News*, 8-3-1880.
48. *Ibid.*, 8-4-1880.
49. *Ibid.*
50. *Ibid.*, 8-4-1880.
51. *Ibid.*, 8-9-1880.
52. *Ibid.*, 11-13-1880.
53. *Ibid.*, 8-9-1880.
54. *Ibid.*, 8-17-1880.
55. *Ibid.*, 8-23-1880.
56. California State Mining Bureau, *Eighth Annual Report, 1888*, p. 355.
57. *Bodie Standard News*, 8-27-1880.
58. *Ibid.*, 9-3-1880.
59. *Ibid.*
60. *Ibid.*, 9-6-1880.
61. *Ibid.*
62. *Ibid.*
63. *Ibid.*
64. *Ibid.*, 9-7-1880.
65. *Ibid.*, 9-20-1880.
66. *Ibid.*, 11-6-1880.
67. *Ibid.*, 10-16-1880.
68. *Ibid.*, 10-16-1880 (reprint from *Sacramento Bee*).
69. *Ibid.*, 9-4-1880.

70. *Bodie Standard News,* 9-27-1880.
71. *Ibid.*
72. *Ibid.,* 10-7-1880.
73. *Ibid.,* 10-5-1880.
74. *Ibid.,* 11-9-1880.
75. Parker kept a bedside vigil (for three days prior to the fire) on a stricken brother engineer, Judd Andrews, who lay at the point of death in the Johnson House.
76. *Bodie Standard News,* 11-15-1880.
77. *Ibid.,* 11-17-1880.
78. *Ibid.,* 11-26-1880.

CHAPTER VII

1. *Bridgeport Chronicle Union,* 1-15-1881.
2. *Ibid.,* 1-22-1881.
3. *Daily Free Press,* 2-12-1881.
4. *Ibid.*
5. *Bridgeport Chronicle Union,* 3-26-1881.
6. Robert de Luce.
7. *Daily Free Press,* 7-2-1881.
8. *Ibid.,* 7-3-1881.
9. *Ibid.,* 7-6-1881.
10. *Ibid.*
11. *Ibid.*
12. *Ibid.,* 7-20-1881.
13. *Ibid.,* 7-23-1881.
14. *Ibid.*
15. *Ibid.,* 8-5-1881.
16. *Daily Free Press,* 8-16-1881.
17. *Ibid.,* 9-1-1881.
18. *Ibid.,* 9-15-1881.
19. *Ibid.*
20. *Ibid.,* 9-20-1881.
21. *Ibid.,* 9-27-1881.
22. *Ibid.*
23. *Ibid.,* 9-20-1881.
24. *Ibid.,* 10-2-1881.
25. *Ibid.*
26. *Ibid.,* 10-11-1881.
27. *Ibid.,* 10-14-1881.
28. *Ibid.,* 10-20-1881.
29. *Ibid.,* 10-23-1881 (reprint from *San Francisco Post,* 10-20-1881).

30. *Ibid.,* 10-30-1881.
31. *Ibid.,* 11-15-1881.
32. *Ibid.,* 11-24-1881.
33. *Ibid.*
34. *Ibid.,* 12-2-1881.
35. *Ibid.,* 12-8-1881.
36. *Ibid.,* 12-2-1881.
37. *Ibid.,* 12-18-1881.
38. *Ibid.,* 12-17-1881.
39. *Ibid.,* 12-13-1881.
40. *Ibid.,* 12-14-1881.
41. *Ibid.,* 12-28-1881.
42. California State Mining Bureau, *Eighth Annual Report, 1888,* p. 396.
43. *Daily Free Press,* 12-30-1881.

CHAPTER VIII

1. *Daily Free Press,* 1-7-1882.
2. *Ibid.,* 1-15-1882.
3. *Ibid.,* 2-10-1882.
4. *Ibid.,* 2-21-1882.
5. *Ibid.,* 2-25-1882.
6. *Ibid.,* 3-5-1882.
7. *Ibid.,* 3-16-1882.
8. *Ibid.,* 3-25-1882.
9. California State Mining Bureau, *Eighth Annual Report, 1888,* p. 392.
10. Formerly known as the Bodie Railroad & Lumber Company.
11. *Daily Free Press,* 9-27-1882.
12. *Ibid.,* 11-22-1882.
13. California State Mining Bureau, *Eighth Annual Report, 1888,* p. 397.

CHAPTER IX

1. California State Mining Bureau, *Eighth Annual Report, 1888,* p. 394.
2. Letter from the editor of the *Evening Miner* (Bodie) to H. Z. Osborne, editor and publisher of the *Los Angeles Evening Express,* 5-20-1886, describing the sad declining trend of the camp's economy.
3. Later a better precipitant, using zinc shavings, was developed.
4. California State Mining Bureau, *Eighth Annual Report, 1888,* p. 397, Table I.

5. From information generously supplied to me by Francis H. Frederick and Philip Bradley, consulting geologists of San Francisco.

6. Samuel W. Matthews, "Nevada's Mountain of Invisible Gold," *National Geographic,* CXXXIII, No. 5 (May, 1968), pp. 668-79.

7. Straight-talking old John Dormer, editor of the *Esmeralda Herald* and former manager of the *Bodie Standard* and the *Lewiston* (Idaho) *Signal,* chronicled a warm tribute to the little lady croupier:

"Esmeralda Herald," Aurora, Nevada, Saturday, September 13, 1879

DEATH OF MADAM MUSTACHE

Last Monday, the dead body of a woman was found about 2 miles south of Bodie on the road leading to Bridgeport. The body was identified as that of Madam Dumont, familiarly known as "Madam Mustache" in almost every mining camp from Utah and Idaho to California.

She was a French woman, very quiet and inoffensive, but with a very strong propensity for gambling. Her favorite game was "21" which she has dealt for many years. . . . With her dead body was discovered an empty poison vial which told the tale of suicide. . . . For twenty-one years, "Madam Mustache" has been a familiar character to the shifting population of the mining camps of the Pacific Coast. From the mines of British Columbia to those of California, and as far east as the Black Hills, the restless little French woman has followed the uncertain growth of mining camps, always pursuing a profession of gambling.

The first known of Madam Dumont, as she was then called on this coast, was in Nevada City in 1854. She arrived one day on a stage coach, a pretty, fresh-faced, dark-eyed woman, apparently about 20 years of age. Her stylish appearance created much commotion among the rough inhabitants of the town. The Madam, at once, rented from the proprietor of a large gambling establishment a table on which she started a game of "Vingt-et-un." The novelty of a pretty woman dealing a game attracted many players to her table; and as she paid strict attention to business and was very lucky, she soon had quite a capital. . . . She was always agreeable and smiling, accepting her losses with a careless shrug and a smile, and her winnings with a true gambler's indifference. . . . She possessed a peculiar power over even the roughest of her customers. One time in Pioche, the room in which she was dealing her game became filled with a noisy, quarreling crowd of miners, mad with drink and flourishing pistols, evidently bound to have a free fight. The barkeepers and Faro dealers were fruitlessly trying to quiet the crowd when Madam Dumont observed their dismay. Quietly she approached the noisiest and laughingly reproved them for their ungallant conduct, succeeding in clearing the room and avoiding a bloody "row. . . ."

No luckless miner ever came broke to a camp where the Madam was installed and asked her for a stake without receiving it. Madam Dumont, despite her strange surroundings and unusal mode of living, possessed the respect, as well as the admiration of her rough companions.

Of late years, what was in her girlhood only an infantile fuzz on the upper lip had developed into the growth of unusual proportions for a woman; hence the nickname, "Madam Mustache."

8. *Bodie Standard News,* 10-9-1880.

Bibliography

Browne, J. Ross. Articles, *Harpers New Monthly Magazine,* Vol. XXXI (June-Nov., 1865), Aug. & Sept. issues.

Bunker, W. M. "From Report Upon the Aurora Mining District," Esmeralda County, Nev., 1879.

Chalfant, W. A. *Outpost of Civilization.* Boston: Christopher Pub. Co., 1928.

Chappell, Maxine. "Bodie and the Bad Man: Historical Roots of a Legend." Unpub. Master's thesis in history, Univ. of California, Berkeley, 1947.

Culcord, R. K. "Reminiscences of Life in Territorial Nevada," *California Historical Society Quarterly,* Vol. VII, No. 2 (1928), 112.

Dana, Julian. *The Man Who Built San Francisco.* New York: Macmillan, 1937.

Davis, William Heath. *Sixty Years in California*: *1831-1889.* San Francisco: A. J. Leary, 1889.

De Luce, Eliza. Diary and Chronicle.

De Quille, Dan (William Wright). *The Big Bonanza.* Hartford, Conn.: American Pub. Co., 1876.

Fremont, John C. *Memoirs of My Life,* Vol. I. Chicago, 1887.

Fulton, Maurice Garland, and Paul Horgan. *New Mexico's Own Chronicle.* Three Races in the Writings of 400 Years, adapted and edited. Dallas, Tex.: Banks Upshaw, 1937.

Irelan, William, Jr. (State Mineralogist). *Eighth Annual Report, 1888,* California State Mining Bureau. Sacramento. Mono County and Bodie districts by H. A. Whiting, E.M., assistant in the field.

Lyman, George D. *The Saga of the Comstock Lode.* New York: Scribner's, 1934.

McIntosh, F. W. *Mono County, Land of Promises.* 1908.

Mining and Scientific Press, issues 1861 to 1902.

Myrick, David F. *Railroads of Nevada and Eastern California,* Vol. I. Berkeley, Calif.: Howell-North, 1962.

Outdoor Life (editors). *The Story of American Hunting and Firearms.* New York: McGraw-Hill, 1959.

Parr, John. "Reminiscences of the Bodie Strike," *Yosemite Nature Notes,* Vol VII, No. 5 (May, 1928), pp. 33-40.
Poughkeepsie (N.Y.) *Journal.*
Russell, C. P. "Bodie, Dead City of Mono," *Yosemite Nature Notes,* Vol. VI.
________. *Guns on the Early Frontiers.* Berkeley: Univ. of California Press, 1962.
Sabin, Edwin L. *Building the Pacific Railway. Phila.*: Lippincott.
Smith, Grant H. "Bodie, The Last of the Old Time Mining Camps," *California Historical Society Quarterly,* Vol. IV, No. 1 (Mar., 1925).
Thompson and West. *History of Nevada.* 1881.
Twain, Mark. *Roughing It.* New York: Harper.
Wasson, Joseph. *Bodie and Esmeralda*: *Complete Guide to Mono County Mines.* 1879.
Young, Edgar Levi. *The Founding of the Utah Territory.* New York: Scribner's, 1923.

Old files of the following California and Nevada newspapers from 1877 to 1902, many of which are on microfilm at the Bancroft Library, University of California at Berkeley, were consulted:

The Alpine Chronicle
The Bodie Chronicle
The Bodie Daily News
The Bodie Standard News
The Bodie Tri-Weekly Standard
The Bodie Weekly Standard
The Bridgeport Chronicle Union
The Daily Bodie Standard
The Daily Free Press
The Esmeralda Herald (Pub. at Aurora, Nev.)
The Mono Alpine Chronicle
The Reno Gazette
The San Francisco Bulletin
The San Francisco Post
The Virginia Enterprise

Private papers and letters were consulted from the personal files of H. Z. Osborne, managing editor of the *Bodie Standard* from May 15, 1878, until he resigned in October, 1879. At this time he became editor and co-publisher with E. R. Cleveland of the highly successful *Free Press.* He held this position until he moved to Los Angeles in 1884.

Acknowledgments

To my wife, Virginia, for her stimulating and sincere criticism, and to Dona de Luce Abt for special assistance and for contributing her mother's diary, and also to the following helpful and wonderful people (some of whom have passed to their Vahalla): John Parr; William H. Metson; Robert de Luce; J. W. Sherwin; J. S. Cain; Judge Pat R. Parker; Bert Dolan; Joe Scanavino; John N. Rosekrans; Spence Gregory; George Parker of Yerington, Nevada; Francis H. Frederick; Philip Bradley; Clarence C. Loose; Grace Crocker; Ella Farrington Mattley; Dorothy Cragen; John Simmes; George Brown; Sadie Moyle Palany; and numerous Bodieites and descendants of Bodieites for their comments and contributions on the Camp's past.

I also express my deepest appreciation to the Bancroft Library at the University of California; Library, Division of Mines and Geology, Department of Conservation, Resources Agency of California; Sutro Library; Stanford Library; Pomona City Library; Marin County Library and to the California Historical Society; Nevada Historical Society; and to the Los Angeles County Museum of Natural History; Tuolumne County Museum; and to Rand McNally & Company; the *San Francisco Examiner;* Frasher Photos; and to all their helpful staffs.

Special thanks are also due to Mr. & Mrs. Raymond G. Osborne for making available to me letters and papers and rare photos of H. Z. Osborne, Editor of the *Daily Bodie Standard* and the *Daily Free Press,* 1878-1884; and to Miss Ruth Mahood, Los Angeles County Museum of Natural History; Richard H. Dillon, Director of the Sutro Library; William A. Sansburn, Librarian, Divisions of Mines and Geology, Department of Conservation, Resources Agency of California, and to his successor, LeVern W. Cutler, Ferry Building Office; and to J. McLaren Forbes for the use of photos from the A. A. Forbes Collection.

Index

Other Books by Nevada Publications

P.O. Box 15444, Las Vegas, Nevada 89114

THE TOWN THAT DIED LAUGHING, by Oscar Lewis. 235 pages. The story of Austin, a rambunctious early day Nevada mining camp, and of its newspaper, The Reese River Reveille.

FREMONT, EXPLORER FOR A RESTLESS NATION, Ferol Egan. 582 pages. This scholar-novelist paints the political, social, and scientific implications of Fremont's expeditions.

MUSTANG, Anthony Amaral. 156 pages, illus. A tribute to a vanishing Nevada legacy, this book describes the life and legacy, this book describes the life and legends of wild horses.

HIGH MOUNTAINS & DEEP VALLEYS, by Lew & Ginny Clark, 191 pages, illus., maps. Coverage extends from Virginia City southward to Tonopah, Beatty, Death Valley, Bishop, Owens Valley. Color maps augment a useful text.

GHOST TRAILS TO CALIFORNIA, by Thomas Hunt. Large 8-1/2 x 11 format, 228 pages, illus. There are sections devoted to all early emigrant routes through northern Nevada. More than 160 color pictures carry captions excerpted from emigrant journals. a large beautiful color map and a portfolio of maps trace the routes of every major emigrant trail.

NEVADA LOST MINES AND BURIED TREASURES, by Douglas McDonald. 128 pages, 6x9, illus. Legends of lost mines in Nevada date from the Gold Rush of 1849 when westbound emigrants discovered silver in the desolate Black Rock Desert. The author recounts 74 of these stories which also include tales of buried coins, bullion bars, stolen bank money, etc. Two-color maps show general treasure localities. Color cover.

HIGHGRADE, THE MINING STORY OF NATIONAL, NEVADA, by Nancy B. Shreier. 150 pages, illus. Detailed account of the rich National district north of Winnemucca, during 1907-13.

THE CALIFORNIA STAR, 212 oversized pages, hardback. In this faithful reproduction of the San Francisco Weekly paper in 1847 are numerous descriptive references to the Donner Party and other northern California pre-state happenings. Prime source material.

FORTY-NINERS: by Archer Butler Hulbert. Subtitled *The Chronicle of the California Trail,* here is an account of the great western migration of 1849 and afterwards. Inferences determined by field work supplement this modern arrangement of emigrant diary material, with facts culled from diaries of gold
rushers, 1849-1853. There is much description of emigrant life interspersed with colorful anecdotes.

FEARFUL CROSSING, by Harold Curran. 212 pages, large 8-1/2 x 11 format, illus. paperback. This book describes the development of the trail and the lives and fortunes of those crossing Nevada. Extensive quotes from emigrant journals and other authorities give intimate insights into daily emigrant living: trouble with Indians, feeding animals, fighting, deaths, food preparation, etc. In addition to giving a history of the main Humboldt trail, Curran also describes the Applegate cutoff. Paperback.

ORDEAL BY HUNGER, by George Stewart. 328 pages, illus. Classic history of the snowbound Donner Party in California Sierra

THE ROCKS BEGIN TO SPEAK, by LaVan Martineau. 210 pages, illus. Nevada and Southwestern Indian rock writing with detailed interpretations.

U.S. Geological Survey Mining Bulletins Reprint Series

These bulletins, issued early in this century, are much in demand as primary reference material for Nevada mining and water sources. All cover extensively mineralogy, topography, history and the various mines. All are 6 x 9 quality paperbacks with pages sewn together.

MINES OF THE GOLDFIELD, BULLFROG AND OTHER SOUTHERN NEVADA DISTRICTS, by F. L. Ransome, 144 pp, maps, index. Color map 22 x 28 laid in. This 1907 Bulletin also covers Searchlight, Eldorado, Crescent and Gold Mountain, The last 42 pages reproduce from Out West magazine two contemporary illustrated articles. "The Nevada Bonanzas of Today" and "Goldfield and the Goldfielders." These capture the flavor and excitement of Nevada's mining era.

MINES OF THE SILVER PEAK RANGE, KAWICH RANGE AND OTHER SOUTHWESTERN NEVADA DISTRICTS, by S.H. Ball. 218 pp, maps, index. Color map 22 x 28 laid in. This 1907 Bulletin also covers Lida-Goldfield Valley, Pahute Mesa, Cactus Range, Reveille Range, Belted Range, Tolicha Peak, the Amargosa Mountain system, Gold Mountain, Death Valley and the Panamint Range.

320 DESERT WATERING PLACES IN SOUTHEASTERN CALIFORNIA AND SOUTHWESTERN NEVADA, by W. C. Mendenhall. 104 pp, illus, index. Color map 14 x 20 laid in. This 1909 Water-Supply Paper covers the Death Valley Basin in Inyo County and the Salton Sink of Imperial County, and numerous places in between. There are descriptions of 323 springs, all numbered and keyed to the colored map. The bulk of the book concerns San Bernardino County; in Nevada the following counties: Esmeralda, Nye, and Clark.

MINES OF CHURCHILL AND MINERAL COUNTIES, 144 pp, illus, map. This report, originally issued in 1937 and 1940, covers many west-central Nevada districts.

An Essential Mining Reference...

MINING DISTRICTS AND MINERAL RESOURCES OF NEVADA, by Francis C. Lincoln. 295 pp, maps, index. This compilation gives a summary of each mining district in Nevada through 1923. There are historical summaries and bibliographies of each mining area, all arranged by counties. Section Two describes Nevada's mineral resources by types. An essential tool for the mining researcher.

MINES OF TUSCARORA, CORTEZ AND OTHER NORTHERN NEVADA DISTRICTS, by W. H. Emmons. 220 pp, maps, index. This 1910 Bulletin also covers Midas, Good Hope, Columbia, Edgemont, Mountain City, Bullion, Safford, Tenabo, Lander, and the Lewis districts. Included is F. L. Ransome's "Notes on Some Mining Districts in Humboldt County" [Pershing County] 1909. Districts included are: Seven Troughs, Rosebud, Red Butte, Humboldt Range, Pahute Range, Sonoma Range.

MINES OF CHERRY CREEK, BRISTOL AND OTHER EASTERN NEVADA DISTRICTS, by J. M. Hill. 214 pp, maps, index. This 1916 Bulletin also includes Gold Butte, the Ruby Range, Mud Springs, Spruce Mountain, Mizpah, Kinsley, Toano Range, Tecoma, Ravenswood, Atlanta, Patterson, Troy, Bald Mountain, Granite, Hunter, Ward, Aurum, Duck Creek, Taylor and Kern districts.

GEOLOGY OF THE GREAT BASIN, by Bill Fiero. 250 pages, illus. A fine treatment complete with maps charts and analysis of Nevada geology. Author covers basic geologic conceptes and processes and complex geologic history. Striking color photographs augment the text.

NEVADA TOWNS & TALES, by S. W. Paher, ed. 2 vols. 224 pages ea. 8-1/2x11. Chapters focus on Nevada's economic, social and geographical factors. Other major sections discuss state emblems, gambling, politics, mining, business and casino entertainment. There is much material on ghost towns, prospecting, legends, early day women, ranching, native animals, industries, banking and commerce, railroads, atomic testing, transportation, etc. Indexed. Color cover. Vol. 1, North, Vol. 2, South.

MY ADVENTURES WITH YOUR MONEY, by George Graham Rice. 334 pages, illus. Here are the memoirs of get-rich-quick financing of central Nevada and Death Valley mines, with interesting anecdotal material. Author capitalized the stocks of Goldfield, Greenwater and Rawhide mines, listed them on the national exchanges, and reaped the profits until convicted of mail fraud in 1911. More than 110 illustrations complement the text.

VIRGINIA CITY'S INTERNATIONAL HOTEL, by Richard C. Datin. 49 pages, illus. Subtitled Elegance on C Street. This book recreates the history, the people and the splendor of Virginia City. The International Hotel typified it all, kings, financiers, President U.S. Grant, and queens of the footlights.

SKETCHES OF VIRGINIA CITY, N.T., by J. Ross Browne. 48 pages, illus. In 1860 the author commented extensively on the miners and their madness over minerals, the Chinese, the Indians, the stagecoach drivers, proprietors, barroom brawlers, etc. Charming, humorous cartoons of these appear in the book.

NEVADA, AN ANNOTATED BIBLIOGRAPHY, by S.W. Paher. 585 pages, 7x10 illus. Here is a researcher's guide and description of more than 2,544 books relating to the history and development of Nevada. The useful 74-page index has 3,550 subjects; listed are 33 other bibliographies referring the researcher to countless Nevada materials.

BODIE...BOOM TOWN. GOLD TOWN! The last of California's Old-time Mining Camps by Douglas McDonald. 48 pages, illustrated, color cover, 7x10 format. Though Bodie was discovered in 1859, no significant mining was begun until phenomenally rich strikes were made in 1877. The height of the boom occurred during 1879-80, though the mines were still active until about 1920. This heavily illustrated book shows the mines and miners, street scenes, important buildings, the mill, bullion, and the crowds which made up this great old mining camp.

Nevada's all-time best seller...

NEVADA GHOST TOWNS & MINING CAMPS, by S. W. Paher. Large 8-1/2x11 format, 492 pages, 700 illus., maps, index. About 668 ghost towns are described with directions on how to get to them. It contains more pictures and describes more localities than any other Nevada book. Nearly every page brings new information and unpublished photos of the towns, the mines, the people and early Nevada life. Now in 10th printing, it is the best seller of any book on Nevada ever published and it won the national "Award of Merit" for history.

MARK TWAIN IN VIRGINIA CITY, NEVADA, by Mark Twain. 192 pages. Twain portrays the life and the people of Virginia City, including the mining litigation, breaking in of a horse, etc. He mined for silver, labored in a silver mill and worked as a reporter for Virginia City's Territorial Enterprise. Drawings and cartoons.

VIRGINIA CITY, SILVER REGION OF THE COMSTOCK LODE, by Douglas Mcdonald. Large 9x12 format, 128 pages, 75 illus., index. The discovery and development of the West's largest silver lode is recounted in an extensive text and both line drawing and photographs. Old and new maps help tell the story.

AN EDITOR ON THE COMSTOCK LODE, by Wells Drury. 343 pages, illus. These reminiscences of Comstock society comprise a vivid cross-section of life. Author portrays the bad men, the law and various personalities as he found them.

MINING CAMP DAYS by Emil W. Billeb. 229 pages, illus. The author provides insights into Nevada and eastern California mining camps after 1905. Dozens of unpublished photographs were taken by this observer-participant, augmenting a good text.

MARK TWAIN, YOUNG REPORTER IN VIRGINIA CITY, by Katharine Hillyer. 92 pages, illus. Informal collection of Twain episodes at the *Territorial Enterprise.*

SILVER KINGS: THE LIVES AND TIMES OF MACKAY, FAIR, FLOOD, AND O'BRIEN, by Oscar Lewis. 286 pages, illus. The story of the Comstock Lode is retold with short biographies of these four men who controlled the richest strike in North America.

PLACER GOLD DEPOSITS IN NEVADA, by M.G. Johnson. (USGS Bull. 1356) 118 pages. County by county summary of 115 Nevada placer districts. Locations, extent of deposits and history.

THE MAKING OF A HARDROCK MINER, by Stephen Voynick. 224 pages, illus. Intimate description of life working underground—the heat, water, dark, constant danger. Much human interest.

VIRGINIA & TRUCKEE, A STORY OF VIRGINIA CITY AND THE COMSTOCK TIMES, by Lucius Beebe, 63 pages, illus., maps, biblio., tables. Few short lines were as familiar to powerful interests and celebrated to the world as the glorious V&T. This fast-moving account describes the mines that furnished ore for the silver mills along the Carson River. After 79 years the rails were ripped up in 1938.

THE COMPLEAT NEVADA TRAVELER, by David W. toll. 192 pages, illus. The author divides Nevada into five regions in order to describe in each of them its history, services for travelers, annual events and assorted trivia. Interesting photographs (some in color) are interspersed amid a lively text.

THE NEWSPAPERS OF NEVADA, by Richard Lingenfelter. 336 pages, illus., index. History of 800 publications issued from various Nevada localities. A thorough study.

TOURING NEVADA: A HISTORIC AND SCENIC GUIDE, by Mary Ellen and Al Glass. 253 pages, illus. Nevada travel descriptions for visitor and resident alike. Maps and color index are definite aids. Color cover.

THE STORY OF CANDELARIA AND ITS NEIGHBORS: COLUMBUS, METALLIC CITY, BELLEVILLE, MARIETTA, SODAVILLE AND COALDALE, by Hugh Shamberger. 200 pages, illus. History of mining in southwestern Nevada; an important study.

COPPER TIMES, by Jack Fleming. 255 pages, Collection of stories on Whte Pine County—its people, towns, copper industry, recreation, education, history.

EUREKA AND ITS RESOURCES, by Lambert Molinelli. 136 pages, illus. Good, short history of the mines, issued in 1879.

RAWHIDE, by Hugh A. Shamberger. 50 pages, maps. Early history, development, and water supply of this mining camp in Mineral County.

A MINER'S CHRISTMAS CAROL, AND OTHER FRONTIER TALES, by Sam Davis. 86 pages. A turn-of-the-century Carson City editor writes of early Pioche, Carson City, Virginia City, and newspapering.

GEOLOGY OF THE GREAT BASIN, by Bill Fiero. 250 pages, illus. A fine treatment complete with maps charts and analysis of Nevada geology. Author covers basic geologic conceptes and processes and complex geologic history. Striking color photographs augment the text.

JULIA BULETTE AND THE RED LIGHT LADIES OF NEVADA, by Douglas McDonald. 32 pages, illus., map. Here is the best written historical sketch to date of Virginia City's famed prostitute who was murdered in 1867. An overview of Nevada prostitution occupies the last part of the book, augmented by interesting photographs.

THE BIG BONANZA, by Dan DeQuille (William Wright). 488 pages, illus., with intro. by Oscar Lewis. Indexed. Subtitled "An authentic account of the discovery, history, and working of the Comstock Lode," the Big Bonanza by DeQuille covers every phase of the epic rise of Virginia City, especially the special technology required to work the deep silver mines. Color cover.

LOST LEGENDS OF THE SILVER STATE, by Gerald Higgs. 142 pages, illus., Obvious, better known Nevada stories are dutifully ignored. Included are stories of Mark Twain being thrown out of Nevada, Civil War days, the $100.00 boulder, etc.

HISTORY OF NEVADA, 1913, by Sam P. Davis. 2 vols. 1344 pages, 60 illus. Originally issued in 1913, this landmark history is a compilation of special treatises on Nevada geography, Indians, territorial life, law and crime, mining history, politics, and biographies of prominent early 20th century Nevadans. The new index has 6,000 subject entries.

DEATH VALLEY GHOST TOWNS, VOL. II, by S.W. Paher. 32 pages, 9x12, illus. Mining camps of the Death Valley National Monument—Skidoo, Panamint City, and Old Stovepipe Wells—are joined by those immediately to the west, including Cerro Gordo, Darwin and Cartago.

LIFE IN THE GHOST CITY OF RHYOLITE, by Betsy Ritter. 64 pages. Here is a lively history of Rhyolite, the schools, the mines, the banks, the railroads, and founder Shorty Harris.

DESERT GEM TRAILS, by Mary Strong. 79 pages, maps. Here is a field guide to gems and minerals of southern California's Mojave and Colorado Deserts. Some sights in Goldfield area included.

GHOSTS OF THE GLORY TRAIL, by Nell Murbarger. 316 pages, illus., indexed. Subtitled "Intimate glimpses into the past and present of 275 western ghost towns," Ghosts of the Glory Trail is a fast-moving chronicle depicting the early-day mining stampedes. All Nevada counties are represented either in the 39 chapters on specific towns such as Aurora, Rhyolite, Candelaria, Hamilton, Unionville, Belmont, Tybo, El Dorado Canyon, Tuscarora, Delamar, etc.) or in the ghost town directory with 275 listings, some in California and Utah. Color cover.

RECREATIONAL GOLD PROSPECTING, by Jim Martin. 138 pages, illus. Basics of panning, use of rockers and cradles, dredges, claim staking, etc. Color cover.

COMSTOCK MINING & MINERS, by Eliot Lord. 451 pages, illus., maps. This comprehensive and well written narrative history of the Comstock Lode traces the birth of the silver mining industry in turbulent Virginia City right up to the original date of publication, 1883.

For a complete catalog of our books write to:

Nevada Publications • Box 15444 • Las Vegas, Nevada

ORDER BLANK

QUANTITY	TITLE	AMOUNT
	SUB-TOTAL	
	POSTAGE	
	SALES TAX	
	TOTAL	

Name ____________________

Address ____________________

City ____________ State ____________ Zip ________

★ ☐ Please send information on new titles.

The chilly, silent background holds Bodie's first stamp mill. The earliest echoes of a steam whistle in the camp first bounced over its brick gothic walls in September, 1865.

Here is the story of men, who faced the wind,
And their struggle in the quest of the "Golden Fleece."

Prospectors and metal barons—gold and silver
Good men and bad.

The prospector and his homely burro led the way
For a maddened march of men following the lure of gold.
Towns, born overnight, died in infancy,
Died in the speed of their own living—
The GHOST TOWNS of today.*

*Excerpts from "This Is My Country," by Frantz Tascher. Copyrighted 1944 by Rand McNally and Co., Chicago. Used by special permission.